T THREE PEAKS RACE

The
HISTORY and
CHARACTERS of

THE MARATHON
WITH
MOUNTAINS

STEVE CHILTON

Foreword by **DAVID WEATHERHEAD**
Chair of the **THREE PEAKS RACE ASSOCIATION**

GREAT NORTHERN

Great Northern Books
PO Box 1380, Bradford,
West Yorkshire, BD5 5FB

www.greatnorthernbooks.co.uk

Design by David Burrill

ISBN: 978-1-914227-62-2

CIP Data
A catalogue for this book is available from the British Library

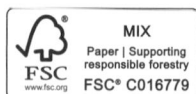

FSC
www.fsc.org

MIX
Paper | Supporting
responsible forestry
FSC® C016779

To Jim Neville, Clive Goddard and Howard Aiken

for the Three Peaks experience, and the many

brilliant training runs we had together.

"Someone once said to me that the
Three Peaks Race is three fell races
and two cross-country races in between –
and I know what they mean."

Dave Hodgson, former chair of the Three Peaks
Race Association, who completed the race 21 times.

CONTENTS

PHOTO CREDITS

ACKNOWLEDGEMENTS

Huge thanks must go to the various people on the organisational side of the Three Peaks Race, and the many competitors, with whom I discussed the event while researching this book. Without their input it would not have been possible to publish this history of the race. I sincerely hope that I have managed to suitably acknowledge them all.

In a similar way to my other books, it was not until I had discussed the idea I had in mind with someone else, and shared the synopsis and approach with them, that I got a feel for whether the idea was a 'runner' or not. In this case it was the enthusiastic response from Graham Breeze that convinced me to start the serious research. He agreed with me that the race deserved a book recording its history.

I wanted to record not just the facts of the history but also the range of characters that have impacted on that history. This involved conducting interviews as widely as possible across a range of people associated with the race, both as organisers and competitors. My thanks go to Boff Whalley, Malcolm Patterson, Ann Bland, and Sheila Walker, who at various times helped me make contact with people that I wished to talk with about the event.

My existing network, and the contacts made through those noted above, allowed me to include a range of experiences and perspectives from Three Peaks Race competitors. One great memory is spending an afternoon in Haworth interviewing four runners who between them had won the race 16 times. For agreeing to have either a face-to-face or an online chat I am eternally grateful to the following athletes (who put in some of the finest performances at the race) for sharing their thoughts and memories with me: Simon Booth, John Calvert, Joan Glass, Carol Greenwood, Mark Croasdale, Ian Ferguson, Ian Holmes, Helen Ilsley, Rob Jebb, Jethro Lennox, Ricky Lightfoot, Shaun Livesey, Jean Lochhead, Linda Lord, Anna Lupton, Sally Malir, Sarah McCormack, Angela Mudge, Jeff Norman, Lou Osborn, Tom Owens, Jasmin Paris, Andy Peace, Vanessa Peacock, Ruth

Pickvance, Mark Roberts, Brenda Robinson, Colin Robinson, Sarah Rowell, Kenny Stuart, Hugh Symonds, Joe Symonds, Brennan Townshend, Dave Walker, Harry Walker, William Walker, John Wild, Mary Wilkinson, and Victoria Wilkinson. Their stories are weaved into the narrative at the appropriate points. Thank you all for your time and interest in the project.

There are also a series of discrete profiles of athletes and officials to give as wide a range of perspectives on the event as possible. Many thanks to the following for sharing their thoughts: Karen Bradley, Steve Breckell, Paul Dennison, Andy Hauser, Tony Peacock, Dave Scott, Jean Shotter, and Dave Weatherhead. Their recollections add considerable depth to the story.

With any work of history there will be multiple sources that are referred to and used. Particular sources in newspapers, magazines and books are noted in the footnotes. I would like to give a massive thank you to the various report writers who have covered the Three Peaks Race over the years, and whose words have often been the source of the basic facts about each year's race. Bill Smith's seminal work on the early days of fell running (*Stud Marks on the Summits*) has been an invaluable source of background information.

Many people have helped me find information, sort out and cross-reference facts, and even point out the error of my ways. I am in debt to them all. Victoria Benn kindly agreed to me using quotes from her book, *Peak Performance: Ingleborough's Sporting Legacy*, and provided an important historical digital image and permission to use it. May Hill readily gave permission to use a couple of quotes from Ron Hill's book *The Long Hard Road*. Malcolm Patterson provided some interesting background for the era that he was active in the sport, and coach to some notable athletes. After conducting hundreds of interviews over the years I finally had an occasion where the audio recording failed to save properly. Only finding out too late to repeat it, my friend Mike Cambray stepped in to repeat the missing interview, and incidentally ask far deeper questions than I usually manage. He also offered his usual full support for the book idea right from the start.

Various people directly connected with the Three Peaks Race Association (TPRA) have offered support and invaluable access to information related to the history of the race. Dave and Shirley Hodgson kindly hosted a lovely half day, with tea and cream scones, which we spent discussing the history of the event and their deep involvement with it. Sadly, Dave Hodgson passed away during the writing of this book. Jon Sharples, and his wife Judy, invited me to visit them even though Jon had just had a tricky operation on his foot. I was excited to look through the 'big blue box' containing the TPRA's archive material and some brilliant early photos of the event. Bill Wade and Dave Scott provided invaluable help in recording the minefield of the various route and course record changes over the years. Douglas Croft shared some reminiscences of his time on the race committee, and in particular his reaction to, and actions after, the unfortunate death at the race in 1978. Janet Wilson helped provide information about the various trophies that are presented after each race, and when they were instigated.

Massive thanks must go to several people who have searched for and identified the many photographs that I hope help enliven this historical record. The individual photo credits are listed separately within the book. Denise Park granted me access to, and extensive use of images from, Pete Hartley's vast photo collection. She also scanned some that were only available as 35mm slides to enable them to be considered for use. Dave Woodhead dug out photos that I was looking for that were deep in his huge archive of Three Peaks material. Dave Weatherhead provided some excellent photos, particularly of the unheralded background support team, and helped with details of the history of the race and the TPRA. Chris Hodgson was exceptionally helpful with sorting photos from his father Dave's collection. Ed Price dug out a John Owen photo from the time he was editor of the Barnet and District AC club magazine. Terry Lonergan readily agreed to the use of one of his photos from a couple of decades ago. Pete Todhunter arranged for me to use photos of, and have a discussion with, the legend that is Joss Naylor. Donella Thompson helped me resolve issues over using

Mirrorpix images and sorted out the appropriate use licence.

Every effort has been made to contact copyright owners, authors and publishers, and appropriate attribution to original sources has been noted.

I must thank two people in particular for giving their time to help me to get this story into print. Graham Breeze was the first person to see the manuscript, and he fulfilled the role of critical friend superbly. He didn't shy away from suggesting things that I would never have considered and helped give me confidence that the structure and approach I was using might work. Dave Weatherhead performed a second critical review of the manuscript, and in addition carried out a diligent check of my spelling and use of language, and used his long experience of the race to fact-check where possible. Both Graham and David stepped up to the plate when I 'needed another set of eyes', as someone may or may not have said, once. Any remaining errors are of course my responsibility.

I will be forever indebted to David Burrill, of Great Northen Books, for taking the book on at a difficult time for publishers. Thanks also to Ross Jamieson for copy-editing the manuscript.

FOREWORD

The Three Peaks Race is one of the earliest known long-distance fell races, certainly in Yorkshire. The first organised race was held in 1954. It has since become iconic, having a fell running 'Who's who' list of winners and is a popular challenge for many outdoor enthusiasts.

Although I only know Steve Chilton by reputation, through my many years involved with fell running and a familiarity with Steve's previous publications, I know he is no newcomer to the sport. As a fell runner himself and author of several books covering various aspects of the sport, he is well qualified to write with experience about this relatively niche activity.

Recognising the popularity of the event, Steve has written a history of the Three Peaks Race which provides a detailed background to the event and personalities involved over the years. There are quite a few guidebooks about the Three Peaks, but few, if any, dedicated to the race itself and certainly none covering the race history in such depth.

Reading the book, it became apparent that a tremendous amount of research had been done by the author. I kept asking myself, 'where has he managed to find all this information?' The Three Peaks Race Association does have a fairly good archive of material, but Steve seems to have delved into many other sources to come up with interesting facts and memories.

I particularly like the interviews. Many of the athletes were from my era, whom I admired and perhaps competed in the same races with. Reading the comments of the top athletes reveals their thoughts about preparation, other competitors and the race itself. Many of the interviews are accompanied by photographs, some going back to the early days of the race. I particularly like the photo of the first six competitors to receive their 21 race awards in 1989.

I ran the race in the eighties and became involved with the Three Peaks Race Association in those days and have been ever since. I have seen the race and the organisation change over the years and the enthusiastic committee has always strived to promote the event in the best possible way.

I know Bill Wade and recall the likes of George Brass, Dave Hodgson and other prominent early competitors and committee members, each serving many years and carrying the Association forward to create the foundation of what is now one of the top fell and trail events in the UK. A couple of chapters in the book feature current committee members who represent the hard-working team promoting the race. The organisation is something Steve covers in more depth in Appendix 1, mentioning most of the individuals responsible for guiding the Association up to recent years. All the appendices give quite detailed information on the race winners and entry statistics together with route changes, which will perhaps help settle the argument about the race now being faster or slower, harder or easier – but I doubt it!

I had the privilege of meeting Fred Bagley, instigator and winner of the first race in 1954, when the Association invited him to present the awards at the 2021 race, a very modest man but a pioneer of the Three Peaks Race. For me, as a club runner, it is and has been an honour to rub shoulders with the elite of fell running, a definite benefit of being involved with the Three Peaks Race Association. Steve's book brings back a lot of memories.

To all fell runners this book will provide an insight into the thoughts of the top echelon of fell runners and a history of a race to which most fell runners will aspire. There is something of interest about all aspects of the event. To anyone with an ambition to run the race, this book will inspire the reader to put on their trainers.

Well done Steve Chilton, on producing this history of the event.

David Weatherhead
Chair of the Three Peaks Race Association, 2023

PROLOGUE

The weather had deteriorated quickly and on the heights it was drizzling, misty and cold. The final slopes were very steep with loose stones and peat. I was climbing on all fours, there were two other runners climbing close to me. Suddenly I lost all energy. It was a baffling feeling. I had to kneel and rest. Pushing up a few feet, I was forced to stop again, sitting this time, looking down to see the other competitors climbing towards me. There was nothing I could do; I was entirely helpless. Another 10 yards, kneel, turn and sit again. "God, I'll never make it." Sleep or semi-consciousness enveloped me for what seemed an age before I crawled that little bit further into the mist and found myself at the top. I stood upright on wobbly, unfeeling legs. Where was the checkpoint? Unexpectedly a runner came from my right. "Where's the checkpoint?" I asked. "Back there," he shouted over his shoulder from the mist.

A dramatic description of reaching the Whernside summit in an early Three Peaks Race (by a top runner).

Chapter 1

BACKGROUND

The Three Peaks is such an iconic race in the history of fell
running, that I wanted to experience it for myself [1]

It has always been a human characteristic to want to challenge oneself, from exploring new territories to setting athletic records. Many endurance athletic events started out as walking challenges. There is a parallel between the extended walks in the Yorkshire hills which led to the establishment of the now iconic Three Peaks Race and the walking rounds in the Lakes which prefaced the establishment of the challenge that is the Bob Graham Round.

By the 1860s there were adventurous individuals, and sometimes groups, testing themselves in the Lake District fells and achieving ever more impressive 'walking rounds'. Possibly the first significant round of the fells was by Rev. J. M. Elliott of Cambridge, who in 1864 departed from Wasdale Head and returned there eight and a half hours later after going over nine of the highest mountains in the Lakes. This round was to become the basis of the Lake District 24-hour Fell Record. This eventually led to Bob Graham's round of 42 Lakeland peaks in 1932, which became the eponymous Bob Graham Round. It is now a rite of passage for endurance fell runners, with its own 'club' for completers (who have achieved it in under 24 hours). It is worth noting that the second successful Bob Graham Round[2] wasn't recorded until 1960, six years after the Three Peaks Race was established.

The Three Peaks Race also has its origins in a classic walk. Two teachers from Giggleswick School, near Settle, J. R. Wynne-

---

1   Quote from Jasmin Paris, a recent winner of the Three Peaks Race

2   The story of the Bob Graham Round is told in *The Round: In Bob Graham's Footsteps,* Steve Chilton, Sandstone Press, 2017

Edwards and D. R. Smith, first completed a walking circuit of some 27 miles over the Three Peaks in 14 hours in 1887. In her book *Peak Performance*, Victoria Benn notes that:

> Following a full morning's teaching they set out over Ingleborough for tea at the Hill Inn, Chapel le Dale. After tea they decided to climb Whernside then Pen-y-Ghent, which they climbed at 10pm, finally returning to Giggleswick at midnight.[3]

Later, the participants said they had never heard of the Three Peaks, or even thought of a Three Peaks Walk.[4]

This circuit, which began to be called The Yorkshire Three Peaks, soon became a standard walk for members of the Yorkshire Ramblers' Club, with other long routes also being developed in the following years. Thornber notes: 'G. T. Lowe, the first president of the Yorkshire Ramblers' Club, writing in their journal in 1932, states that the formation of a Three Peaks Club came into his mind while on a walk at Whitsuntide, 1892. Later in that year the title of the Yorkshire Ramblers' Club was selected after several other names had been considered, and the club founded.' The Three Peaks Walk was never a qualifying walk for membership of the Yorkshire Ramblers' Club, although it was once suggested that it should be.

Gradually the circuit of the Three Peaks became an accepted feat of endurance and times of between five and six hours were claimed during the 1920s and early 1930s. A comparison with the Bob Graham Round is only partially valid as that is significantly longer at approximately 62 miles, and initially took over 23 hours to complete.

Within a decade, competitive runners had started to run all three of the Yorkshire peaks and had established new records for the round. It seemed that a time of less than five hours was now becoming the target.

---

3 *Peak Performance: Ingleborough's Sporting Legacy*, Victoria Benn, Tickled Trout Press, 2020.

4 For this detail, and much more on the history of the Three Peaks Walk, it is recommended that you read Norman Thornber's booklet *The Three Peaks*, a Dalesman Pocket Book, published in 1949.

It was now being seen as an athletic challenge, rather than a walking one, and in 1948 a fast attempt was made by three climbers from Leeds: Des Birch (Leeds University Climbing Club), Arthur Dolphin (Fell and Rock Climbing Club) and Jack Bloor (Yorkshire Climbers Club). They were also all members of the Leeds athletic club Harehills Harriers and had walked the Three Peaks several times. Birch was an international cross-country runner, Dolphin a county-level runner, but Bloor something of a novice athlete.

In his book, *Stud Marks on the Summits*, Bill Smith gives details of the effort, which took place in frosty conditions:

> In December 1948 this trio set off on a clockwise circuit from Chapel-le-Dale in frosty conditions and Birch finished in a time of 4 hrs 27 mins. Bloor was dropped by his companions coming off Whernside, then Dolphin got dropped by Birch crossing the boggy moorland to Pen-y-Ghent. Dolphin then retired, while Bloor struggled on over Pen-y-Ghent and down to Horton. At a farm near the village, he was given a pot of tea and a beef sandwich, which helped to revive him, and he then continued over Ingleborough to reach his starting point in 5 hrs 20 mins. [5]

They had started and finished at the Hill Inn and were dressed in the running gear of the day. The trio later reported a few things they had learnt which they thought might be of help for future attempts on the record:

> We came to the conclusion that summer is the best season for running in shorts and shirts; and that training over the actual hills is the best form of training. The route would be better run in the reverse direction. It is easier and faster, when tired, to take the short steep uphill sections than the long sloping ones. Running downhill would be far more rhythmical if over a gentle slope. We all enjoyed ourselves, and if the run were taken seriously the time could be cut down below 4 hours. [6]

Bloor and Dolphin returned in January 1949, taking their own

---

5   *Stud Marks on the Summits: A History of Amateur Fell Racing 1861–1983*, Bill Smith, SKG Publications, 1985.

6   The quote is from Norman Thornber's *The Three Peaks* booklet.

advice and trying an anti-clockwise attempt, again starting from the Hill Inn. With snow and ice underfoot, Dolphin knocked 25 minutes off Bloor's previous time, finishing in 4 hours 55 minutes. Bloor did not make the final climb up Whernside. These efforts, and the times taken, were reported in the regional newspapers, in effect throwing out a challenge to others. Preston Harrier Fred Bagley was one of those who rose to the challenge. In *Peak Performance*, Victoria Benn notes Bagley saying:

A group of us from Preston Harriers used to go off for weekends; we'd hitchhike or get a bus up to Ingleton and have a walking weekend. On this particular weekend we did the Three Peaks. We were all in our walking gear wearing boots and long trousers carrying rucksacks and a picnic, camping stove and so on, but I remember we did it in just over the five-hour mark – we were pretty fit in our early twenties! We were aware of the 'running record' of four and a half hours as we'd seen it in the paper, so we thought we could beat it if we organised a race.

Chapter 2

FIRST RACE

Fred Bagley deserves recognition for being both a good runner and also an innovative event organiser. He took on the task of organising the first Three Peaks Race,[7] and also chose to run in the race. Bagley was a keen fell walker and had already competed in the Lake District Mountain Trial.[8] On 24 April 1954, an anti-clockwise route was chosen for the Three Peaks Race, starting at the Hill Inn, Chapel-le-Dale. Initially the start was outside the Hill Inn but was later moved to the field behind the Inn.

There was virtually no publicity, except word of mouth. It attracted 11 entries, with just six starting, for a 23-mile romp over Ingleborough, Pen-y-Ghent and Whernside. It would have been very different to today underfoot, in that it included many miles of trackless ways. As already noted, it was felt that breaking the existing record for the round was a definite possibility.

The best way to get a feel for that first race is by studying the report of the event. The following seven paragraphs are from *The Dalesman* of June 1954, from an article written by H. W. Eccles (who was one of the timekeepers for the race):

> A similar route to that taken on the previous occasion was chosen, the result being that the first two men home succeeded in finishing the course in well under the existing time. The winner, F. Bagley, of Preston Harriers, reduced it by no less than 39 minutes, and so became the first man ever to complete the 23-mile circuit in under four hours, his actual time being 3 hours 48 minutes.
>
> Following him closely home was Stan Bradshaw, of Clayton-le-Moors Harriers, who ran a fine race and clocked a time of four hours six minutes, thus clipping twenty-one minutes off the old record. The third man home was clubmate Alf Case in five hours two minutes.

---

7   Co-organiser was Bagley's fellow Preston Harrier, Malcolm Withnell.

8   The Lake District Mountain Trial (a 'navigation event' over 15 to 20 miles) first took place in 1952. Fred Bagley came 6th in the second edition of the Trial, in 1953.

The race was started by M. T. Withnell (Preston Harriers) from the Hill Inn, Chapel-le-Dale at 11.10am. The weather was fine and reasonably clear, but a strong easterly wind made the day extremely cold, a fact noted both by competitors and timekeepers on the peaks. The peaks were occasionally veiled by light mist, but ground conditions proved fairly good because of a recent dry spell.

The times recorded on the peaks were as follows: On Ingleborough (timekeeper – A. Bibby, Lancaster Primrose Harriers and Athletic Club) all competitors were timed in at 11.37am (actual time twenty-seven minutes[9]). On Pen-y-Ghent, the race was beginning to open out, although the leading three were still close together as the following times show. In first position was F. Bagley, who reached the summit at 12.58pm (actual time one hour forty-eight minutes), followed by S. Bradshaw at 12.59pm (one hour forty-nine minutes) and third A. Case at 1.00pm (one hour fifty minutes). Timekeepers were H. Eccles and C. G. Shorrock.

From Pen-y-Ghent F. Bagley steadily increased the lead after resisting one challenge by S. Bradshaw and topped the third summit, Whernside, at 2.38pm (three hours twenty-eight minutes) with S. Bradshaw at 2.50pm (three hours forty minutes) and A. Case 3.27pm (four hours seventeen minutes). Timekeeper was M.T. Withnell. These positions were held to the finish when F. Bagley clocked home at the Hill Inn in a very fresh condition at 2.58 (three hours forty-eight minutes) with S. Bradshaw at 3.16pm (four hours six minutes) and A. Case 4.12pm (five hours two minutes).

F. Bagley, the new record holder, is a keen cross-country and track athlete. He was Cross Country Champion of the Club for the 1952-53 season and is the 1953-54 three-mile Club Champion. He is also a keen fell walker and a regular visitor to the Three Peaks country and the Lake District.

The event was very successful and Preston Harriers and Athletic Club are thinking of making this an annual event. Although the entries for this race were modest in number, they are hoping to increase the entry in future.

No mention is made in *The Dalesman* report of the three starters who did not finish.[10] Bill Smith noted some extra detail of how the race unfolded, in the 50th anniversary race booklet, including the route choices taken (rightly or wrongly):

---

9   In a report in the *Yorkshire Evening Post*, in which Bagley is quoted extensively, he claims he 'went up Ingleborough in 26.5 minutes, and the others took 27'.

10 The *Lancashire Telegraph* reported (in 2004): 'Although held in Yorkshire, the origins of the race are firmly in Lancashire with all six of the runners in the first race of 1954 hailing from the county.'

Bagley reached the mist shrouded summit of Ingleborough but then headed too far south, hotly pursued by his rivals, before eventually getting back on course at Sulber Nick. The route from Horton to Pen-y-Ghent then took a more direct line over the intakes and up the fell's steep southwestern flank, between the crags. Bagley and Bradshaw took different routes beyond Nether Lodge, Bagley taking the road whilst Bradshaw kept to the fields. Bagley arrived first at Ribblehead but then struck a bad patch on the steep ascent of Whernside, reached via Winterscales Farm. This did not deter him, however. Bradshaw took second after descending from Whernside too early and emerging into rough boulder fields.

The *Yorkshire Evening Post* carried an article shortly after the race, that quoted an interview with Fred Bagley, whom they claimed, 'rather hid his light under a bushel'.[11] Some of Fred's thoughts on the day are reproduced below. They suggest a confident and reflective man, who ended with what might seem a provocative inter-county challenge. The article also listed the other three starters in the race as: 'B Cottam (Barrow AC) and W Airey and Smith (Lancaster Primrose AC)':

Cottam retired on the top [of Ingleborough] with cramp in the thighs. There was a little cloud as we ran off Ingleborough, and I went too far south, missing the Shooting Box altogether. The others followed, and we very nearly ended up in Crummock. Luckily, I realised in time and, after a detour of about a mile, I managed to find Sulber Nick.

Despite this mistake, we were in Horton before we were expected, and missed the refreshments. Case had caught me up at Beecroft Hall, and we ran together till about a mile before Pen-y-Ghent, where he dropped back to run with his friend Bradshaw. Airey and Smith retired on Pen-y-Ghent.

Bradshaw took a slightly different route after Pen-y-Ghent, and I was surprised to see him just in front at High Birkwith. I ran with him to Nether Lodge, but he complained of fatigue and told me to go ahead.

At Ribblehead I was told my time so far had been 2.5 hours, which greatly refreshed me, but going up Whernside I began to feel shaky at the knees. There was a cold wind, and a black cloud blew raggedly across the ridge. I was glad to shelter in the lee side of the cairn on top and chat with the markers. I finished in 3hr 48min.

11 'Three-Peak challenge to Yorkshire harriers', *Yorkshire Evening Post*, Tuesday May 25, 1954.

On the whole I found the run very enjoyable and apart from the final climb up Whernside, I did not suffer from exhaustion. Taking into account the stops I made, and one or two route errors, I think it should be possible to go round in 3.5 hours or less next year, though much depends on the weather on the day.

Anyway, the Harriers intend to make this an annual event, to be held on the first Sunday after Easter. We are looking forward to a bigger entry next year. The fact that the record now belongs to Lancashire should provide a challenge to the Yorkshire clubs.

He was also asked about his training, which he outlined. 'I have a daily training run of about four miles before work, amounting to about 1,400 miles a year, and casual walking on the fells at weekends makes up another 1,400 miles roughly.'

In an article that looked back on his time on the fells, Stan Bradshaw added some more detail on how that first race panned out. It shows how little some runners knew of the route, and that a variety of route choices were clearly available in those days:

I lost sight of Fred Bagley on the summit of Ingleborough in the mist. Dropping out of the mist, Alf Case and I had no idea where to go next, but we were lucky to see the small figure of Bagley in the depression leading down to Gaping Ghyll. He had got too far south but we followed him and must have got too far south of Sulber Nick.

I went direct to the summit of Pen-y-Ghent via the buttresses, following the lefthand side of the wall to the checkpoint. I must have passed Alf on the climb and was by myself on the descent. I had heard of Black Dub Moss and avoided it by going to the right over the 'bedstead' at the gap in the wall. I had never been over this ground before. I found myself in front of Bagley at High Birkwith, where I asked the farmer the way to Ribblehead.

I eventually hit the road near the cattle grid at Ribblehead. Under the viaduct, then cut off up the cart-track to the right of Gunner Fleet, then to the right of Winterscales and directly up Whernside. I reached the summit via a grassy ridge with 'steps' in. Bagley must have been in front now, and not knowing the correct way off Whernside, I cut down to the left too soon and found myself on a steep boulder field where I must have lost a lot of time.[12]

Stan Bradshaw's full Christian name was Stanley, and he

---

12 'Sixty years a fell runner', *The Fellrunner*, June 1990.

1. *Organiser of the first Three Peaks Race and winner of that first race, Fred Bagley*

was named after Accrington Stanley football club, for whom his father Ernest played. When he entered and ran in the first Three Peaks Race that year he had never been on Pen-y-Ghent or Whernside. He obviously got a liking for the Three Peaks circuit though, as in the 1980 race he achieved his ambition to complete 100 circuits of the course, including racing, training and walking. He also took a turn on the Three Peaks Race Association committee.

Alf Case later became honorary secretary of the Three Peaks Race Association (and chairman of the Fell Runners Association), and he noted in a short historical article on the race (in the spring 1972 issue of *The Fellrunner* magazine) that 'there was virtually no publicity except word of mouth that the event would be held on the last Sunday of April'. Fred Bagley did place a small advert for the race in the *Lancashire Evening Post*. Alf Case added that 'the checkers on Ingleborough were able to cross over and do like duty on Whernside'.

Bill Smith comments, in *Stud Marks on the Summits*, that 'another athletic circuit of the Three Peaks took place during the spring of 1954 when John F. Bell, a professional runner from Giggleswick, went round in about 4 hours from Chapel-le-Dale as part of his training for local sports meetings'. The race was held again in 1955, with an increase of ten competitors over the inaugural year.

Chapter 3

THE EARLY YEARS

1955

George Brass was one of the finest runners of his time. He had an indomitable spirit and was known for his generosity. George Brass loaned Bill Smith and his co-publishers the financial support needed to help get their iconic book *Stud Marks on the Summit* published.[13]

Brass, of Clayton-le-Moors Harriers, came home 1st in the second race (on 25 April 1955) in 3-28-45, nearly 20 minutes faster than Fred Bagley's time from the first race. Stan Sykes (Longwood) was second in 3-43-21, with Joe Hand (Border) 3rd in 3-44-00. As well as Brass setting a new race record, the other two medallists were also inside Bagley's time from the first race. Some entrants unfortunately had checkpoint/navigation issues, and two runners were not checked in at the final peak of Whernside.

THREE PEAKS FELL RACE.

Held on Sunday 24th April, 1955.   Official results as follows:-

			hrs.	mins.	sec.
1.	G. Brass	Clayton-le-Moors	3	28	45
2.	S. Sykes	Longwood Harriers	3	43	21
3.	J. Hand	Border Harriers	3	44	0
4.	G. Thornton	Oxford City A.C.	3	51	15
5.	F.C. Bagley	Preston Harriers A.C.	4	9	30
6.	J. Morris	Staveley Works Sports Club	4	11	15
7.	K. Heaton	Clayton-le-Moors	4	18	15
8.	E.W. Horrocks	Leigh Harriers A.C.	4	26	0
9.	B. Lister	Clayton-le-Moors	4	38	45
10.	F. Whitehurst	Sheffield United A.C.	5	2	45
11.	A.G. Page	Preston Harriers A.C.	5	10	45
12.	F.W. Rawlinson / W.F. Hill	Unattached / Clayton-le-Moors	5	52	0

2. The full result from the 1955 race

---

13 Subtitled 'A History of Amateur Fell Racing: 1861–1983', the book was published by SKG Publications (Smith, Knott and Gildersleve) in 1985. Out of print now, it is an invaluable resource for researchers. The FRA also made an interest-free loan to help make the book happen. The loan was repaid, and Bill Smith donated the profits from the book to the Three Peaks Race Association, Lake District Mountain Trial Association, CFRA, and the Bob Graham 24 Hour Club. He also donated £1,000 to the FRA.

3. *The Hill Inn start in 1955*

These early races were all run anti-clockwise from the Hill Inn, Chapel-le-Dale. That second event saw a small increase in numbers, having 16 starters, of whom 13 finished. Fred Bagley was the only runner from the first race to finish this time, in 5th place. B. Cottam also started, but dropped out again (along with P. N. Dent and N. Lindsay, two unattached runners), this time reaching Ribblehead. For this year full splits were recorded for each runner at Ingleborough, Pen-y-Ghent and Whernside and were included on the results sheet.

In his reminiscences, Stan Bradshaw tells of an amusing incident that happened at the start of the race: '16 of us were lined up in the road outside the Hill Inn when the whistle or gun went: half of the field ran down the road to the lane that leads to the Post Office, while the other half, including myself, ran up the road to the stile about 20 yards on. I can't remember which of us took the quicker route!'

1956

Twenty-three runners started in 1956, of whom 13 finished and 6 retired, proving that it was a tough challenge. Four runners had completed the course but were not seen by the marshals manning the Whernside checkpoint. Jack Bloor (Leeds Harehills Harriers), who had been part of the timed runs in 1948–49 and helped establish the race, led all the way to win in 3-33-15, half a minute ahead of Joe Hand. Jack Bloor[14] was a pioneering climber and fell runner, a coach of orienteers to world-class level, and had many rock climbing first ascents in Yorkshire and the Lakes. Alan Heaton was 3rd in 3-37-35 after working his way through the field all race.

Alan Heaton was a modest man who delivered some extraordinary running achievements without fanfare. He was 422nd out of 467 finishers in the 1956 English National cross-country championships. But that cross-country race was far too short for him, being only a few miles long. Heaton had massive endurance capability, which he put to good use in the event that he will probably be most remembered for. In 1960, just four years after that unremarkable cross-country race, he became only the second person to run the 42 Lakeland summits of the Bob Graham Round in less than 24 hours, a feat first attributed to the Keswick hotelier Bob Graham in 1932.[15]

In 1985, at the age of 57, Heaton was the first person to run the Wainwrights[16] – the 214 Lakeland fells listed in the seven guides by the famous hillwalker and author Alfred Wainwright. Heaton ran continuously, stopping only to sleep occasionally, and have a septic toe treated in hospital. He completed the 320-mile route in 9 days 16 hours and 42 minutes. More recently several athletes have reduced the time for this feat, and the record stands at five and a half days at the time of writing.

---

14 The Jack Bloor Fund was established in 1985 to commemorate the life of Jack Bloor. He had a heart attack and died after he finished the Leeds University relay, in 1984. He was only in his late 50s. The Fund awards grants to those who want to improve their physical and/or technical skills in any recognised outdoor adventure sport.

15 The Bob Graham Round website has details of this classic endurance rite of passage: http://www.bobgrahamclub.org.uk/

16 Details of the Wainwrights Round can be found at: https://www.anewfoundcompendium.com/wainwrights

4. *Alan Heaton finishing the race in the 1980s*

1957

The Three Peaks Race was beginning to attract the very best fell running exponents of the era, with Stan Bradshaw, Jack Bloor, Eric Beard and Ken Heaton also among the 17 finishers in the 1957 event. Alan Heaton came 2nd, to Clayton-le-Moors clubmate Peter Dugdale, who romped home in 3-33-50, over three minutes ahead of Heaton, with Gilbert Bradshaw (Benwell Harriers) 3rd in 3-43-25. Alan Heaton once said that the Three Peaks was one of his three absolute favourite races, along with the Lake District Mountain Trial and the Pendleton Fell Race. He also gave a philosophical take on being out in the hills: 'I would say that the 25 years of endeavour on the hills has brought me much frustration and disappointment, but these are far outweighed by the rewards I have had; one of which is the satisfaction that comes from testing yourself and succeeding in mastering your fallibilities in an environment where you like to be.'[17]

1958

Entries for the race had reached 29 for the 1958 event, and all bar three finished. George Brass won for the second time with a superb new record time of 3-08-25, which was 20 minutes faster than his 1955 winning time. Dave Hodgson (Leeds St Marks) held the lead at Ribblehead but struggled on Whernside, and Brass took a large chunk of time out of him there. Hodgson eventually dropped to 4th, with Ian Watson (Stockport) taking 2nd and Ray Shaw (Border) 3rd. Dave Hodgson shared a memory of that race, which was his first time of running the Three Peaks Race:

> I hung on to a group of Clayton Harriers from the first summit, Ingleborough, including George Brass, Stan Bradshaw and, I think, Alistair Patten. Conditions were misty and I had only the vaguest idea of the route. There were none of the well-blazed paths that now exist. The group gradually thinned out until Nether Lodge, between Pen-y-Ghent and Ribblehead, when George and I were on our own. George didn't know me, but I was aware of him as a

---

17 In his report on his own Bob Graham Round.

5. *Dave Hodgson leads George Brass in the 1958 race*

previous winner, and I had also beaten him the previous year in a one-mile track race. I felt pretty confident but had no experience of racing more than nine miles cross-country. George was doing all the route-finding, and after passing Winterscales at the foot of Whernside, turned to me and asked how I felt. I said, 'I am a bit tired.' George immediately shot off up Whernside to win! I crawled up on hands and knees to finish 4th – and learned a few lessons.

George Brass had won the Three Peaks Race twice in the first five years and brought the record time down by a massive 30 minutes. Not into high mileage, he trained much of the time over Pendle hill. He completed the Three Peaks Race 39 times in all and was a top fell runner with some brilliant performances. He won the prestigious Lake District Mountain Trial twice, in 1961 and 1962. The first one was based at Wasdale Head and was a fairly routine win by almost 30 minutes in a time of 4-54-58, from Des Oliver, after Joss Naylor got unaccountably lost on Seatallan.

6. *Crossing the railway at Horton-in-Ribblesdale*

The second Mountain Trial win by Brass was far from routine. Based that year in Glenridding, the Trial was run in icy winds, in low cloud and driving rain. The conditions were so severe that Brass was in fact the only competitor to complete the course. Known hardman Eric Beard commented at the time that, 'I've never been so cold in my life. I just had to give up'. George Brass described the conditions as the worst he'd ever known. He finished after 6 hours 50 minutes, carrying one of his shoes as it had disintegrated on him.

1959

Frank Dawson (Salford) won the 1959 Three Peaks Race in 3-13-25, having worked his way through the field. Forty-four competitors had set off, with Dawson arriving at the summit of Ingleborough in 9th place. By Whernside though he had a minute lead over Bert Bradshaw, with the gap remaining the same to the finish. George Brass came in 3rd, nearly five minutes later. Frank Dawson was from Ambleside, in the Lakes, and had a good pedigree, with an uncle who had been a guides (professional) racer.

1960

Frank Dawson triumphed again in 1960, knocking another big chunk off the course record, as the race report notes: 'He created a stir by completing the course in under 3 hours, after being 5th on Pen-y-Ghent, 4 minutes down on Dave Spencer who was then leading. Dawson took 2-58-33 to beat the eventual runner-up Dave Hodgson by 3-47, the latter being in contention throughout.' This was the first time that certificates were divided into 1st and 2nd classes: 18 competitors having beaten 3.5 hours, and 27 competitors the 4.5 hours target, respectively.

7. Race programme cover, 1960

CLAYTON-LE-MOORS HARRIERS

SEVENTH ANNUAL

THREE PEAKS RACE

(Under A.A.A. Laws)

Horton Church and Penyghent

STARTING at 11 a.m. and FINISHING at

Hill Inn, Chapel-le-dale

on

Sunday, 24th April, 1960

PROGRAMME AND MARKING SHEET PRICE 6d.

Chapter 4

DECIDED TO GIVE IT A GO

In 1961 **Ron Hill** was a research student at Manchester University and was just beginning to find his way in the various branches of athletics. He liked to test himself over all running surfaces. That year he had already finished 2nd at cross-country in the British Universities' Championships; gained a 3rd place in the Windermere to Kendal Road Race; and won the Rivington Pike fell race. At this time he often raced twice a week.

As his club, Clayton-le-Moors, used to attend the Three Peaks Race he was tempted to join his clubmates that year. The day beforehand he won a track 3-mile race, and he was up early for the two-hour coach trip to Chapel-le-Dale. That year there were 86 entries of whom 64 started. It was a cool and dry day. He had little idea what he was in for. At 11am they set off for Ingleborough, with Ron reaching the summit in 4th place. He lost some places by dint of a poor route choice off the top, but he got back up to 5th place by Horton-in-Ribblesdale.

There is a long description of the race in Ron Hill's autobiography (*The Long Hard Road – Part One: Nearly to The Top*), where he describes the issues he had on his traverse of Pen-y-Ghent that day:

I followed the man in front, took the lead and headed for what I thought was the peak. Mistake. I heard a call, 'Ronnie, wrong way!' I was way off course. I had to catch the bunch again; finally climbing steep steps cut into the side of the hill with hands pushing down on thighs and knees to force my body upwards. I emerged on the grassy peak in 4th position once more, just behind the leaders. Round the knot of spectators and recorders and off in the direction of Ribblehead. On this free running stretch I took the lead only to find when I got to the bottom I was completely lost. It was a low area of tufted grass and heather covered hills, hiding the far horizons and landmarks to head for. There weren't even any footpaths. I stopped, cursing again, until the following runners came down.

Dave Hodgson came along first but Ron waited for Frank Dawson as he had won the last two years, and presumably reckoned he was the best bet. Soon Dawson admitted he was lost! Setting off hard after Hodgson the good running allowed him to catch him again and he optimistically took the lead just as the gradient got really steep. At this point the reader might like to re-read the prologue, as that is Ron Hill's description of the difficulties he had in surmounting Whernside and locating the checkpoint. He then describes the final descent:

> My number was recorded; back down the ridge I went, no idea where I was heading in the mist. My legs were very weak. Alan Heaton, an expert on the course, caught me. I followed him across the bogs and peat hags, down the precipitous slopes on to the smooth farm roads until with about ¼ mile to go he just ran away from me. I ended tired and very, very hungry in 5th position with a time of 3 hours 11 minutes 55 seconds, nearly 7 minutes behind the winner Geoff Hodgson of Blackpool.

Ron Hill never did win the Three Peaks Race. He came back in 1963 when the weather was atrocious, with visibility about 50 metres, and finished 9th in 3-41-47. In 1964 he was 4th, having tripped over a dog ten yards from the finish.

In 1966 Hill reckons he had his best ever cross-country season and had big ambitions on the track and road for that season, but still he ran the Three Peaks again, coming 9th in 3-15-26. He was a truly great runner, but destined not to win the Peaks. Finishing just ahead of Ron Hill that day was Peter Leviston, who wasn't an official entry as he was aged 17 at the time. Leviston recently added this detail of his memory of the day. 'I travelled up with Dave Spencer [who finished 5th] whose picture was on the race posters that year. I took it steady up Ingleborough but was leading through Sulber and into Horton. There was a group of five runners around me heading for one of the many stone walls. On one I struggled to climb it, got on top and got cramp in my legs. From there it was hard work through the coarse grass, gullies and bogs. I got to the Ribblehead Viaduct in reasonable shape though, and saw Dave [Spencer] with his wife having a

8. *Ron Hill at Ribblehead*

cup of tea at the side of the road, which he offered me. I declined, thinking I had got the beating of him. Climbing Whernside my back was hurting, my legs had gone, and I spent a lot of the time going up backwards. Dave caught me. I was caught by Radley at the top and I managed to run with him to the end. I didn't go through the finish funnel as I was under-age.'

Ron Hill was an inveterate racer, and two comments he made in his autobiography suggest that his very frequent racing hindered his chances of doing really well at the Three Peaks. Of 1961 he said, 'Even the Three Peaks Race, my longest ever run, didn't prevent me racing the day before.' Recalling the 1964 race he noted:

> I started to build up the mileage in preparation for the track season and ran the Three Peaks once more. It was really just for training and the challenge. After my first couple of attempts I had never attacked the race seriously but run it more for training and the sense of achievement at the end. This year I ran the Manchester and District Harriers road relay on the Saturday, and the Three Peaks on the Sunday.

I consider **Joss Naylor** as being up there amongst the finest fell runners we have ever seen. Despite being virtually unbeatable at events like the Lake District Mountain Trial at his peak he also never managed to win the Three Peaks Race. He did have ten attempts at it between 1966 and 1978, with his best placing was 3rd in 1973 in 2-44 on the old course from the Hill Inn.

For his first Three Peaks in 1966 Joss says he knew a few of the people who were planning on doing it, so he decided to give it a go. The winner that day was Mike Davies, who Joss had a number of good races against in Joss's early days, especially in the Mountain Trial. It was a day off from farming for him too. He had no chance to get to know the course in advance, as he recalls now. 'There was no time as a farmer to travel down for a look round the course. I just thought I'd try to hang on to front guys and see what happened.'

I asked him about it not being his kind of terrain. 'Don't get me wrong. I did enjoy the race and the craic afterwards. However, it was not long or rough enough ground for me to dig in and get away from the rest. It also came at a busy time on the farm, with lambing and sorting out sheep to get back on fell. It is also a bloody long way from Wasdale to do a race.' When he did race it, he recognised it as one of the biggest longish English races, although acknowledging that at the time when he first ran it there weren't as many of them as there are now. He called it a good way to get a long fast run in your legs early on in the year.

Being Joss, he spiced up his responses to my questions with a couple of amusing anecdotes. 'Once I was coming off the fell to the road near the finish and was told that Ron Hill was not that far in front. So, I changed up a gear and caught him just before turning into the finish. That made both of us smile and gained me a few choice words off Ron. Another time we had a bit of a scare getting there when the car decided to overheat. But a trip to the nearest beck with a bottle to get some water soon had us back on the road again.' He also adds that, 'If you were up in the front of the race it was sometimes difficult to find a quiet spot for a pee if you needed one, especially when there was normally a lot of walkers also on the route.'

9. Joss Naylor, 1976

I also asked Joss my standard question about how he thought the Three Peaks Race fits in to the wider fell/mountain running picture. This was his measured response. 'It has always been a popular race, although these days the numbers trying to get a spot are amazing. Maybe it has become too big, and I know it takes some organising, plus the cost of putting it on is substantial. It is a good job a few sponsors help with the cost. The increase in trail running numbers is now filtering into this type of fell race where, unless weather is crap, the route is fairly easy to follow. It is still a good race to do and if you are fit that early in the year on a good day you can bag yourself a good fast time, but you have got to be fit as it's a course that can catch you out on those tough climbs. It is good that there seems to be an active committee putting in the hours to put the race on as it is one of the well-known fell races up there with the likes of the Ben, Fairfield, Borrowdale and Ennerdale races. I hope it keeps being run for a good few more years.'

Another absolutely top runner who never ran well at the Three Peaks was **Billy Bland**. He was Fell Runner of the Year in 1980 when he was at his peak, and he had consistently superb results in the Lake District classic long fell races. The Wasdale and Borrowdale fell races are reckoned to be two of the toughest on the calendar. Billy Bland won Wasdale nine times and Borrowdale ten times.

When interviewed for his biography[18] he originally suggested that the 1977 race was his first attempt at the Three Peaks Race. The results from that day show Billy finishing in 34th position in a time of 3-09-20, some 18 minutes behind winner John Calvert. Billy said that he 'didn't like the experience, but maybe did go back once. I was just no good at it. It was too runnable in between the peaks for me to do well. Maybe I should have persevered a bit more. I doubt if I would ever have won it. But it was nowt to do with travel.'

But here is a thing. As he talked through his career for my book, Billy Bland's recall of detail from specific races was pretty amazing. But here he had something of a blip. His memory of

18 *All or Nothing at All: The Life of Billy Bland*, by Steve Chilton, Sandstone Press, 2020.

10. Billy Bland training in the Lakes

maybe going back, possibly in 1978 or 1979 as he recalled it, is not correct. Some enquiries on social media uncovered the fact that he had in fact run the Three Peaks Race the year *before* that, i.e. in 1976. This was a surprise as he was only just getting into his stride in long races by then, and Ann Bland noted that, 'he didn't win Borrowdale till 1976 and I don't think he would even think of doing the Three Peaks till after that.' Then, on being told he had done it earlier, she mischievously added, 'he must have thought he was better than he was!' But run he did in 1976, coming a lowly 91st in 3-17-10.

When reflecting on the Three Peaks Race, Hugh Symonds commented that, 'It is a totally different race to Ennerdale, Borrowdale or Wasdale. Like different sports really.' That partly explains why Ron Hill, Joss Naylor and Billy Bland never won the Three Peaks, despite each of them trying to do so more than once. There are similar examples from the modern era.

11. *The start line in 1961*

Chapter 5

TWO HODGSONS

1961

The sixth different runner to win the Three Peaks Race was Geoff Hodgson (Blackpool), who was not related to Dave Hodgson. Geoff Hodgson won the Three Peaks Race in both 1961 and 1962. In the first of those years there was really bad weather, resulting in a 3-05-10 winning time and 16 retirements (from the 65 starters). Geoff Hodgson's strategy was to move through the

12. *Frank Dawson and Geoff Hodgson*

13. *Geoff Hodgson*

field as the race progressed. He was 12th on Ingleborough, 7th on Pen-y-Ghent and in the lead by the top of Whernside. Dave Hodgson was 2nd by nearly three minutes. Peter Booth took 3rd place, with Alan Heaton just beating Ron Hill into 4th place by 12 seconds, with record holder Frank Dawson 6th.

1962

Geoff Hodgson used the same tactic in 1962, pacing himself well again, going from 8th on Ingleborough, to 6th on Pen-y-Ghent, until he took the lead again on Whernside. He came home in 3-00-07 to win by over three minutes again from Dave Hodgson, repeating the positions from 1961. Dave Hodgson had been nine seconds down on Martin Cranny on Whernside, but descended better than him. Cranny was 3rd, with Eric Beard 4th. This time there were 12 retirements out of the 66 starters.

1963

There was a new race winner in 1963. Dennis Hopkinson (Clayton) ploughed through the classy field to win in 3-18-37 from Bert Bradshaw. Once again there were a significant number

14. Dennis Hopkinson

of dropouts, with only 45 finishing from 110 starters.[19] In his autobiography,[20] Ron Hill noted that he 'followed Alan Heaton again coming off Pen-y-Ghent, but it didn't pay off as we got lost, at one point meeting a group heading up Pen-y-Ghent!'

1964

A startling new course record was set in 1964, by Barrow's Peter Hall, who won in a bold front-running style in 2-53-00, taking a hefty five and half minutes off the old record from four years ago. Peter Hall was considered one of the finest and most consistent runners of this era, having many wins over different distances and surfaces. As well as winning the Ben Nevis Race four times in a row (1962 to 1965), he also won the Lake District Mountain Trial in 1963 and 1964, and came back to the Three Peaks for a 2nd place in 1965 and a 4th in 1967. He later turned professional.

The description of the race in Ron Hill's autobiography gives

---

19 40% of starters finishing is the lowest percentage ever for the race, lower than the 50% in the first event.

20 *The Long Hard Road – Part One: Nearly to the top*, Ron Hill Sports, 1981.

a good idea of racing at that time. Getting there just in time, he changed in a barn at the rear of the Hill Inn, into a red Spanish vest he had previously swopped at a race and strapped on a wrist compass he had bought to help him navigate. He takes up the story, after following others early on:

> Off the second peak, Pen-y-Ghent, in 8th position, I put my foot on what looked like a patch of green velvet moss and found my left leg buried in mud past my knee. I had a bit of difficulty getting my leg out, and when it did come out, there was no shoe on the end of it. I had to fish down in the black mire for the studded shoe, then found that neither shoe would stay on with all the suction from the muddy moorland. There was only one thing for it, bare feet: but anyone who has run on heather in wet, bare feet will vouch for the fact that it is a prickly, painful experience.

Losing sight of the runners in front, Hill put his studs back on for the limestone chipping farm tracks and gained some places to catch up to 4th-placed Colin Robinson going up Whernside. Hill continues:

> I wasn't interested in a fight for 4th place, so I let Colin go, stopped and had a drink and a wash in a beck. I just took pot luck on the route, largely guided by loud-speaker voices penetrating the mist below and to the left. Blessed relief, on to a tarmac road and the last smiling hill to the finish. Fourth. Where was Colin? He arrived 1.5 hours later in a car. In the mist he had gone down the ridge and ended up miles from the finish.

But these performances aren't the real story of this period. For that we need to look in more detail at **Dave Hodgson's** record at the Three Peaks Race. I recently spent a wonderful morning with him reliving his peak racing times and subsequent commitments to the sport, and this race in particular. Referring to his training diaries, Dave Hodgson recalled the nine years that he had top-10 finishes at the Three Peaks Race, as well as coming 2nd place a frustrating four times.

We have already heard his description of his Three Peaks Race in 1958, which was his first time at the event. The longest training run he had done prior to that was 13 miles over Ilkley

15. The Hill Inn start, 1964

Moor, eight days before the race. In the race Dave Hodgson had the lead at Ribblehead. He says he didn't know the route very well, but that the Clayton lads all did. He followed a group of Clayton runners off Ingleborough and on to Pen-y-Ghent, then he and George Brass pulled away. They had the fateful discussion about feeling tired and Dave chuckles, 'That was the last I saw of George'. Fourth was not bad at all, though, for a first attempt.

In 1959 he was 10th after being in the lead at the top of Ingleborough. He recalls vividly what happened next. 'The mist was really bad, and it is easy to go on a wrong bearing off the plateau. I went off on my own charging through the mist, coming out of which I saw Crina Bottom Farm, which is on the Ingleton side. I turned round and went back up to the top and got there the same time as the last runner. I got through to 10th place by the finish, but I reckon with the fitness I had by then it was one of the years I should have won it.' There is a theme running through our conversation about not ever having won this race that means so much to him.

The next three years were his other three 2nd-place finishes. His diary again tells the tale. In 1961 he notes: 'Second to Geoff Hodgson. Faded a bit on Whernside but was reasonably satisfied. Was in winning position at Ribblehead. If only I had been stronger.' The 1962 entry was short and to the point: 'Very tired on Whernside. A bit lucky to be second at the finish.'

The 1963 race was another that Dave looks back on, again thinking he should have won. He comments: '[Dennis] Hopkinson may have been a better cross-country runner than me, but he wasn't as good a fell runner. Conditions were very bad. I was reasonably satisfied and felt good on Whernside.' He laughs at the irony of this, as he *never* felt good by Whernside. His diary shows that he, 'did a recce 2 weeks beforehand. Went round in 3-30 on my own. Windy with snow on the tops. Very tired over last mile.' He says that recce is one of the reasons for what may seem to be under-performances in the race, adding, 'that is only 7 mins slower than my time in the race 2 weeks later. Ridiculous!'

Dave suggests that 1964 was also a year that he sometimes thinks he should have won, but tempers that thought when talking about it now. 'Actually no, Peter Hall was a better runner than me. He was a better climber than me normally, but I out-climbed him on Whernside that day, and dropped him. I was a better climber than descender. I did train to improve my descending. I feel I was a better descender than Peter Hall, but I think I ran out of steam on the descent. Just before the track to the finish at the Hill Inn, Peter appeared on my shoulder and I was amazed. On that last track he dropped me to win.' His diary notes: 'Probably my best race ever. Disappointed at not winning. Fairly pleased with my performance.' He then shares a bit of fairly harsh self-analysis: 'I think that was the trouble, I was too often pleased with finishing second.'

His diary entries summarise the next two years. 1965: 'Warm. Perfect weather. Very disappointed with 8th. Just died after Ribblehead.' 1966: 'Reasonably satisfied considering shortage of distance running in training.' His diary shows a 20-mile run in

16. *The top three in 1964. L to R: Dave Hodgson, Peter Hall, Mike Davies*

17. *Second man, Dave Hodgson, with sons Michael and Ian, 1964*

the build-up, but which Dave had to turn back on halfway.

In one of the several videos about the Three Peaks Race, Dave Hodgson comments that, 'Some say that it is like running three fell races with two cross-country races in between, and I know what they mean by that.' Dave Hodgson never did win the Three Peaks Race. A look at his training and preparation may give further clues to his performances in this period and help explain that annoying fact.

Chapter 6

DAVE HODGSON

Dave Hodgson gave huge amounts of his time to his own running, and later to various administrative roles in the sport. Earlier though, neither of his parents encouraged his interest in sport. He recalls his early life and his own interest in sport. 'My father was interested in boxing, and to be fair he taught me the value of a straight left. I went to Scarborough High School for Boys and was there in the war years, so sport was very restricted. At the end of the war, they organised a school cross-country, actually more of a road race, and I finished 3rd. The winner was a friend called Alan Beagent, and we found out that the school was entering a team in the North Riding Schools cross-country champs. We decided we would do a bit of training for it. We used to meet before school on a couple of days a week and do a 20-minute run. In the champs Alan won and I came 2nd, possibly because no one else had done any training.'

A year later someone came up with the idea of starting an athletic club, and Dave and Alan joined the fledgling Scarborough and District AC. 'We had a team in the Yorkshire Champs, in Graves Park (Sheffield), and I was in the Junior category. We got the train there, went for a fish and chip lunch, and Alan finished 4th and I finished 6th. We both spewed up afterwards.' From then on Dave was a cross-country runner in winter and in summer he did track, going to the local grass track meetings.

After leaving school and doing National Service, Dave Hodgson worked for Yorkshire Bank. Banks were open Saturday mornings, closing at 12.30, so getting to meetings in and around Leeds could be a problem. 'I was more a cross-country runner than anything else. The important events were the Leeds and District Champs and the Yorkshire Champs. Rotherham and Sheffield were the top cross-country clubs in the country at that time. I ran two or three times at the National Cross Country

Champs, once in Graves Park and just got in the top 100. I ran best on a muddy course or when the weather was bloody awful. I had some great battles with Pete Watson at this time.'

Harden Moss was a sheepdog trial that had a short fell race, which Dave won in 1954 and 1955. He adds, 'In the summer I used to do mile handicaps and 2-mile team races on the track. I had one very good year when I won a lot of prizes. Bear in mind the top prize might be seven guineas.[21] But I accumulated a lot of clocks and canteens of cutlery as well.'

Dave adds that he thinks, 'in those days the only two fell races (around here) that were under AAAs Laws were Burnsall and Harden Moss. Kilnsey was a pro race and occasionally some of the Bingley lads used to run at Kilnsey under assumed names. I never did, because the sanctions for running in a race not under AAAs Laws were quite vicious. You might get away with it once, but if you did it again you would be banned from representing your club.'

Dave found out about the Three Peaks Race through Harry Croft, who was from Leeds St Marks AC. Croft knew that Dave was interested, having done a lot of fell walking. 'He knew I was running at Burnsall and Harden Moss. Harry Croft was close to the Northern Counties AAAs and he must have told me about it.'

On hearing about the race, Dave walked the Three Peaks for the first time with a couple of friends from Leeds St Marks AC. 'None of us had cars so we had to get a bus from Leeds to Skipton, change to a bus to Ingleton and we walked the Peaks from there, which is not a good starting point. We set off from our B&B at about 7am on Sunday with the intention of getting back to Ingleton for the last bus, but it took us a long time and we missed it. That was a couple of years before I ran the race in 1958.'

Dave then launches into a discourse on why he thought he should be winning the Three Peaks, by comparing himself with rivals, and also offers more thoughts on why he did *not* win. 'The year before I did my first Three Peaks there had been an athletic

---

21 Converted to today's values this would be worth around £200, so a significant amount for prize money then.

18. Dave Hodgson winning the Burnsall Classic in 1958

match which was Leeds and District against Northwest Lancs. I did the mile and George Brass was running for Lancs and he was nowhere near me, and he never beat me at cross-country. I also used to run against Geoff Hodgson a lot, and he never beat me on the track or at a short fell race. But he did marathons too and had more endurance than me, and regularly beat me towards the end of the Three Peaks.'

He then illustrates his training and racing regime, admitting it wasn't particularly sensible. 'In general, my routine was to do the Leeds and District cross-country in early March, then step up my mileage to 60 miles a week before the Three Peaks. The Burnsall race is in August. I liked it because it was the first fell race I did and was reasonably close to Leeds. They gave me an award for running it 40 times. After each Three Peaks I would have a couple of months where I just ran but didn't train seriously and didn't race till Burnsall.'

One year his diary shows that he did 51 miles in the week before the Three Peaks. 'I always went round the Three Peaks a couple of weeks beforehand and it didn't really give me enough time to recover. I wouldn't dream of doing that now. I didn't have a coach and frankly I thought I knew it all, and I didn't. For ages I had a scorn of coaches. But I lacked a bit of advice.' Dave admitted that his favourite training ground was up and down the Chevin. Sessions like 10 x 100m up the Chevin. Then comes something he mentions more than once, including in his diary, and that was his pre-race nutrition strategy. 'I got this idea that I had to be like a boxer. They ate steak before a fight. For several years I used to get Shirley up at the crack of dawn, so she could be doing me steak for breakfast. I am sure it was why I ran out of steam on Whernside so often. If I had had my porridge, which I normally had, it would have been a lot better preparation.'

Dave never thought of himself as a brilliant navigator. But on one occasion local knowledge around the route choices paid off for him. 'It was the year when I came 3rd [1963]. I was 13th at Horton-in-Ribblesdale because I had gone adrift between Ingleborough and Horton and lost a lot of places. I never saw anybody from Horton to Ribblehead, but when I got there, I was somehow in 3rd place. I had picked up 10 places without seeing anyone. We used to go over Black Dub Moss. The route from Pen-y-Ghent went over Black Dub Moss as it was the most direct route. I knew it well, like which bit of the stone wall to climb. I knew the way to Nether Lodge. It was misty but I must have found my way well over that section of the race.'

Dave Hodgson listed what he thought were the two performance highlights from the Three Peaks Race. 'First, I was most impressed by Anna Pichrtova (in 2008) because although we marked the course as it was World Trial that year she came over and ran it on sight in a new record. Victoria Wilkinson later beat that record, but she spent a lot of time reccying that course and she had all her breakdown times by timing herself over all the sections. She knew just what she had to do to beat that record. Secondly, I have to mention Jeff Norman's course record

19. Dave and Shirley Hodgson, 2022

(in 1974). I never knew Jeff that well, but he was a top athlete doing the Olympics as well. Jeff brought the record down in big chunks, which was tremendous.'

Dave Hodgson finishes this part of our chat with an explanation of how his 21st Three Peaks came about. 'I think I was chairman at the time. George Brass was on the committee as well. George suggested that we should give a special trophy to anyone that had finished the race 21 times, because the Ben Nevis race did that.' The first year they were presented was in 1988, and recipients that year were (with number of years in brackets): Alan Heaton (31), George Brass (25), Stan Bradshaw (23), Alistair Patten (22), Dave Scott (21) and Clifford Huck (21). Alan Heaton had only *not* run in four of the races between 1954 and 1988.

Dave adds: 'I looked up my records and found I had done the Three Peaks 16 times. I thought I had better do another five. So, I started doing it again. I did my last (and 21st) one in 1993 at 61. I had no problem meeting cut-off times. I had won the FRA v60 championships. Looking back, I hadn't done much racing in my 50s. I probably did more races in my 60s than I did in my 20s and 30s.' So, a long and successful career of racing at the Three Peaks, but you can tell that it still rankles with Dave that he didn't manage to win the race that he had put so much of himself into.[22]

---

22 Sadly, Dave Hodgson died during the preparation of this book, on 10 April 2023 at age 91.

20. Dave Hodgson after finishing, 1990

Chapter 7

FOUR IN A ROW

Mike Davies was something of an outlier in the fell scene, as he was a member of Reading AC and taught at a school in the flatlands of the south of England. Bill Smith described him as 'one of the most revered athletes in the history of amateur fell racing and one of the very few not born and bred in the North'. Dave Hodgson adds that, 'some of the regulars thought Mike Davies coming up from Surrey to recce the course was giving him an advantage but that is silly.'

Having been in contention throughout the 1964 Three Peaks Race and having finished 3rd that year (within the previous fastest time), Mike Davies proceeded to go on a winning spree and dominated proceedings for the next four years.

Davies loved the Three Peaks and trained on those hills whenever he could. His regular training routine included going up to the Yorkshire Dales during his Easter vacation and staying at a youth hostel. His specific race training involved starting at Ribblehead to do a full round of the Three Peaks, then climbing Whernside for the second time, to finish at the Hill Inn. Describing his own training he said that he used to train in heavy boots to make up for the lack of nearby hills where he lived. His training intensified when school was out in the summer, and he used to do twice-daily sessions on the South Downs.

Mike Davies competed in the Three Peaks Race 12 times, winning four times and finishing 3rd twice. His last race there was in 1977 when he recorded a time of 3-12.

1965

The first of his four wins was 1965, on a hot and sunny day, when he took exactly six minutes off Peter Hall's record from the year before. Davies had left Hall in his wake on the ascent of Whernside and stretched his winning lead to nearly eight

21. *Mike Davies at the Hill Inn*

minutes, finishing in 2-47-00. Finishing 3rd was Derek Lawson, and 4th was another southerner, Chris Fitt (from Mitcham AC), as a healthy 97 of 115 starters finished.

Mike Davies wrote a long report, very lyrical in parts, on the race which appeared in *The Fellrunner* to celebrate 30 years of the Fell Runners Association. Dave Hodgson declared it to be, 'a masterpiece of mountain running literature.' Two short extracts give a feel for the occasion and the course conditions of the time. First this, about the start:

> At the gun I sprint for the top of the slope only to find Peter Hall and David Spencer already ahead of me through the gate. I settle for third berth as far as the limestone crags, once across that we become a quintet as Dave Hodgson and Derek Lawson join us. Peter leads us across the dry tussocky grass. Crossing the long wall beyond Wife Hole, Dave veers off to the right whilst the four of us spearhead the main field in a direct line for Swine Tail. The gradient is easy, but the long tussocky moorland makes it heavy work. Peter and David alternate in the lead. I hold them despite walking the steeper inclines. We negotiate the network of gullies forming Humphrey Bottom and turn towards the base of Ingleborough.

Then his thoughts on the final run-in to the Hill Inn:

I'm glad there is no late challenge as my legs feel so weary. Stepping on to the final roadway is like a sailor coming ashore – I'm all at sea, and the dreaded cattle grids require every ounce of concentration. At the second one a spectator calls, 'One forty-three and … record'. What is he on about? I had forgotten all about time, since 10.59am. A walker opens the next gate. Violent cramp contorts both calves. Oh no! Not now. Don't stop. I urge myself on. The spasms ease and I gather for the final drive slightly uphill. Phew. The bumpy field has me all over the place! Done it. I am thrilled; incredulous of the record time but mainly pleased to have got round the course. It has been quite a battle. And on such a lovely sunny day.[23]

1966

The weather was completely different in 1966, with heavy cloud shrouding the peaks. The same two southerners led the way on to Pen-y-Ghent, and Mike Davies led Chris Fitt by a minute over a snow-covered Whernside summit. The distance apart stayed the same on the descent and Davies won in 2-53-22, with Fitt finishing in 2-56-03. In 4th place was Bill Wade, who later was to become an active committee member for the Three Peaks Race Association.

1967

The same two athletes again dominated the 1967 race, although Davies was in control throughout, having taken the lead over Ingleborough. He finished in 2-47-19, just missing his own record. Fitt was challenged by Pete Watson and Pete Hall for a while, but held them off to finish 2nd with a couple of minutes to spare. His effort took him to within a minute of Davies by the Hill Inn.

1968

In 1968 Mike Davies was full of confidence and decided to front-run the race. He was tracked by Ricky Wilde up until

---

23 'Three Peaks. The 1965 Race – as one competitor remembers it', October 2000 *Fellrunner*. It was actually a reprint of a previously unattributed article which had first been published in the spring 1972 issue.

22. *Dave Hodgson at Ribblehead in 1966*

23. *L to R: Jeff Norman, Mike Davies and Pete Watson, 1968*

Ribblehead but, on the ascent of Whernside, Davies proved to be much stronger, taking four and a half minutes out of Wilde as he began to suffer. Davies came home strongly to set a spectacular new course record of 2-40-34. Three other runners were able to overtake Wilde who struggled home in 5th place, behind Pete Watson (who also came in inside the old record), Jeff Norman and Colin Robinson. We will hear more of the latter two in the next chapter.

Ricky Wilde was something of an enigma, admitting to being a lazy runner and not always running to his full potential at some races. In a profile in *Stud Marks* he tells the story of his introduction to fell racing, which was at the Three Peaks the year before (1967):

> I had no particular ambition to do a fell race. It was just a natural step, having already taken part in track, road and cross-country races. Quite a few members of my club, Manchester and District Lads Club Harriers, used to tackle the Peaks, mainly as a training run. I can't remember where I finished, but I think my time was around 3 hours 20 minutes. It was misty and I got lost coming off Ingleborough, the first peak in those days. I worked my way back through the field to some extent but was shattered on the last climb up Whernside.

As noted above, Wilde was back to run the Peaks again in 1968, but with no more specific training. Wilde commented that he had 'chased Mike Davies all the way, but was stopped in my tracks at Winterscale and crawled up Whernside', thus dropping to 5th place. 'Again, I fell apart,' he concluded.

Wilde ended up doing a good number of fell races and left his mark on the sport. Two particular races from 1977 stand out from his *palmarès*. In July he rocked up at the second ever Snowdon race and won in 1-06-07, nearly six minutes faster than the winner the year before. Wilde, who was a renowned descender, started steadily and was up to 2nd place by halfway up the mountain. He caught the leader, Dave Francis, further up and led to the summit. Despite falling on the descent, he won by over a minute from a fast-finishing Jeff Norman.

Later that year Wilde ran in the inaugural Lantern Pike fell race, which is more of a severe cross-country event. In fine weather Wilde triumphed in 29-12, saying he 'ran hard all the way', finishing a minute and a half ahead of Jeff Norman. Wilde's record time that day has not been beaten since.

Just after those two Three Peaks races (in 1970) Wilde had a tremendous season and placed 6th in both the National and the International Cross-Country races, the two biggest races in the cross-country calendar at that time. That winter he also broke the world record for 3000m indoors (with 7:47.0), when winning the European title, having already won the UK title. He also won a marathon in the USA in 1979 in 2-14-44. This was Grandma's Marathon, in Minnesota. He went back the next year and ran three seconds faster, this time finishing 4th.

Ricky Wilde ran in a very different era to that of today. Rather than huge sums of money, a typical prize would be a tea set. On one occasion, having won a race overseas, he was presented with a shotgun which he brought home on the plane.

In addition to his Three Peaks exploits, race winner Mike Davies also had good results in many other events. He won the Ben Nevis race, the Lakeland Mountain Trial three times, and absolutely loved travelling to races, often taking in classic races in Scotland. Davies thought nothing of driving up overnight on a Friday to run a race on Saturday, sleeping in the car after a full week's work. He was also involved in the setting up of the Fell Runners Association (FRA) in 1970, was the first Editor of the FRA magazine, and devised the original FRA's 'Fell Runner of the Year' scheme in 1972.

Although he disappeared from the running scene in later life, his obituary commented that Mike Davies, 'will be remembered as a modest winner, courteous in defeat and a true gentleman of the sport'.[24]

---

24 *Mike Davies 1933–2012*, Dave Hodgson, spring 2013 *Fellrunner*.

Chapter 8

REFLECTIONS
FROM DAVE SCOTT

Dave Scott has had a love affair with the Three Peaks Race. He holds the record for the most appearances at the Three Peaks Race, having completed the race an awesome total of 48 times, after first competing in 1965.

He was born in Burnley in 1943 and joined his local running club, Clayton-le-Moors, in 1959 at the age of 16, after running well at school. He had run for the Lancashire Schools team and won various local Youth Club races in the Burnley area. He was encouraged by Stan Bradshaw, who was the president of the club and, according to Dave, a true legend. 'He noticed that I had won a couple of local races. I call it headhunting!' Dave recalled to me recently that Stan Bradshaw had called and talked to his mother, at their shop in the centre of Burnley, about him joining Clayton. 'Two weeks later he called again to talk to her and that evening she asked me why I had not joined. I said that I only had 5/- (25p) pocket money a week and couldn't afford the bus fares. She said that she would pay them, so the next Saturday I caught the bus to Padiham, where I waited on the town hall steps to be picked up by Stan in his red Volvo to go to the club run. These were held from working men's clubs in the local area, three of them in Clayton.'

Dave had loved running since he was a small boy when he used to run everywhere. 'I think that I started training for the Burnley Grammar School sports day when I was 14. Even now I still enjoy training and racing. If it is a running day I go whatever the weather, although since retiring I might delay by an hour or two if it is supposed to stop raining!' He also reveals that in 1985, along with Eric Birtwistle, he decided to see if they could run every day for a year. They did, and he continued for five

24. *Dave Scott at Little Dale Beck crossing in the 1997 race*

years twenty-nine days until a badly twisted ankle forced him to have a break.

When he first joined Clayton, Dave Scott looked in awe at Alan Heaton, George Brass, Stan Bradshaw and Alistair Patten, who had all run the Three Peaks. 'George Brass had actually won it twice. I thought when I was old enough (you had to be 21 then) that I'd like to have a go at the race. I was away at college when I was 21 so had to wait until 1965 when I was 22. What a baptism of fire that proved to be! No advice, no long training runs, no support, no food, no drink. It is little wonder that I bonked and had a lie down on Whernside for about 20 minutes before I managed to continue to the top, with some nuts and raisins from the Mountain Rescue guys. They had approached me, asking if I had seen a body lying down nearby which they had been watching through their binoculars! I walked to the summit and jogged on. The following year I went on a mountaineering course in North Wales, little knowing what a huge influence the race would have on my life over the next 50 years, so it was 1967 before my next race. Not surprisingly I knocked 58 minutes off my time!'

Having run his first Three Peaks in 1965, Dave Scott proceeded from 1967 onwards to compete in 49 consecutive races. The second time he just wanted to do a better time. 'People asked if I might do it again and I said yeh. Little did I know! I didn't realise after I had done quite a lot how many it had been. Then George Brass said to me that I was one of only six who have run it 21 times. He said there will be a second presentation after the race for you, me and the rest of us.'

Dave has a good recall of his Three Peaks experiences and proceeds to tell me some of the highlights. 'My best time was 2 hours 59 minutes in 1974. One year Clayton finished 3rd team. The prize was a toast rack. I ran once the week after running the London Marathon. My legs were not good that day. I just ran to finish. I was ill in 1994 during the race. It was diarrhoea and I had to go to the loo at Stainforth on way to the race start. Looking back to 1965, I doubt that I ever imagined the part the Three Peaks Race would play in my life.'

In the years Dave Scott has run the weather has varied from blizzards, hailstones, torrential rain, and thick mist to blazing sun. He recalls 1978 for me. 'In really bad weather, Ted Pepper died on Ingleborough getting lost in the mist, and leaving the summit in the wrong direction. This resulted in the tapes that now lie along the plateau to the checkpoint. In the bad weather I always used to run down the line of upcoming runners.'

Dave reflects on changing times. 'Because of the weather, the underfoot conditions, changes to the course, new paths, boards and paving stones, it is difficult to compare times. There have been at least seven course changes whilst I've been taking part. The route from Pen-y-Ghent to Ribblehead is now defined, but originally there were numerous options. Some were better than others, so going for a recce was key then.'

Reflecting now on the range of weather conditions he has run the race in, Dave Scott notes now: 'I remember discovering that hailstones hurt at 2,000 feet when you have less hair.'

Dave is rightly proud of the achievements of his Clayton clubmates and noted the club's leading times in an article on the club website (in 2022). 'The men who have finished in under 3 hours are: Andy Churchill 2-50-02, Clifford Waddington 2-56-02, Keith Windle 2-59-14, David Scott 2-59-48 and now after a gap of over 30 years, Chris Holdsworth 2-54-49.'

Dave also provides statistics on the club's winners of the race. Over the years four Clayton men have won the race: George Brass 1955, and 1958; Peter Dugdale 1957; Dennis Hopkinson 1963; and David Walker 2003. Four ladies have also won the race: the phenomenal Vanessa Peacock 1985, 1987, 1988 and 1989, Ruth Pickvance 1990, Jean Rawlinson 1995 and Beverley Whitfield 2003.

Away from the Three Peaks Race, Dave Scott also has some impressive achievements. 'We were the first club to run a relay on The Pennine Way in 1970, and whenever I look at the photo of the 24 of us on the green at Kirk Yetholm it brings back many memories of that weekend. In later years I've been a member of Clayton teams in the British Vets Road and Cross Country Relays, at which we've won gold, silver and bronze medals with some super performances.'

He says his best achievement was doing the Bob Graham in 1972. Also doing the Welsh 3,000-footers with Alan Heaton and John Haworth. 'I was the least experienced of the three, and it was the only time I ever saw a Brocken spectre going along Crib Goch.'

Dave also set himself some personal targets when he reached 40, all of which he achieved. 'These included running from John o' Groats to Land's End in 20 days – not consecutively I might add – and then the following year cycling the other way in two periods of five days; climbing all the Wainwright Peaks in the Lake District; and running the Pennine Way in six days.'

Unbeknown to him, his daughter (who lives in Denver, Colorado) organised a new 'David Scott Trophy' in the form of a glass decanter to be presented to the oldest finisher on the day, male or female. 'In 2015 I was very proud to be its first recipient and four years later was equally proud to present it to Wendy Dodds, as the oldest finisher that year.' He relives that first occasion for me. 'On the 69 years and 364th day of my life I ran the Three Peaks. So, to run as a 70-year-old I had to run it again the next year. My daughter secretly decided her elderly dad should have been recognised with a prize. When I finished, I was hurriedly taken into the marquee and my wife was up on the stage. What is she doing, I thought? She announced I was to be the first winner of the David Scott Trophy. I have presented the trophy once or twice and I did it once for your clubmate, John Owen (from Barnet and District AC). A lovely guy.'

Unfortunately, Dave was timed out in 2016. 'The gate at the bottom of Whernside was frozen and they couldn't get it open. I had to queue for ten minutes. The weather was lousy. I realised going up Whernside that I wasn't going to get the cut-off time. If it had been better weather, I would probably have carried on as it was my 50th. But I didn't want to go against the rules. So I ran 50 times altogether, but sadly was timed out on my 50th.'

Dave Scott said in 2017: 'It was the first time for 50 years that I hadn't stood on the start line feeling nervous and apprehensive. However, it was really interesting to watch the race for a change, especially the section from the bottom of Pen-y-Gent to Ribblehead AND I actually saw the winner finish!' He adds now, 'I love the Three Peaks, it was the pinnacle of fell running at that time, and for many people it still is. It is a challenge for anyone. Of course, you had more route choice in the early days. No boards in the boggy section, no flag stones to go up any of the hills.'

Chapter 9

LANCASHIRE RIVALS

1969

Two runners from Lancashire dominated the next seven races, between 1969 and 1975, having classic battles against each other on three occasions. In 1969, Rochdale Harriers' Colin Robinson came out on top after a race-long battle with Altrincham and District AC's Jeff Norman. They came to the summit of Whernside together, one minute ahead of the previous year's winner, Mike Davies, and Pete Watson. Robinson showed his strength by getting away on the last descent to beat Norman by 13 seconds (the tightest finish thus far) with a winning time of 2-44-44, also leading Rochdale to the team prize.

In an entertaining report on this race in the Clayton-le-Moors newsletter, Dave Scott describes his shoe dilemma: ripples or studs? He also notes that he decided to wear, 'two vests and a t-shirt, a good idea for most of the race but hail stones still hurt at 2,000 feet.' He collected (from friends *en route*) a drink and fruit pastilles and Dextrosol, his method that day for avoiding dehydration and the dreaded 'bonk'. He suffered severe post-race stiffness from the cramp he experienced in the latter stages of the race, which only cleared by the Wednesday afternoon afterwards. He decided that he would take salt tablets next year.

Colin Robinson and Jeff Norman had a strong, yet friendly, rivalry on the fells for a number of years, with two further tussles to come at the Three Peaks. Looking back on that 2nd place in 1969, Jeff Norman recently said, 'I remember it well, because I thought I'd got away from him. We were on the descent, but he had a few yards to catch on me. He then passed me and tore away from me to the finish. I was never any good at the finish. I thought by then [*having already run the race four times*] that it was winnable if I only got it right.'

Colin Robinson is hailed by his club (Rochdale Harriers) as

25. *The 1969 podium. L to R: Jeff Norman, Colin Robinson, Mike Davies*

the greatest athlete ever to run for them, winning many races and helping the club to win multiple championships. Colin joined Rochdale Harriers as a teenager in 1956 and became the club's cross-country secretary whilst still a teenager in 1959, a job that remarkably he held for over 60 years. In 1961, he won the Junior (U23) title at the National Cross Country Championships, which was held at the 'home of cross-country', Parliament Hill (London). He next won the Junior International title (a precursor to the World Cross Country Championship) at Nantes in France, also in 1961. In addition to his own win, he led England to the team gold.

We have already seen that Colin ran in the Three Peaks Race in 1963. He says it just seemed a good idea at the time. 'It was a club decision to take part, as no one had competed in it before. In fact, no one had visited that part of Yorkshire. Joe Salt, Alan Hughes, Roger Carter and I decided to give it a go. As we stood in the start field, we didn't know which direction to face, and the mist was right down. I had to follow other runners, one being Alan Heaton, who had a map and compass. Fell running was all new to me. I did finish 5th though.'

Fell running was opening up by the end of the 1960s as more races were introduced, particularly in Colin's local area. At that time, he was competing on track, cross-country, road and fell. Then he came back to the Three Peaks for the 1969 race. He says now that looking back it was an interesting lead up to the race, as the following breakdown to the week shows:

Sun April 20:	won the Keswick Round the Houses race in a new record time of 21 minutes 33 seconds. It was approximately 4 miles.
Mon 21:	ran 10 miles doing laps of the local golf course.
Tue 22:	club night at Springfield Park. Did two sets of 6 x 400 on the track again covering 10 miles.
Wed 23:	did a steady 10-mile road run.
Thu 24:	travelled to Cambridge. Represented the AAAs against Cambridge University and Middlesex. Was 2nd in the 5000 metres to John Thresher in 14mins 23.4. Six miles in total.
Fri 25:	2 Laps of local golf course 5 miles.
Sat 26.	Local road circuit 5 miles very wet.
Sun 27:	Three Peaks 1st in 2.44.44. Rochdale were first team with 1st, 5th and 9th.

Colin adds that it must have been bad weather as he ran in a long-sleeved shirt but didn't carry anything else. 'I can't remember much of race. As we approached Whernside Jeff Norman, me and Pete Watson had pulled away. At the top there was just Jeff and me. We descended together in hailstones, and I got away from him along the track to the finish.'

Racing and training were not always as hectic as that period illustrated above, as Colin explains. 'I averaged 40 to 60 miles per week in training. The most I ever did was 80 miles when unemployed. Fell training was done in the weekly long run around Ashworth Valley and Knowl Hill in my local area. Some steep descents in the Valley and a highest point of 1500 feet.' He adds that he could both climb and descend reasonably well, but that his navigation was not brilliant, despite doing some basic orienteering events for practice. As to Dave Scott's shoe quandary, Colin's answer was: 'Shoes for the fells were Reebok studs. Geoff Foster of Reebok was just down the road from me at Bury and I used to visit his factory.'

Colin Robinson didn't run in the 1970 Three Peaks Race as he was injured. Despite coming 2nd to Jeff Norman both times, Colin says that he can't recall any details of the 1971 and '72 races, which are described in the next chapter.

Colin has been an exemplary club member, serving in an official capacity (including being club president), but also offering to athletes of all abilities his wisdom gained over the years, and he has encouraged everyone from beginners to international athletes. He was present at the setting up of the Fell Runners Association in 1970 and was FRA member number 12. Interestingly, he concluded our discussion by saying that he 'did enjoy winning the Three Peaks, but consider my best fell result to be coming 3rd at Langdale in 1973'.

At the 2019 race, to mark the 50th anniversary of his victory, Colin Robinson and wife Brenda (who was 4th in the first ladies race in 1979 forty years previously) were invited to present the prizes. A nice touch from the organisers.

1970

For the 1970 race there was snow on all three of the summits. Jeff Norman was alongside Trevor Proctor on Ingleborough, with guides racer Fred Reeves and Steve Edmunds just behind. Steps had to be kicked in the steep snow on the slopes ascending Pen-y-Ghent, approached via the intakes from Horton. Norman was the first to scramble up between the summit crags, with a one-minute lead over Proctor, with Pete Watson now 3rd. Norman was running in road shoes, which was giving him

26. *Jeff Norman, 1970*

some problems on both snowy and boggy terrain. But Norman ascended Whernside well, and went on to win in 2-48-11, from Pete Watson (2-53-41), with Proctor 3rd.

Jeff Norman explained the shoe situation recently, referring to a long feedback report for himself that he wrote after each Three Peaks Race he competed in. 'Yes, I was running in road shoes on a snowy course [Tiger Cubs, which he had used in every Three Peaks Race so far]. It is just that I didn't have fell shoes then. I changed to fell shoes in later races there.' Checking that report again, he notes that he got it wrong coming off Ingleborough. He went through Horton in 3rd place, with Trevor Proctor leading. 'By the top of Pen-y-Ghent I had a lead but was taking it cautiously in my racing flats. Pete Watson caught me later on, but I started to get away on Whernside.'

27. *Jeff Norman takes the win in 1971*

Chapter 10

NORMAN CONQUESTS

The early 1970s were a real purple patch for Jeff Norman. He won the British Fell Running Championships in 1974, and for six years in a row (1970–75) won the Three Peaks Race, setting new records in four of those wins. Writing about Jeff Norman in *The Dalesman* magazine, Bill Smith called him 'King of the Peaks'.[25]

1971

In fine weather in 1971 Jeff Norman had a fantastic battle with Colin Robinson. Going through Ribblehead together, Norman pulled away going up Whernside to give himself a one-minute lead at the summit. He extended this on the descent to win by just over three minutes. Norman's 2-36-26 took more than four

---

25 'Runners on the Three Peaks', pp966-968 *The Dalesman*, March 1976

minutes off Mike Davies's record from 1968. Colin Robinson was 2nd in 2-39-32 (also inside the previous record), with Harry Walker 3rd in 2-44-15. Harry Walker had entered the Three Peaks Race for the first time that year, when he was just 22. 'I was ready for it,' Walker says, 'as I had trained for six weeks specifically for it. I used to run from Colne to Pendle on a Sunday and sometimes on a Monday too.'

Jeff Norman recently re-lived that race for me. 'I was level with Harry Walker going up Ingleborough. Another runner caught me coming off Ingleborough and we ran together into Horton. Then Colin Robinson joined us. I got away from Colin over the top [*of Pen-y-Ghent*] and then he came back at me. I didn't find the best route across the bog, but Colin followed me. Coming to the bottom of Whernside I had a 50-yard lead, which was quickly turned into a 10-yard deficit. But I was feeling strong so not worried and went away after that to take the win.'

1972

Bill Smith briefly tells the story of the 1972 race in *Stud Marks on the Summits*:

> The first three positions in the race were the same as in 1971, though the weather was quite different, with rain, sleet and low cloud to harass competitors. Jeff Norman led through Horton, Pen-y-Ghent and Whernside checkpoints and cruised home an easy winner in 2-36-27, missing his record by a mere second. The next arrivals were Colin Robinson 2nd: 2-45-00, and Harry Walker 3rd: 2-50-38.

Harry Walker was 2nd in the British Fell Champs that year, then won it in 1973. He recalls that he had got married on a Monday and went to the Lakes on his honeymoon. 'We came back, and I had my first win in the Pendle on the next Saturday. A couple of weeks later it was the Three Peaks Race. It was hard, as I got cramp at the bottom of Whernside, chasing Jeff Norman.'

Consulting his diary, Jeff Norman explained that he suffered from cramps that day too. 'I had a slow start and worked my way through to 7th at the bottom of the climb [Ingleborough]. Harry

28. Jeff Norman leads Harry Walker

was leading at the top along with Dave Cannon. Colin Robinson caught us on the descent. I started to get a gap going up Pen-y-Ghent. I had a six mins lead by Ribblehead. But I started to get twingeing pain in my legs every now and again, and cramp on the road section, so was nursing my legs a lot. I reckoned afterwards that I could have run two minutes faster without the leg issues. It was an event I looked forward to every year. I had a better run-up to the race that year, as I had started marathon training by then.' Apparently, he was heard beforehand to say that he was determined to win that day.

1973

The weather for the 1973 race was cool, clear and sunny. Reckoned to be ideal for a new record and Jeff Norman duly reduced it by over four minutes. Norman took the lead going up Ingleborough, and then gradually pulled away as the race went on, despite a tumble coming off Pen-y-Ghent. He beat Harry Walker by over seven minutes, with Joss Naylor coming home next. In his report Bill Smith comments that, 'Surprise of the day was the 3rd position attained by Joss Naylor, who sliced

29. *Jeff Norman approaching Ribblehead, 1973*

14m 15s off his previous best time in 1971 and moved up 11 places as well. Possibly Joss has always found the Peaks course a little too smooth and fast by comparison with the more rugged terrain over which he excels.' It turned out to be a race that Joss Naylor never managed to win, despite his dominance over similar distance races at this time. Commenting on being beaten by Jeff Norman again, Harry Walker reckons Jeff was always a better runner than him.

Joss Naylor recently recounted how that day had gone for him, explaining it really wasn't his type of course. 'Aye, I had a good run that year and all seemed to click in the race. I had managed a couple of long fast runs at home, and I was with the leading runners over the tops, especially on the climbs but they got away from me coming off the last top. I tried to pull them back on the downhill and if there had been a bit more climbing, I might have caught them. But it was a good run for me over a course that really was not my type of ground.'

Jeff Norman reckons he had a good run-up to the race and felt very confident. Conditions were perfect, with no wind on the day and no rain for a week, and the course the driest anyone could remember. Jeff described it as warm but not too warm. 'I went to the front early on with Harry Walker and Alan Spence for company. I had a small lead at the first summit but allowed Harry to get back to me. I opened a gap on the descent, and that was the last I saw of anybody. I had got my route over the bog sorted now.' Overlooking his diary, I note that he did 81 miles in the week of the race, and 71 miles in the following week, so was training and racing hard.

1974

The Fellrunner reported the next year's momentous race result in its November 1974 edition, with Jeff Norman achieving his fifth straight win and a fabulous new record time, in a field of 251 runners. Reporter Bill Smith wouldn't have known then that this time would never be bettered, due to the course start moving to Horton the following year:

> Jeff Norman made Yorkshire Three Peaks history in this race by at last breaking the two and a half hour barrier, despite the poor conditions resulting from rain and sleet, high winds and low cloud. Harry Walker was disappointed to only finish second again and promises Jeff stiffer competition next year. The two reached Pen-y-Ghent summit together, along with Martin Weeks, and Harry was leading on the descent but had a nasty fall on the way down. Jeff had a two-minute lead at Ribblehead which he increased to six minutes at the finish. Meanwhile, Weeks was maintaining a strong challenge for second place, but Walker finally shook him off over the last section from Whernside to the Hill Inn.

Harry Walker was climbing really well that year, when the last race from the Hill Inn was run. He caught Jeff Norman up

Programme and Marking Sheet 10p
All proceeds to the Three Peaks Race Association

11am Sunday 28 April 1974
Start and finish at
Hill Inn Chapel-le-Dale Ingleton Yorks.

Daily Mirror SPONSORED

THREE PEAKS RACE

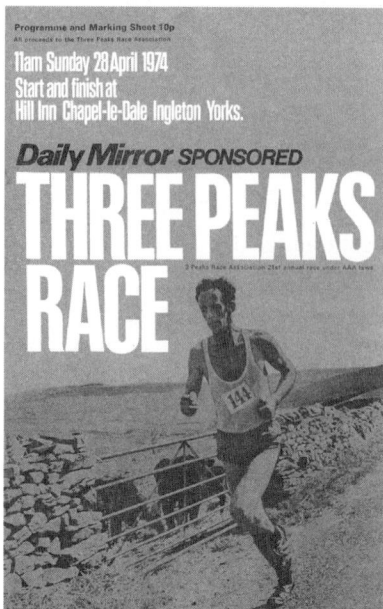

30. Joss Naylor on the race programme cover, 1974

on the buttresses going up Pen-y-Ghent and was right behind him on the track going down. 'Then I fell, and got up and thought I'd better get after him. Martin Weeks came past me just before Ribblehead, but I got back to 2nd. I was bruised from the fall, but it is all part of the game, isn't it? I don't think I would have beaten Jeff, but I would have been closer to him. Would that record have stood the test of time if the course hadn't changed? I wonder.'

Martin Weeks was a runner on the rise in 1974, and he went on to win the British Fell Championships in 1976, which was a great season for him. He had entered the Three Peaks in 1972, having joined Bingley Harriers. He finished 34th and said shortly afterwards that it was probably one of the best races he had run, at the time. Weeks finished 6th in the Three Peaks in 1976, but never managed to win the race, having a best of 2nd place in 1978.

It was interesting to hear Jeff Norman as he reflected back on his brilliant time that year, which is the fastest that any of the versions of the course has been covered. Intriguingly he states that his preparation for the race was the worst he had ever had. He had a trawl through his own race feedback and expanded on the event from that. 'I had had a fall whilst training so missed plenty of days. I had a sore throat and felt rough on the day, with some sort of cough as well. I didn't feel too bad once we started and found myself in the lead on Ingleborough. Mike Short came up to me for a while and then took the lead. I was feeling easy as we went along and opened a gap on the descent. Running strongly but relaxed, I felt great. I was well rested up [*laughs*] due to missed training. I did have a moment of worry approaching Horton as there was suddenly hail and strong winds. My thighs became very cold. Going up Pen-y-Ghent my climbing muscles seemed too cold to work well. Harry closed on me and caught me on the summit. I was more a descender than an ascender. As soon as we got over the top, I took him back and started to stretch out. The bog was exceptionally dry. I felt great along the road. Relaxing up the steep part of Whernside, I then started to tire towards the top. Eased off coming down to make sure I didn't fall.'

1975

After 21 years the race was first run over the new course, starting at Horton-in-Ribblesdale, in 1975. The new course added an extra 1.5 miles to the distance as it no longer took a direct route across walled pastureland to Pen-y-Ghent. As the route to the first peak was now prescribed this meant that there was a decreasing need for navigation skills from competitors.

It was a warm and sunny day, with good going underfoot. Mike Short led to the summit of Pen-y-Ghent, with Harry Walker a tight five seconds behind, and Jeff Norman a further 40 seconds back. By Whernside, Norman was ahead of Walker by 30 seconds, with Short a further half-minute back. Norman and Walker dropped Short going up Ingleborough, with Norman ahead by a minute at the summit. He opened up a gap descending to the finish, bursting into the sports field in Horton in 2-41-37, a record for this new course that would last seven years, until John Wild smashed it in 1982. Harry Walker came in 2nd in 2-45-05, with future winner John Calvert overtaking Mike Short late on for 3rd in 2-50-48.

Jeff Norman is from Leigh in Lancashire and started running cross-country and track for Altrincham and District AC when he was 17 (in 1962). Within two years he was running on the fells too, coming 14th in his first race at Rivington Pike, which he says he and two clubmates just decided would be good to have a go at. He was inspired by stories of the Three Peaks Race, which he first entered in 1966, his first really long event. He says now that he entered on very little training. 'I was desperate to do the Three Peaks. I had been injured and wanted to do it as soon as

I was 21. Injury affected my build-up, but I ran anyway. It was hard work, but I got round, in 54th place. I had not recced any of the course, but I enjoyed it.'

He swiftly progressed to 27th the next year, having been 7th at one point, and then died a death. Again, he had not done enough training for it. As noted, he was 3rd in 1968, had been a close 2nd in 1969, and then won six in a row from 1970 to 1975. He only did one other race after 1975, as he was more of a marathon runner by then. That was in 1979, on 29 April, when he was 10th in 3-06-10. 'I have no further details of this race, other than that Harry Walker won in 2-53-11 as I had stopped keeping a detailed diary. So, I can't explain why I ran so badly. I can't have been injured as it was sandwiched between two marathons, both of which I ran well in: Boston on 16th April (2-15-44) and the European Team Championship in Brussels on 9th June (6th in 2-17-43 on a very hilly course).'

Having only run the course starting in Horton twice, he says: 'I always had a liking for the original course. Possibly because I won it a few times and had really got used to the course. I very rarely went to the front till quite late on.'

Jeff Norman won the British Fell Champs in 1974, in the years when there were points for every race. 'I thought it wasn't fair because I couldn't afford to go to all those races', Jeff says now. On the suggestion of 1974 being his peak year, Jeff argues otherwise. 'I remember 1970 as a good year for me. I was very pleased to win the Ben Nevis Race that year. I wasn't expecting to win it as it is not my sort of race. It had a massive road finish then, as it finished in the centre of town.'

Jeff did quite a few international mountain races. In 1974 the Fell Runners Association sent a team to race at Sierre-Zinal. Harry Walker was 3rd, Jeff Norman 5th, Joss Naylor 8th and Pete Walkington 23rd. The first three entered as an FRA team and they won the team prize. Jeff Norman was quoted afterwards, saying he didn't especially rate it, as it is basically all run on paths. He says now that it doesn't sound like him, asking if perhaps it was a Joss quote, before admitting he might have said something like that.

31. Jeff Norman and Harry Walker after the 1975 race

One of the keys to his racing success was his endurance. He admits that each year he would do a couple of outings over the Three Peaks in around four hours – getting the endurance in, as he puts it. He did these with Trevor Proctor a lot. An interesting fact about Jeff Norman is that he won the Snowdon race, as well as Ben Nevis and the Three Peaks. On the male side that makes him one of a unique set of four runners. The others to win all three iconic 'national' races are Kenny Stuart, John Wild and Ian Holmes. Some quartet that is.

When asked to compare his Three Peaks wins to his Olympic marathon in terms of achievement, Jeff Norman came back very quickly with: 'My Olympic performance was crap, in terms of what I was capable of. I did better in the trials than the Olympics and Commonwealth Games. But winning the British Championships was special.' The Three Peaks was very special to him though, as he notes: 'I was 21 when I first did it, and I had always wanted to do it as soon as I could.'

Chapter 11

BLACKBURN BUDDIES

The second half of the 1970s was dominated by two class runners from Blackburn Harriers. John Calvert won in 1976 and 1977, with Harry Walker coming home first in 1978, 1979 and 1981. Horwich's Mike Short broke their run with his win in 1980.

1976

As we have seen, Jeff Norman had been on a run of six victories but was not entered for the 1976 race, as he was bidding for selection for the Olympic marathon team and had a trial race to concentrate on. Harry Walker had already been 2nd in the race three times and was considered the favourite. It was a cool but sunny day with dry underfoot conditions, possibly disadvantaging fell specialists. The hard ground played havoc with Walker's shoes, and they fell apart early in the race, necessitating a mid-race change and restricting him to 7th place.

John Calvert had a different view to Jeff Norman, and said he was using the race as part of his own preparations for the marathon trial, with coach Joe Lancaster's approval. This was the second running of the race from Horton-in-Ribblesdale, with Ingleborough now the final peak. Calvert was 8th at the summit of Pen-y-Ghent, with all his main opponents ahead of him. He worked his way through the field and was up to 5th at Ribblehead. Seeing the lead runners over Ingleborough, Calvert suddenly thought he could win and pushed the pace, breaking away across Simon Fell and Sulber to take advantage of the fast moorland run-in to win in 2-43-59. Speaking afterwards, Calvert commented that, 'It's rotten for Harry. He should have won today.'

John Calvert says now that he had done some recces with Jeff Norman, Trevor Proctor, Colin Robinson. 'We all used to meet up to recce the Peaks course, particularly to try to get the best way to go over Black Dub Moss. If you went up there now you would find a few pairs of trainers lost in the mud. You used to think that if you could see the bedstead then you were on a good line [*the farmer had made a gate out of an old bedstead*]. I did the marathon trials in 1976 as well as the Three Peaks. I never really trained specifically for the marathon.'

John also says he didn't know in advance about the filming of the race in 1976. He laughs now, saying, 'Have you seen the video? When we were going up towards Pen-y-Ghent the helicopter was directly above us. It whipped all the dust up over us and it looks like we are waving to them but we were giving them the sign! We later heard it was for Yorkshire TV.' Interviewed in the film after finishing, John Calvert said, 'I feel tired [*laughter*]. I didn't think I would win, I thought Harry Walker would. The conditions were good underfoot which I think spoiled it for Harry. It was maybe too fast for him, and he looked tired going up Ingleborough. I just saw a chance and took it.'

Harry Walker gives a little more detail about the shoe issue. He had set off thinking he could lead all the way, and possibly had gone too fast. 'I was with Mike Short, and I think we knackered each other up. Mike dropped back and I was running with Alistair Blamire. My shoes were falling apart, and I passed Stan Bradshaw (who was spectating) and I had to put one of his shoes on, which was two sizes too small. Then I got to my wife Sheila, and she gave me a pair of my shoes. I may have over-trained that year. On the little downhill before the big up for Whernside my legs just went.'

1977
Conditions were vastly different in 1977, with rain and sleet on the day making the going underfoot very heavy after a week's worth of rain. John Calvert was equal to it though and ploughed through the mud to finish in 2-51-04, two minutes ahead of Mike Short. Ricky Wilde was 3rd, with Harry Walker in 6th.

John Calvert admits that he wasn't an out-and-out fell runner, but that it was definitely pleasing to have won the Three Peaks Race twice.

32. Harry Walker (no 58) in the lead pack in 1976

'I wasn't that good at boulder running or climbing steep fells though. The Peaks was a tough running race and suited me. My main aims were road and cross-country. But it was a strong aim that I had to win the Peaks.' He also says that Bill Smith had written in *The Fellrunner* that Calvert, 'had only won the Peaks because he was a road runner. I had this thing in my mind that I wanted to prove myself, which I did.'

John did cross-country at school, which he hated. 'Three of us used to stop in the park and play football and wait for them to come back and join in the run again. But one time I had a go, and it went OK. The PE teacher said, "Do you want to start running?". I made the school team for races, and eventually finished 9th at the English Schools.'

He continues by explaining that George Kirby (chairman of the Blackburn club) signed him up at a meeting at school. 'I signed a form that I thought was to go to a school race, but it was for Blackburn Harriers [*laughs*]. I didn't find out about that until 12 months later when I ran for the Youth Club in Accrington in a race organised by Clayton-le-Moors Harriers. I won and the winner got a free membership to Clayton. Then there were arguments as Blackburn said they had already signed me. The funny thing was that in 1968 we left Clayton to join Blackburn anyway. We tried to get them to amalgamate, but they wouldn't.'

John Calvert says that initially they just went out and did their own thing for training. Then in 1975 Joe Lancaster started coaching him. 'When I started with Joe Lancaster he asked me what my ambitions were. I said, "To win the Three Peaks". He geared my winter training to that aim. I used to train round Widdop and places

33. *John Calvert after winning in 1977*

like that. I would try and do 20 miles on a Sunday, and when it was lighter might also do 15 miles or so on a Wednesday night. I was also trying to get in the national team at cross-country. I got a couple of trips abroad from that.'

Early on John did the Junior race, up to Ingleborough and back from the Hill Inn. 'One time I did a different route up to others, which I thought would be faster. Instead of following the track by the fence I went straight up the middle to come out almost bang on the cairn. The cloud was down, and I ended up with a bit of rock climbing towards the top. I got to the top and thought I was in the lead. Coming out of the cloud on the way down the normal way I looked down and they were all there in front of me.'

John Calvert admits that he had done the Three Peaks Race a few times before coming 3rd to Jeff Norman in 1975. Then, it was just a case of trying to get round. 'We did it when we were about 18, with no number. [*Harry Walker, who I was interviewing together with John, chips in with, 'you did it, I didn't.'*] I was 31st in 1973, 13th in 1974, and then finally 3rd in 1975, before winning in 1976 and 1977.'

1978

John Calvert had been hoping for a treble in the 1978 Three Peaks Race. 'The Commonwealth Games were in Edmonton, Canada, and my sister lives out there. She said I should try for the team. I did the marathon trial at Sandbach. I trained for that and couldn't do the Peaks as well, as they were too close. I was sponsored by Reebok, and I had some light racers from them. At about 18 miles [in the marathon] my Achilles just went. So, I didn't run the Peaks that year.'

The weather for the 1978 race day was thick mist, fierce winds and light drizzle. Harry Walker triumphed over the conditions, and all the other runners, coming home with a nine-minute margin over Martin Weeks, the largest winning margin at the time. John North led onto the Pen-y-Ghent summit, but by Whernside Walker had a lead of four minutes, which he stretched over Ingleborough. Ian Roberts was 3rd, with North holding on for 4th.

There were 410 starters in the race, and the thick mist resulted in many of them going off course, and over 70 retiring. Ted Pepper (of Blackheath Harriers), a newcomer to fell racing, sadly died from exposure after going astray coming off Ingleborough, and was only found after an 18-hour search by the rescue teams, who conducted the search in equally bad conditions. The race has always attracted runners away from the normal fell running fraternity, and Bill Smith (in *Stud Marks*) commented heavy-handedly: 'Hopefully, these once-or-twice-a-year fell runners will have taken warning from this tragic accident and now pay more attention to the weather, protective clothing, route-finding and their own fitness for the fells – as distinct from cross-country or road-racing fitness.'

A letter from John C. Frankland (Medical Officer with the Cave and Rescue Organisation) gave further information on the situation on the day and after.

[Pepper] died from hypothermia on a small British mountain on a spring day. Perhaps some would have thought this improbable, but they have sadly been proved wrong. Conditions on the Three Peaks on April 30th were as bad as at any time in the Race's twenty-five-year history. Visibility was no more than a few yards and although the air temperature was above freezing point the wind speeds of sixty miles per hour provided circumstances which are as chilling to the body as an air temperature of -30 degrees with no wind.

Navigation on the summits was difficult and following a competitor who was confident of the route was not always feasible. Of those who became lost on Ingleborough a number understandably ran down wind and finished up miles off course in Clapham. Edward Pepper was found down wind and perhaps thirty minutes run away from where he last checked in on Ingleborough summit. He was on a vast featureless fell above the mist level in an area searched by both the very experienced RAF Mountain Rescue Team and trained Search Dogs[26] on the evening of the race. It is probable that he may have been dead before the race ended officially.[27]

It did cause the Three Peaks Race Association, and the Fell Running Association, to think carefully about how to respond, and in particular what measures to put in place to avoid any similar situations from occurring in the future. Soon after this the FRA made the provision of navigational skills training a priority. Arguably the Three Peaks Race became a leader in race safety following Pepper's death. The measures taken by the TPRA are explored further in Appendix 1.

Harry Walker said in a post-race interview that he had 'finished 2nd three times and 3rd twice and I thought I was never going to win it. But I took heart from the fact that Colin Robinson was 29 when he won.' So, Harry Walker finally won the race, eight years after he had first entered, and he did lead most of the way. He recalls now that, 'Some of the runners chose a different route to go up Pen-y-Ghent. They went on what turned out to be a shorter route. I pressed on and asked at the top how many

---

26 In 'Edward Pepper Obituary', Peter Knott, *Fellrunner* spring 1978, it was noted that during the 18-hour search which continued throughout the night over 300 persons and some 20 dogs were used with air search facilities being provided by the RAF.

27 'Death of Edward Pepper. Three Peaks Race 1978', John Frankland MO, CRO, *Fellrunner* Christmas 1978.

had gone through. They said one, John North, and I passed him going down. I was on my own all the way home. Martin Weeks said he was waiting for me to die. I had a great run. There was a cold east wind, and I was wearing a hat because of that.'

Born in Colne, Harry Walker has never moved far away. Like his friend John Calvert, Harry was spotted in a school race and joined Clayton-le-Moors in autumn 1964. John Calvert was already a member. Walker's introduction to fell running was at Thieveley Pike, at Stan Bradshaw's instigation. He found that he was better at climbing than running on the flat.

Harry Walker says things were different then. The Clayton club had a whole programme of training around the Three Peaks Race. 'But I had never heard of the Three Peaks Race until I joined Clayton, and then of course it became important to do it. The Horton route didn't suit me as well as the Hill Inn one as we used to go through the buttresses on Pen-y-Ghent, but they stopped that from 1975.'

Harry was injured before the race in 1977. 'I had won the Edale Skyline Race and I had a bit of a cold and went out for a long run a couple of days after Edale. I shouldn't have done, because Edale was hard. I got to a stile, and I twisted something and couldn't run properly. For six weeks I could only jog. The week before the Peaks race I went to Pete Walkington's wedding and Joss Naylor was there. He said, "I will sort you." I went up to Workington to see a man Joss recommended. By golly, I was able to run with Joss the day after. It was my hip that was displaced, and he put it back. Since then, I have had a new one.'

Harry Walker concludes that he didn't really finish running competitively, but because he was building the house that the interview took place in, and was short of time to train, he ran races locally to save travelling time. 'A local Grand Prix had arrived by then, so there were plenty of races to do. John Wild had appeared on the scene and was breaking records for fun. He was favourite in 1981. But I trained really hard for four weeks and got the win, my third, that year.'

Chapter 12

REFLECTIONS FROM ANDY HAUSER

Andy Hauser's first Three Peaks Race was in 1977, and his most recent 2019, for a total of 39 completions, which is the third most of any males, after Dave Scott and Bill Wade. He recently shared his background and some memories of over 40 years of involvement with the race.

Andy was born in Huddersfield in 1955. He considers his greatest achievement in the sport as his 3rd place at the Three Peaks Race in 1991, but also his six wins in the Manx Mountain Marathon (plus a win in the half mountain marathon). He has also had some good road race results having represented Yorkshire in the Inter Counties 20-mile race twice.

Andy was at Lancaster University and a few of the staff there used to do the Three Peaks. 'I thought, that is the sort of thing I want to do. At the first opportunity I did it. I was 21. I'd walked it, but not as a recce. I didn't think I needed to recce with it having about 400 runners. When I first did it, in 1977, there were little shortcuts you could take. The big change was going straight up Whernside, now you follow the railway and cut across the river and straight up from there. That extension was done in 1987, and it was further. Also, you didn't see anyone walking along the route on race day in the old days, but now it is crowded.'

He adds that before he did the race, they used to cut across the fields from Nether Lodge to get to the Ribblehead to Dent road and miss out the Horton to Ribblehead road altogether. 'Coming off Ingleborough has got a lot worse too. The path has got very stony. The worst fall I ever had was dropping down to the shooting hut. When Ted Pepper died in the race, in 1978, there was no path visible at all. The small trods weren't visible as it was snowy and misty. Even on a clear day the path wasn't very clear then, as not many people did the race or even walked the route.'

He recalls that in 1990 the conditions were mild and dry, but there was a very thick mist throughout and underfoot was very wet and slippery. The race report after the race suggested that times were typically 10 minutes slower than normal. 'It was a period where I was very confident and set off at the front until the final part of Pen-y-Ghent, where Gary Devine and Shaun Livesey broke clear and I arrived at the summit in about 8th place. By Ribblehead, I'd grouped up with Ian Ferguson and Paul Sheard. We ascended Whernside together in thick mist in 3rd place. Failing to take out the compass (and I knew the bearing), we veered off course, but corrected our route to find ourselves at the summit just a few seconds behind Shaun and Gary. I've never been a great descender, so I lost sight of all of them coming down to Chapel-le-Dale. Despite having run up Ingleborough from Chapel about 30 times at that time, it was very confusing. The grass is very short near Chapel, and the path wasn't visible in the thick mist. Fortunately, I knew it well enough not to get lost, but I slowed due to doubts. The others all arrived at the summit together two minutes ahead and raced to the finish. Gary Devine (Pudsey & Bramley), ahead of Shaun Livesey (Rossendale), Ian Ferguson (Bingley), Paul Sheard (P&B) and me (Holmfirth, in 3-05-18), clear of Andy Trigg (Glossopdale). I always thought that it's one I could have won if I'd been more confident in the mist and used the compass going up Whernside, which I normally do, but I followed Ian Ferguson who was striding out confidently.'

Andy says that the older he's got the harder it has become to race the Peaks. 'I used to think it was perfect for a decent road runner like me, because it seemed to have a lot of fast running sections (especially the tarmac bits), but now it seems very stumbly and challenging. In late December 2017 I'd had an operation to remove my prostate gland (which had an aggressive cancer). I targeted doing the 2018 race but was unable to do the desired training. It was a miracle getting to the start line, but I really suffered a lot of pain, and my fitness was lacking, so I recorded my slowest time ever.'

He was always serious about the event. He admits to what I think of as a fabulous obsession, which he shares with Sarah Rowell. He always checks the percentage of his time against the winning time. 'I have a spreadsheet with the times and percentages all recorded. It shows that I am deteriorating very fast now. But I have had bad luck recently. One year I had a pulmonary embolism about two weeks before the race. This year I had a back problem and haven't run for a year. I have never had such a long layoff, ever. I hope to fix it and then go again, definitely. Three more to get my 42 is looking a bit more difficult after these setbacks.'

He also shares a couple of memories of amusing situations encountered. 'In training, we were once crossing Black Dubb Moss (the old route) which always used to be very boggy, but on this occasion was full of deep fresh snow and we were trying to swim across it because you couldn't stand up and walk/run across it. On another occasion, after completing a training run, we were washing in the Ribble when one of our runners disappeared downstream. We noticed him doing the front crawl, but still going downstream. We all thought it really funny, but when he finally got to the side, we discovered that he was really panicking.'

Strangely, he reckons that in 1991, when he came 3rd, he was never really in with a chance. 'I always set off at the front but took it easy to begin with. They seemed to get away that year. I paced it well but never really saw the first two. I also seem to take loads of people, even now, going up Whernside. People tend to go too fast too early.'

The Three Peaks has always been the race that Andy wanted to do. 'It seemed to be a great achievement to complete it. Then I found I was getting faster and higher in the field, so that sparked my motivation, and I thought I might be able to win it. Then I targeted 21 completions. From that point, I basically really enjoyed running on the fells, so why not continue. I have suffered some serious injuries, but I'm still enthusiastic. I will try to get back to it. If I got 42 completions it would result in a second award. Dave Scott is the only male to get two awards. I'd like to be the second. Wendy Dodds has got two awards for her 30 completions.'

34. Andy Hauser finishing the 2015 race

Andy views the Three Peaks Race as a challenging 'A' class race. 'It disappoints some of the Lakeland runners because there are too many fast bits and not enough ascent and descent per mile. For me, the runnable bits play to my strength and can catch runners out, because they run too fast early on, whereas I know how to pace it right. It's also the best time of the year for a long 'A' class race, after all the high mileage in winter, followed by the early racing in the spring.'

Andy Hauser was very consistent at his peak, having nine top-10 places. 'I have been second v60. As I have got older, I have struggled to get the awards, but I did win the v50 category twice.'

As we finish talking, he mentions another incident from his peak years. 'Yorkshire TV interviewed me in 1992 because I was doing the Manx Mountain Marathon and then the following week the Three Peaks, then after that the Scottish Island Peaks. They were impressed and came to film me at work and then filmed me up on the Three Peaks. They were meant to do a piece about me on the Monday night after the Three Peaks. It got dropped for a parrot walking across a tightrope. So, I guess I was less interesting than a performing animal!'

Chapter 13

FIRST WOMEN

At the time the Three Peaks Race was established women just weren't expected to be interested in such events.[28] That had begun to change in the 1970s and the Three Peaks Race Association duly addressed the issue. The race secretary (Douglas Croft) said the following in a letter published in *Athletics Weekly* on 20 November 1976:

> Fell running is now gaining increasing support from ladies, and I have received a number of enquiries. This matter has been considered by my committee, who take the view that the factors [the location, facilities and the provision of rescue and first-aid services] preclude extending the present race to include lady competitors. We and our sponsors would, however, be prepared to consider a separate race, provided that sufficient support was forthcoming.

He concluded by asking interested women to write to him. They did just that, and the first women's race took place a couple of years later but was *not* separated from the men's.

1979

Confirmation came that the Three Peaks Race was accepting women, with the following being noted at the Three Peaks Race Association AGM: 'It was decided that there would be a Ladies Race in the 1979 event, covering the full distance with a common start time but separate result list, prizes, etc. Women entrants had to prove that they had completed 2 category 'A' events of at least 12 miles in the last two years.'

On 29 April 1979 women ran the Three Peaks Race for the first time, on a misty and windy day, with light drizzle. Bill

---

28 The story of the pioneer women fell runners and the struggle to be accepted is told in *Voices from the Hills: Pioneering Women Fell and Mountain Runners*, Steve Chilton, Sandstone Press, 2023.

35. Winners John Calvert and Jean Lochhead, 1979

Smith reported briefly on this auspicious occasion, in *Stud Marks*: 'There were eleven starters, of whom three retired. Jean Lochhead was first back in 3-43-12, ahead of Bridget Hogge (4-03-27), Joan Glass (4-07-25) and Brenda Robinson (4-09-42).' The other four finishers were, in order, Anne-Marie Grindley, Anne Bland, Janet Sutcliffe and Jean Dawes.

Jean Lochhead thinks now that she might have got an even better time that day. 'The time would have been faster had I not climbed too early and got on to Simon Fell and straight into a headwind all along the top to the summit of Ingleborough. I ran the Three Peaks about five times, for fun really. The thing that sticks out in my mind is what a long way it is down from Ingleborough.' She also recalls an incident that happened to her on the Three Peaks, in a different year. 'One time, whilst crossing a deep bog between Pen-y-Gent and Whernside I thought, "I had not noticed that boulder there before" and leapt on to it and my foot went through a dead sheep!'

36. Brenda Robinson on the way to 4th place, 1979

Before taking up fell running Jean Lochhead had been keen on cycling and middle-distance track and cross-country racing, reaching international standard at both disciplines. Her fell running had started with her first race, at Pendle in 1978, after a decade of running in the other disciplines. She continued running on the fells till she stopped being competitive in 1985, as she was more into orienteering by then.

Brenda Robinson reflected recently on her time on the fells. She competed that day and says that she was very pleased with her run and was proud to have run in the first Three Peaks Race that included women. She says her main memory of that day is being stuck in a bog, with a similar story to that related by Jean Lochhead (above). She explains the situation, which could have ended badly. 'We started in Horton in front of the men and had climbed Pen-y-Ghent and were on the way to Ribblehead. I was in the leading group when the men started to catch up with us. We were all heading for a stile, and a queue formed. To the right was a wire fence that I thought I could climb through. I left the track and jumped onto a rock in the middle of a wet patch. The rock turned out to be a dead sheep in the middle of a bog! As I sank down into the mud the girls ran on, and the leading men glanced at me and continued running. I am five feet tall and as I sank further the bog was up to my waist and I couldn't move. I shouted but there was no one around except the runners and I couldn't expect them to stop. Some of the men did eventually shout advice like "lean forward and swim out", but I was well and truly stuck and still going down. Someone in the race must have told the next spectators he passed, and a man eventually came running back to me. He lay on the ground and held out his hands which I was able to reach, and it took some time to wriggle out and get free of the mud. I hope I thanked him. Amazingly, my shoes didn't come off and I was able to finish the race, coming in 4th. I stayed calm during the experience because there were people around even if they were not stopping. Afterwards I did have a few anxieties about it all.'

Brenda also recalls how poor the weather was. 'I ran in my technical gear, which consisted of an Army and Navy large cagoule and a scarf. I was confident of getting round as I had done some recces with Colin. I was pleased to pass some of the male runners I knew. A seasoned runner pulled out at a road crossing which spurred me on after my bog episode. Colin went from 3rd on Ingleborough to 23rd at the finish due to hypothermia. I was just tired at the finish.' She also adds that, 'The distance wasn't right for me, as I enjoyed shorter, faster races. Importantly, I felt the women gave a good account of themselves that day.'

Talking with **Joan Glass** recently, she admitted to having great memories of the Yorkshire Three Peaks but noted that it may probably be for the wrong reasons. For the race in 1979 she had tried out a carbo-loading diet for the first (and only) time. 'I had read about this relatively new diet that was allegedly good for long races, and if done correctly, it probably is. Alas, I rather overdid the carbo-loading the day before the race, including a couple of pints of Guinness the evening before, not something I normally drank but, hey ho! It was going to work wonders. How

I got up Pen-y-Ghent with legs that felt like lead and my gut complaining so much I'll never know. Staggering through the bog along to Ribblehead was no better, but I kept telling myself it had to improve. At Ribblehead friends had a flask of water with honey in it and a honey butty (the legendary Eric Beard swore by honey butties), but I don't think I had the butty. Going up Whernside was slightly less painful, but I came through it when descending Ingleborough where I took satisfaction in passing quite a few of the men. I just wish I had felt that good earlier!' The other reason Joan remembers the Yorkshire Three Peaks is because that is where she bought her new trainers. 'I liked the Walsh studs. They were brilliant and I used them immediately after purchasing! Not recommended normally but fell running shoes were not readily available in North Wales at that time, so it was a case of buying and wearing, and it is testament to Walsh shoes that I never had a problem with them. It was immensely satisfying being able to prove that we ladies were capable of running the longer routes.'

The bad weather for the Three Peaks Race certainly didn't faze Harry Walker, who came home 1st again, in a time of 2-53-11. Ian Roberts was 2nd, with Harry Jarrett 3rd, and Brian Robinson 4th. Colin Donnelly won the shorter Junior race and came back to feature strongly in the Senior race the next year.

1980

Nine women ran in the 1980 Three Peaks Race, the second year for them. Bill Smith described the action: 'Véronique Marot was three minutes ahead of Sue Parkin on Whernside, but the Yorkshire girl closed rapidly on the descent so that she was only one minute adrift at the Hill Inn, and then forged ahead going up Ingleborough to arrive at the summit with a two-minute lead.' That lead stretched to over seven minutes by the end, with Joan Glass closing Marot down rapidly in the last few miles. Parkin's time was 3-35-34, beating Lochhead's from the first year by nearly eight minutes. Lochhead had been unable to defend her record due to illness.

Sue Parkin came to fell running from orienteering. Her first

37. Sue Parkin finishing, 1980

fell race was at the Wasdale Horseshoe in July 1978. With its 34km length and 2750m of climb it is regarded as one of the hardest races in the fell running calendar. Sue often trained at Holmfirth with Wendy Dodds and other runners of a similar standard. Parkin maintains now that orienteering was always her main focus, even though she loved running on the fells.

Véronique Marot had wanted to run the race for years. Her diary records how that day went: 'I was leading most of the way and I knew Sue Parkin was fitter and better at descending.

38. Linda Lord running in the 1990 race

She overtook me after Ingleborough. I was 2nd in 3-42-40.' Véronique's problem was that she wasn't fell-fit. 'That undid me at the Three Peaks. I had natural endurance but hadn't trained on proper hills. There was only one hill where I lived, and I used to run up and down that hill, often in the pouring rain.'

Linda Lord enjoyed the longer challenges in the early days, including that Three Peaks Race in 1980, which she completed in 4 hours 2 minutes, for 5th place. She adds now: 'It was only the second year that women were allowed to enter, and it felt like it was a real achievement, as I had watched the race several times.'

Linda Lord was a fell walker in the 1960s and 1970s, and before she began running had walked the Three Peaks a couple of times, taking about eight hours. 'I had watched the race when it started at the Hill Inn, marvelling at the speed and athleticism of the competitors. Then as a runner, my first Three Peaks was in 1980, although women had only begun to be accepted as competitors in the race in 1979. I didn't qualify for that first women's race, not having the requisite number of long 'A' category races under my belt. But I remember feeling so pleased to have finished the race, halfway down the women's field, and surprisingly beating my clubmate and mentor Anne-Marie Grindley.'

She concludes that, 'Ingleborough was the first mountain I climbed as a 15-year-old, and the Three Peaks area has a special place in my heart. It's about an hour's drive from home and it is my favourite place for a training run. I avoid weekends – especially in the summer when hordes of sponsored walkers are on the route and prefer to keep to the lesser-known ways up the three individual hills. I was on Ingleborough on a bitterly cold but fine day last March, only a handful of walkers and the odd runner about. Just me and the dog, that's how I like it.'

Being a new name on the scene, 20-year-old Colin Donnelly proceeded to surprise a few seasoned watchers with his run at the 1980 Three Peaks. Andy Styan's well-constructed report in *The Fellrunner* (July 1980 issue) is a good read and gives a feel for how the race panned out. An edited extract is included here:

Arriving late, I spent 10 minutes trying to decide whether to run or just watch. I'm glad I decided to watch, because I saw the most exciting finish I've ever seen in a fell race. It was a perfect day for the event. Perhaps a little hot, but visibility was excellent, and it was as dry underfoot as it is likely to be. Would there be a record? Would Harry Walker get his hat-trick? Would Colin Donnelly continue his phenomenal start to the season? By Whernside there were only three in it – Mike Short, Harry Walker and Colin Donnelly. I had asked Mike at Pendle if he was going to win the Peaks, and after hesitating, he replied, 'Well, yes I am'. He must surely have felt

39. *Pete Hartley with Denise Park, TPRA committee member and commentator at the race*

his chances go as Donnelly pulled away coming off Ingleborough. Colin had beaten Mike at Pendle and Kentmere, and looked a safe bet for a win at the first attempt, with Harry dropping way back. As they came to the last stile with 300 yards to go, Colin had a 30-yard lead over Mike, and both looked exhausted. Mike took an age to get over the stile and that really looked like the end for him. Not so! Reaching the last short hill before the drop to the finish, Colin went legless, and Mike, seizing his chance, put in a tremendously gritty burst to pull back the gap and forge a 20-yard lead. It was a wonderful piece of running by Mike Short, which after many years, gave him his first win at the Peaks. The crowd at the finish had missed the real spectacle.

This turned out to be Mike Short's only win (by just five seconds), and, despite an otherwise brilliant career, Colin Donnelly never had a Three Peaks win. Rightly there is a mention in the report for Pete Hartley, many of whose photos grace this book, who had his highest ever finish in the race (4th), one behind Harry Walker.

Chapter 14

REFLECTIONS
FROM TONY PEACOCK

Tony Peacock first entered the race in 1979 after having done the enforced apprenticeship of doing at least two other Category 'A' long fell races. The following are his thoughts about how things were around that time:

To qualify, it usually meant that you had to have done two of the long Lake District classics like Borrowdale or Wasdale – far more serious undertakings in my opinion. There was a certain arrogance displayed by the organisers of the Three Peaks at that time, probably born of its long history and popularity. On the other hand, all they wanted in the Lakes races was your money! Once you had passed the entry criteria your name went into a draw and if you were lucky you got a number for the Three Peaks.

At that time the race was sponsored by the *Daily Mirror* and you had to wear the un-loved orange plastic bib, which was emblazoned with the paper's logo and your race number. On hot days they were very uncomfortable.

At that time kit was very basic. Cotton T-shirts prevailed and on sweaty days they rubbed runners' chests, causing their nipples to bleed. Trail shoes were not available then, but would have been unsuitable anyway on the course at that time. There were only two suppliers making fell running shoes, Walsh in Bolton and Reebok in Bury. I think I wore Walsh Ripples which weighed in at about a pound each foot; perhaps a slight exaggeration, but they were heavy. Someone took a photo of me popping a Dextrosol tablet in my mouth for a sugar boost during the race. Jelly babies would have been a lot cheaper and probably just as effective.

1979 was sometime after the free-for-all route of the early

40. Comparing notes after the 1990 race. L to R: Walter Wilkinson, Alan Heywood, Tony Peacock

days when runners took the shortest route, climbing walls and crossing farmers' fields, and an accepted 'standard' route had been established. After Pen-y-Ghent most people crossed Black Dub Moss to rejoin the Pennine Way. Avoiding being sucked into the bog was tricky and, of course, you also had to keep clear of the dead sheep floating in the morass.

The route from Ribblehead went under the viaduct to Winterscales then straight up the open moor to the summit of Whernside.

After the Hill Inn there is a large area of bog which today is crossed completely by duckboards. In 1979 there was a token ten yards of wooden walkway, after that you were on your own. There was no path up the steep hillside leading up to the Ingleborough plateau and you hauled yourself up the slope using the wire fence. Generally, there was little in the way of prepared footpaths and the route from Ingleborough to Sulber Nick was no exception, following peat groughs and drainage ditches.

Walter Wilkinson was a charismatic character who would lead runs on Clayton-le-Moors (my club) training nights. Wherever Walter led, others would unfailingly follow. We were also quite adventurous, and by the early 1980s Stan Bradshaw (Jnr) and I had competed in various two-day mountain marathons together, including the Swiss Karrimor. We had completed the Bob Graham Round and competed in the Three Peaks Yacht Race.

Chapter 15

THE WILD YEARS

1981

The weather had its own ideas about the timing of the 1981 race. On the Friday beforehand harsh blizzards virtually cut Horton off, with snow over six feet deep in places, and huge drifts on the fells. The race secretary noted, 'the road beyond Horton towards Ribblehead had been closed by a general depth of 5 or 6 feet [of snow] and an avalanche had occurred at Selside, and electricity lines were down.' Farmers reported depths of snow up to ten feet, with drifts of up to 18 feet high on the fells. The race was postponed till mid-October, eventually being held on a cold, clear day with strong winds and driving rain early on.

Fiona Wild admits now to having no particular memories of her win that year. 'No, I have no recall of this, though I did enjoy the course. I see I was just under four hours [3-59-16]. I didn't know the only other female competitor.' Fiona Wild's introduction to fell running came through competing in mountain marathons, both at home and abroad.

The other competitor that day was Anne-Marie Grindley, whom she beat by over thirty minutes. It was taking a while for the race to fully grab the imagination of the leading women fell runners. Not just content with running in the race, Anne-Marie Grindley had also already taken positive action to change the situation with regard to female entries, as she explains. 'With the help of Stan Bradshaw, Jean Lochhead and I had got ourselves on to the Three Peaks Race Association committee to convince them that ladies were quite capable of navigating the course and completing the event in a reasonable time. I am proud of that contribution to women's fell running.'

In the build-up to the 1981 race John Wild was being touted as favourite. He had set course records at Pendle, Kentmere and Rivington Pike in preceding weekends. John says now that he did one recce in 1981 in preparation for having a go at the Three Peaks that year. 'I did the recce with an old friend called Al Tomkinson, whom I was at RAF Cosford with. We drove up and decided to register that we were doing the Three Peaks in the cafe in Horton, as many walkers did. They said: "How long do you think you will be?" When I said, "Less than three hours" they thought we were taking the mickey.'

John Wild says he doesn't remember what time they did but reckons it was a half decent day and they jogged round. 'It is an obvious course which you can't really go wrong on, not like one of the long Lakes courses. The funniest thing was that we were going up Whernside and a bloke came towards us on his cyclo-cross bike. He shouted at me and stopped. It was a man who used to be a member of my old athletic club. So, we had a bit of a natter, and he went down, and I went up. We found no problems with the course. The only thing I remember was how steep it was going up Ingleborough. I was mindful of that. Then there were the big stiles you had to get across.'

Jack Maitland had travelled all the way down from Aberdeen to do the race in the spring, but arrived in Settle to find it had been cancelled due to the snow and so travelled back again the same day. John Wild lost his chance to run the iconic race that year. John did not do the revised date as he was chasing British Championship points elsewhere. The Three Peaks didn't fit in to his plans anymore.

On the rescheduled day the heavy going underfoot resulted in the slowest time since moving the start to Horton. Harry Walker gained his third win in four years. Harry adds that if the race had been run in the spring, John Wild would probably have won. 'I went to the Ben Nevis Race in September 1981, and had a bad run. I thought I would sort myself out for the Three Peaks, so trained hard and managed to achieve my third win. Bob Whitfield was favourite to win, as he'd won the Ben and the Three Peaks was his home turf. I won the race in 2-56-34, the only person under three hours that day. The conditions were cold and windy, and boggy underfoot. In April 1982, only six months later, and following an injury at work, I ran 2-55-59 for 16th place. The conditions were good, showing how much weather conditions affect race times.'

1982

Sunny skies turning overcast and a coolish breeze greeted the runners for the 1982 Three Peaks Race. Jane Robson won, with Linda Lord less than three minutes behind, and Wendy Dodds in 3rd. The report noted that from the organisers' point of view, 'support for the women's event was disappointing and it appears that the growth in enthusiasm for ladies' fell racing has temporarily ground to a halt. In the absence of many of the better-known runners, the race was won by 21-year-old Jane Robson of Leeds University Orienteering Club in the good (but not record) time of 3-40-54.' The race programme showed that twelve women had actually entered, but only three finished on the day.

Jane Robson (now Morgan) confirms that her background was in orienteering and she was a member of the British Orienteering Squad at the time she did the Three Peaks Race. She adds: 'I started at Leeds University in 1979 where I was introduced to fell running and also started to do the Karrimors. It was a great place to train and the fell running was a supplement to my orienteering training. I can't remember how I came to decide to enter the Three Peaks, but it was obviously an iconic race in Yorkshire and was always going to be one to do. I'd run a road marathon the previous year, so had obviously trained for the distance too. I also trained with a few past participants of the Three Peaks at Leeds including Wendy Dodds so guess it just sounded a great race to do.'

Reflecting on her win that day, she recalls that she remembers having a bad cold the week before. 'I was thinking of not running, but my transport and support team persuaded me otherwise. I remember feeling very slow and sluggish up Pen-y-Ghent, but then started to feel OK (I think a week of not much running the week before helped) and gradually started passing people. I was surprised to be told I was the leading lady (but there were not too many in those days) at the top of Ingleborough and was delighted to take an unexpected win.'

41. *Winners John Wild and Jane Robson, 1982*

Looking back on that year now, Linda Lord adds a reflection on her own performance. 'My 1982 race was a real let down for me. I was having a good year of racing and had finished the London Marathon in 3-13 two weeks beforehand, and had turned out some good results in several long fell races. I was the first woman through Ribblehead and at the Hill Inn, and coming down Sulber Nick was surprised to be passed by Jane Robson, even though I was going well and overtaking male runners. I finished a frustrated 2nd, and to this day it rankles as one of my most bitter disappointments. My mum was watching the race. She died a few months later, and I never placed as high again in the race.' She adds she completed the race seven times, and eventually became disenchanted with the route, especially now as it's referred to as a *marathon with three hills*. 'There's too much paving and prepared paths now, like many other walking and race routes in popular places. Also, I'm not keen on all the hype and commercialism that's crept into fell running in general. Despite all that, I have happy memories of the races, and treasure my 1984 2nd-place medal, and the glass trophy for 1st LV40 in 1995.'

John Wild had his eye on a win at the Three Peaks Race in 1982, having been disappointed about having been in superb form the previous year when it was postponed to the later October date. Back in 1981 the race sponsors (the *Daily Mirror*) had requested a photo of Wild, and went down to RAF Cosford, where he was stationed, to meet him. According to Wild, they wanted a photo of him with a kit bag in front of the jets he worked on. They put an article about him in the paper and then, of course, it was cancelled because of the snow. They came back to the race in 1982, saying, 'What are you going to do if you win?' Wild said, 'Have a beer', and the newspaper guy was there at the end of the race with a pint of beer for him.

For the race it was completely different to the previous year, the weather being sunny with a coolish breeze. John was perhaps the favourite in a strong field. John Reade took an early lead going up Pen-y-Ghent, followed by Mike Short, who was coming back from injury. At the summit these two were joined by three others, including former British fell champion Alan McGee, with Wild not far behind. Coming off the summit in the lead, Mike Short lacked fitness and soon faded, whilst Wild joined the leaders on the way to Whernside. Then Wild took the race on and won in a new record of 2-37-30, having taken five and a half minutes out of Alan McGee in 2nd place. The picture of him with his pint was on the back page of that Monday's *Daily Mirror*. John notes, 'It was quite weird seeing my picture in a national newspaper, but my mum loved it.' In his files John has a copy of that Monday's *Daily Mirror*. Whilst the back page has his photo in the report on his Three Peaks win, the front page has a headline that screams 'IT'S WAR – says Argentina', with a subhead saying that Britain had taken back South Georgia.

42. *John Wild's post-race pint, 1982*

John says now he did no more recces before going back in 1982, and that he didn't do any specific preparation or training for the Three Peaks, mostly because he was challenging for the British Champs again. 'To be honest I think I was captivated by the fuss the *Daily Mirror* made of me in 1981, and I felt obliged to go back and do it.'

On the start line John felt very comfortable. 'I knew that like other races I could let others go and see how it panned out, feeling confident I could take them on later in the race. I took the lead going up Whernside and I felt great. I had got quite a lead before we got to Ingleborough. But I was getting cramp on the high stiles, that is getting down the steps. I was a touch worried about that. I enjoyed that pint of beer at the end. I didn't go back to the Three Peaks again because by the end of 1983 I was thinking about doing the marathon.'

He thinks he was really lucky that year as it was as dry as you like. Even the bogs between Pen-y-Ghent and Whernside were absolutely dry, and that was why it was such a fast time. He was told it was a record and that it went in the *Guinness Book of Records*.

The race has a fine tradition, according to John. 'There are very few routes that so many want to do. It is a tick in many people's book. Whether it is a category 'A' race is another matter. It is not technical running like Borrowdale, for instance. It is not easy. I am not trying to belittle it. It was hard.'

John finishes by describing what was a typical approach to the race by him. 'Anne and I turned up in our van the night before and went to a pub near Ingleborough. It was full of Hell's Angels. I had a few pints of Old Peculiar and slept in the back of the van in the car park, and then turned up to do the race next morning. We had sausage and chips in the pub too. Perhaps it wasn't the best preparation, but we had a great time.'

During the presentation the announcer made some comment because the Marines had just invaded South Georgia, as part of the Falklands War. John Wild was in the RAF, and the announcer said something about him 'being busy in the near future'.

In his report on the race, Dave Hodgson made the bold suggestion that Wild's time was relatively better than Jeff Norman's record for the shorter course from the Hill Inn (in 1974). 'Comparison with the giants of the past is always contentious, not to say dangerous, but after due consideration I would say that John's 2-37-30 represents around 2 minutes faster than Jeff's Hill Inn time of 2-29-53.'

Chapter 16

IT WAS NOT A
SURPRISE TO WIN

1983

The weather conditions at the time of year that the race is
held can vary from year to year. For 1983 it had reverted to
wet weather in the build-up, but it was fine on the day. Dave
Hodgson's race report notes that: 'The leading ladies chose to
run in together after being close together for most of the race.'
Carol Walkington/Campbell commented on that agreed tie,
which was with Wendy Dodds. 'It was Wendy's suggestion
to run in together, after we had run down from the summit of
Ingleborough more or less together.' Reflecting on it in 2004,
Wendy Dodds said: 'I fell over several times on the descent
from Ingleborough and was helped by other runners. Carol and
I passed each other several times on the descent, until a mile or
so from the end we agreed to finish together.'

Carol and Wendy's time of 4-08-01 was a *de facto* record
because of the course changes in effect that year. Wendy Dodds
has obviously taken a liking to the event, as she has run it 37
times in the last 41 years.

The year 1983 was a good one for Carol Walkington. She hoped
to compete well on the fells. She was surprised to find herself as a
contender for the British Fell Championships and finished runner-
up to Angela Carson/Brand-Barker. Over the years Carol won a
number of races all over the Lakes, with many of her wins being
more local in northwest Cumbria. She also supported and paced
many Bob Graham Round attempts in the 1970s and 1980s, but
although she recced and planned her own attempt, the time was
never right, which she is very sad about looking back now.

The first five women's Three Peaks Races had produced six
different winners (including the tie). Take up was slow though,

43. Carol Walkington descending Pen-y-Ghent in 1986

as there had been eight, nine, two, three and six finishers in those five years. The data in Appendix 5 shows how the numbers picked up slowly and reached very good numbers in recent years.

In 1983 the Three Peaks Race was the third race in the British Fell Championships, and the third weekend in a row that championship races were held. Championship status usually resulted in larger entries than normal and often provided a really strong field too. The field of 381 was in fact only the fourth largest ever at that time, but it was stacked with top runners.

The race was run at the end of one of the wettest Aprils on record, and the times were affected negatively. The *Daily Mirror* sensationally suggested in their report that, 'Four runners broke legs – the result of going shin deep into treacherous wet areas and losing their balance.' Hardly.

Kenny Stuart moved into the lead going up the second peak (Whernside), stretching out to win by nearly four and a half minutes, proving he could now win the long races, after formerly having been a 'guides' racer. Hugh Symonds came in 2nd, ahead of 20-year-old Shaun Livesey. Livesey had won the Junior race (up Pen-y-Ghent and back) in 1982 and he asked the organiser if he could run the main race in 1983, even though he was too young technically. The organiser agreed that he could. Livesey adds now that, 'Typically by then I would be doing 1-45 to 2 hours on a Sunday. Dave Cartridge had taken me round the course too. But the Peaks was the only time by then that I had ever run that distance'.

Kenny had only been reinstated as an amateur runner in August 1982, having had a very successful career as a professional runner. In the 1981 season he had won 30 out of his 32 races. He had already had several wins in 1983 by the time of the Three Peaks Race. He was still excited about being reinstated and was looking forward to races, including this one. He adds that, 'in those days people thought that because someone was coming from the guides races then you could only run short races, and that was why you were doing them. But for me it wasn't like that. I was training for longer races for at least six months, between applying for reinstatement and getting it. I knew I could do well in 1983, but I wasn't banking on winning the champs.'

He also went down to recce the Three Peaks course. 'I went to recce it midweek and took a day off work, I think. I drove down there in my Mini 850. I could see Whernside and reckoned I would probably be with someone when I got there. I thought I would recce between the bottom of Whernside and Ingleborough and also the long finish run-in. So, I ran all that and ran back again. I didn't have time for any more. That way I knew how the finish was, and the last third of the race if you like.'

His results had obviously been noticed, as the *Daily Mirror* (also the race sponsor at that time) made him favourite for the race, and sent a reporter and photographer to interview him a week or so before the race. 'A bloke from the *Mirror* came here (Threlkeld) to interview me. That sparked a bit of nervous tension in me. I was careful of being too confident, because of the hype and because of the distance of the race, and the speed it might be run at. I knew well enough what the race was going to be like. I had seen the reports. After recceing that finish, I knew it would be a fastish course.'

Kenny adds, 'one big recollection I have of the race is that the night before I went to bed early to get some good sleep in. We had to travel down the next day. I remember not being able to get to sleep, and at one o'clock in the morning I came downstairs and took a bottle of Guinness out of the fridge and drank it to relax. I went to sleep OK after that! I was tired the next day though. It caught up with me a couple of days later.'

Kenny commented on the race, 'I knew I could get round. Still, I didn't want to go it alone and went out with Hugh Symonds. Following Hugh was fine. He is a really nice bloke, and that is how races are run. There is a photo of us going alongside Ribblehead Viaduct and he is around 6ft something and I was 5ft 4.5ins. The going was heavy, and I was bothered with cramp in the later stages, and a bit scared I'd have to ease up. I should have respected the race a bit more than I did. It was just little twinges which you think are going to get you, but it didn't. I'd have liked a better time, but they told me after it was the heaviest going for years and the course was a mile longer, but then I wouldn't know as it was my first time there!'

44. Kenny Stuart, 1983

Kenny also offered the thought that it was not a surprise to win the race. I challenged him to justify that statement, as it was his first, and only, go at the Three Peaks. He calmly replied, 'it was really wet, it was terrible. I was very fit at that time, and it wasn't a surprise. I had done the long training runs. It was more of a cross-country style race than a traditional Lakes fell race. I was slightly worried about the cramp, which I got on Ingleborough, but I got through that.'

The cramp proved to not be a problem that day, and he wasn't stiff after the race. However, two weeks later there was another championships race at Ben Lomond. Kenny had run so hard to challenge John Wild at Ben Lomond [*Wild won*] that he had very severe stiffness after that.

Kenny explains now that for the whole season he was probably trying to do too much. He was too intent on trying to cram every sort of training session in. 'I should have been on a two-week cycle rather than worrying about every week. If I did a hard session of hill reps one week, then I didn't need to do them the next. You live and learn, but runners often don't. You can't actually see where you are going wrong because you are so obsessed with getting it all done. Now I look back and think I could have done it differently.'

He was not getting enough recovery between races, not having a single rest day from 11 April to 8 May that year (with the Three Peaks in the middle of that period). His diary indicates the intensity of training he was doing at that time. The week before the Peaks he did 68 miles in total, with six days being double sessions. The week of the race he did 80 miles, including the 14-mile recce of the route plus another three double days, and a taper of six miles and three miles on the Friday and Saturday prior to the race. The week after the Three Peaks he did 72 miles in seven double session days, and then had a 69-mile week with four double days before racing at Ben Lomond on the Saturday. 'I went out on the Sunday after Ben Lomond trying to run with the lads, including Dave Woodhead, and I'm thinking this nine-mile run is killing me. I might normally have done two hours on the fells that day but just couldn't do it.'

From his position in 9th place in the Three Peaks Race,

Malcolm Patterson concluded that Kenny Stuart was in a class of his own that day. Patterson remembers it as a disappointing race for him. 'I had heard so much about this race and dreamt of doing it long before I took up fell running. I lost touch with the leaders before even reaching Ribblehead that day. I had not got enough speed endurance. It was too much of the "cross-country style" and too many flat bits in between the hill climbs!'

He adds, in looking back, that he only raced the Three Peaks that one time. 'I finished in 3-07, some 14 minutes adrift of the winner, Kenny Stuart. I had grown up knowing about the Three Peaks Race. I remember watching the classic Yorkshire TV documentary about the race, with its footage of winner Harry Walker (or John Calvert?) gesticulating (shall we say) at the helicopter, which was filming him and getting so close to him that the downdraft was impeding his progress, hence the reaction! So, I was excited to do it, relishing the atmosphere, the large number of spectators *en route* and the sense of history surrounding the race. Sadly, my memory of the race is not a happy one. I tracked the leaders on the first climb to Pen-y-Ghent and was in the lead pack as we descended, but when we turned onto the flatter, faster section towards Ribblehead the leaders just ran away from me, and from there onwards I struggled to maintain form and focus. Running from Ingleborough through a slippery Sulber Nick was interminable!'

It was certainly a field loaded with talent, as evidenced by the 4th, 5th and 6th places being filled by Bob Whitfield, Jon Broxap and Jack Maitland respectively. Evidence of the quality is that 2nd-placed Hugh Symonds and 3rd-placed Shaun Livesey won five of the next six Three Peaks Races between them.

The previous year's winner John Wild wasn't even able to be there, as after the National cross-country championships he had broken a bone in his foot – at work, helping organise a sports competition. He wasn't able to train for six weeks, the worst injury he had ever had. The injury meant that John missed not just The Three Peaks, but also Kentmere, and Blisco. John can laugh now, saying, 'That was a real ball-ache. I had missed the first three races of the Championships.'

He described the slightly bizarre circumstances of how the injury happened. 'We had a *Superstars* competition at work. I had donated a trophy I won in Spain from a cross-country race, so I agreed to be part of the organising team. I was goalie in the football shootout where the guy dribbles towards you and shoots. I dived one way and the ball hit my foot and broke a bone, one of the metatarsals. It was the most painful thing. I had to hobble home without a shoe on.'

The injury didn't stop John Wild having a good season though, as he was back running fairly quickly. He was always chasing Kenny Stuart for the championship title, as he had to make sure he covered his ten events. Having missed the first three, he had only two to spare.[29]

Kenny Stuart's 1983 winning time was a new record for the Three Peaks Race, as the course had been slightly lengthened for that year. He concludes that, 'the race was important to me, as it was an ambition to run it, and an even greater thrill to win it, like. In those days it was a truly iconic race. It has slipped back a bit now. There is less hype now perhaps. Our newspapers rarely give good coverage to fell races. But the Three Peaks Race would be up there in my highlights, along with the Ben Nevis Race.'

Kenny also adds, 'I wasn't one of those people that thought I needed multiple wins at races. There were other races I had to run to get championship points the next year. I had really wanted to run the Three Peaks Race anyway, and it happened to be a championships race when I did it. It was always a big race.'

Kenny Stuart's final comment was on the 'fell race or not' discussion. 'It is a fell race – it is just a different type of fell race. I can understand why they say marathoners can do well on it, there is a lot of runnable stuff between the peaks, which is quite unusual for a long fell race. A lot of fell runners might not do it. Some people might have the stamina but not have the speed.'

---

29 For the full story of that year and the rivalry between John Wild and Kenny Stuart see *Running Hard: The Story of a Rivalry*, Steve Chilton, Sandstone Press, 2017.

Chapter 17

TREBLE FOR SYMONDS

1984

With the course having been changed significantly the year before, rumours were abounding about further changes for the 1984 race. But it was run over the same course as 1983, with really good ground conditions being conducive to fast times. A highish temperature was moderated by the cool breeze.

For the women, **Bridget Hogge** finished in a time that was only 5 minutes 26 seconds slower than Sue Parkin's 1980 record. Dave Hodgson reckoned that, 'Allowing for the Sell Gill diversion, Bridget's performance was probably superior.' Karen Mather was 2nd, just three minutes behind. Bridget recently said that she didn't have too many memories of the race but made an interesting comparison with the Lakeland Classics. 'I recall enjoying the Three Peaks, although there was not much chance to slow down; whereas at the Wasdale, Langdale and Borrowdale events you used to have to slow down at times.' Bridget Hogge had been 3rd in the initial British Fell Championships in 1979, and runner-up (to Pauline Haworth) in 1980. Later, in 1984, Bridget completed the Bob Graham Round in 23-45.

Hugh Symonds proved that he was on top form, coming home as the 18th different winner of the race (in its 31st running). Symonds was dominant, being in a lead group right from the start, and pulling away coming off Whernside. He finished in 2-50-34, beating Kenny Stuart's record for this new course by exactly three minutes, and with a gap of over five minutes on 2nd-placed runner, a young Shaun Livesey. Symonds had improved on his 2nd place from the year before, having run over seven minutes faster than he had in 1983. Reflecting on the race recently, Shaun Livesey said: 'I completely blew up on Whernside and dropped to about 9th by the Hill Inn. Somehow, I came back to finish 2nd. It was a hot day, and Hugh just went

45. *Hugh Symonds and Shaun Livesey at Ribblehead Viaduct, 1984*

away from me on Whernside. I had come 3rd the year before and I was one year stronger so I thought it would be good to stick with Hugh. I was pleased to pull it back after faltering so badly. Even now it surprises me how I did that at that young age.'

1985
Before the start of the 1985 Three Peaks Race there was a tribute to Jack Bloor, who had recently died. Bloor was one of the race's founders, who also won the third version of the race and was chairman of the Three Peaks Race Association for a number of years.

Vanessa Brindle/Peacock, who went on to have a remarkable run of races over the Peaks, strode out for the first of her four wins. There was a record field of 18, as the women started showing their strength in depth. Vanessa finished in 3-38-10, a new record by nearly three minutes. She was well clear of Jacky Smith and Rosie Naish, in 2nd and 3rd respectively. The race report again explained the effect of the recent change in the course. 'The time must be worth two or three minutes less than Sue Parkin's 1980 race record, set before the Selgill diversion was introduced.'

Hugh Symonds won for the second time, in another new record, but did not have things all his own way, as the race report indicates:

> By the top of Pen-y-Ghent the race was beginning to take shape, with Jack Maitland, Hugh Symonds, Mike Short, Steve Breckell, Bob Ashworth and Andy Harmer moving ahead of the field of 389 starters. At the Ribblehead checkpoint a quartet, comprising Breckell, Maitland, Ashworth and Symonds were clear, with scarcely the depth of a chest between first and last of the bunch. The same four were ahead at the top of Whernside, with Jack a minute ahead of Hugh. At Chapel-le-Dale Jack continued to lead by over a minute, a lead which he held all the way to the top of Ingleborough. In the final run-off, however, it was Hugh Symonds who sped away to a clear-cut win, with Jack Maitland a little over a minute behind, clocking 2-50-16 to the winning time of 2-49-13.

A discussion I had when researching another book revealed

46. *Hugh Symonds leading the 1985 race*

the true drama of that finish. Hugh Symonds still remembers that race vividly. 'We got to the bottom of Whernside, and Jack starts running away from me. It was one of those moments when I thought, "I can't go with that, I will die." So, I let Jack go. OK I thought, "Second today, I won it the year before." Going up Swine's Tail, on Ingleborough, it gets really steep by a fence. People were saying, "Jack is finished, you can get him". I thought great, I feel really good and strong. More than one person said you can get him. At the top you pass runners going the other way and you can see them. I looked Jack in the eye, and I thought I can beat you, Jack. It would be a mile from the finish when I passed him. I wrote in my diary: "First, just!".'

At the same time Jack gave me a fairly good reason for him fading at the end of that race. That weekend he attempted a tough double – to run the Mow Cop Killer Mile and the Three Peaks Race on successive days. All went well at Mow Cop as he set a new record of 6-31 for a race that has a gradient of 1 in 4 in places. There was a prize for the first runner to get under 6-30. Maitland was close, recalling, 'I won in 6-30 point something. There is a great photo of me finishing. The next year Roger Hackney turned up and took the time under 6-30 for the

*47. Jack Maitland climbing Pen-y-Ghent
ahead of M. Freer and Chris Hirst*

prize.' Possibly no surprise then that Jack found Hugh Symonds too strong for him at the Three Peaks, after Jack had led for much of the way.

Jack Maitland never did manage to win the Peaks, saying that Hugh was something of a *bête noir* for him. He said, 'Hugh beat me when I thought I should have won the Ben Nevis Race. Then I also finished 2nd behind him at that Three Peaks Race.'

Hugh Symonds grew up in the Manchester area and joined Altrincham and District AC in 1968, a club with some absolutely top athletes. 'Alan Blinston was an Olympian, and at 15 I just looked up to him, and Jeff Norman (who started his Three Peaks winning streak in 1970). I genuinely thought I could never be that good. I did the odd fell race in those early years. I did Burnsall at 17. There was something in the back of my mind that said, maybe one day I could be a proper fell runner.'

48. *Hugh Symonds and Bob Ashworth*

Hugh went to Durham University in 1972 to read Mathematics. 'But I wanted less track and more off the beaten track. I was coached by Alan Storey at the time. He had us doing ridiculous mileages – I maxed out at 140 miles a week once. I had always wanted to do the Three Peaks as I had grown up and seen Jeff Norman as some kind of superstar, who kept winning that race (1975 was his sixth win). I had done the Junior fell race, the Whernside, coming 5th. So, I went for it in 1975, coming about 30th. I was fit but had done virtually no fell training. Alan had me do the carbo diet. I took it to extremes, and was so hungry and was almost ill. Not sure it was the best preparation. My diary entry reads: "3-26. Very disappointed. Cramp and leg pains."'

He recalls a really memorable event where he went with Jeff Norman and some others to recce the Three Peaks course. 'The big question mark was how to get from Pen-y-Ghent to Ribblehead. We ended up at the Hill Inn and bumped into Joss Naylor, who was also doing a recce. He seemed to be dressed in a sack held together with safety pins, and had hair all over the place,' Hugh chuckled.

Hugh didn't run the Three Peaks again until 1982. By then he had moved to Sedbergh and had changed from being a road runner to a fell runner. His diary entry reads: '9th. 2-48. Good race.' 'I had no idea then that I was destined to win the race,' he adds now. By 1983 he was running for Kendal AC. Again, he gives a succinct summary in his diary: '2nd. Very pleasing. 2-58.' Commenting now on Kenny Stuart tagging him in that 1983 race, and out-running him to win, Hugh explains that it hadn't bothered him. 'I would have been so happy to be at the front end of the race, as it was new to me. My mindset for all long races was that this race doesn't really start until a certain point. In the Three Peaks it was Ribblehead. If you are not relaxed at Ribblehead you will probably hit trouble.'

Hugh went one better in 1984, to win in a time faster than Kenny Stuart had run the year before. Significantly, he adds: 'Kenny didn't do it that year. I felt that if Kenny wasn't at a race at this time, then perhaps I could win it. Probably because of the photos, I remember being together with Shaun Livesey by the Ribblehead Viaduct. There is a longish bit of road before you get to Ribblehead Viaduct. That mile or so is awful. But you suddenly need to be heading along at about five minutes a mile there. I am not sure exactly where I pulled away from Shaun that day.'

During our discussion of his Three Peaks races Hugh admits to one major regret, concerning what happened after he had won the race for the first time in 1984. 'Afterwards I went off for a pint or two with Dave Hall and missed the prize-giving. Pauline had to take the trophy while I was in the pub. I came back after the presentation was all over. I was gutted. A lady told me my name was mud. I was SO embarrassed. I took the trophy home, hung it on the wall and vowed to go back and win it properly the following year. I think Dave Hodgson was the organiser at the time and after 1984 he was always very careful to make sure that the winner was present for the prize-giving.' Hugh seemed embarrassed still, as he described those events to me recently.

That second win in 1985 is described in detail above, including the tussle with Jack Maitland, whom Symonds points out had some major successes, winning Sierre-Zinal one year, for instance.

There is no sign of Hugh Symonds in the leading results for the 1986 Three Peaks Race. He explains that it was the year that he got very involved in a barn conversion. 'My training was affected, but I did run it and I finished 25th in 3-18. Very disappointed.' Hugh ran the Three Peak Race again in 1989. He says he now had a 'Munros mindset', as he was working towards his continuous round of the UK's mountains, starting in Scotland. For this he was in what he describes as big training. 'My last good races, ever, were in 1988. I did have some success as a v40. In the Three Peaks in 1989 I was 18th in 3-10. My diary comment was that I was not in the race. I did run it again as a v50, in 2004, and was thrilled to get under four hours.' Hugh looked it up and soon after the interview passed on the information that he had finished 101st in 3-59-42.

Hugh Symonds finished our discussion with his thoughts about the Three Peaks as an event, and its place in the sport and in his own career. 'The Three Peaks is a one-off. It is more like an Edale or a Three Towers, being nothing like any Lake District Classics or the Scottish hill races. Being one of the oldest long-distance fell races it is certainly one of the classics. To me, if you want to be a fell runner, and you want to win races, then the Three Peaks would be one of them. Ben Nevis another, and Wasdale (sadly that one – well, Billy Bland twice – beat me). The Three Peaks has always got a lot of publicity. Winning the Three Peaks is up there for me in my career highlights, along with the Ben, and Ennerdale, and Vignemale in the Pyrenees.'

1986

For this year there was a minor adjustment to the course. The section from Ribblehead to Whernside was altered, giving a shade more fell running to relieve the monotony of track and road running.

First woman home was **Carol Walkington** in 3-49-12 from Jacky Smith in 3-50-41. Carol Walkington (now Campbell) says that she trained hard during 1982/83 (when she tied with Wendy Dodds at the Three Peaks) and in 1985/86. She says it was the first time she kept a diary and trained properly, and that she often

49. *Wendy Dodds passing the viaduct at Ribblehead, 1992*

trained with the men at Horwich. Jacky Smith set the course record for the Pen-y-Ghent race that year and went on to win the British Fell Championships the following year.

Jack Maitland had been on good form early in the year but had pulled out of the Three Peaks through injury. On an equally good spell of racing was Shaun Livesey, who beat Brent Brindle by a couple of minutes, to lead his Rossendale team to a win over Brindle's Horwich.

Shaun Livesey has a good recall of the event. 'I was 23 and became the youngest to win the race at that time. Hugh Symonds was competing, but strangely enough I never doubted for one moment that I'd win that day. That was the first time I had ever felt that. It was based on my training and my form. I had done it twice, and I knew that on both occasions I was strong towards the end and had not blown up. I was confident in my ability, plus Bob Ashworth and Dave Cartridge were running, which helped as I wanted it to be fast, and that would make it a small lead group, which I preferred. Also, I could hopefully run on from that. Us three ran fairly fast to Ribblehead and I believe that we got there in

50. *Shaun Livesey crossing the line to win in 1986*

the fastest time up to that year. I decided to go for it and broke away running towards Whernside. Coming to the top of Ingleborough, Harry Walker was there and he shouted that I was miles in front by then, and nobody was in sight. I think I might have been five minutes ahead. As I came back down off the top and passed him again, he said, "Slow down and enjoy the victory." I remember I let my arms drop and physically relaxed because there was no way I wasn't going to win. I remember smiling quite a lot over that last four miles. The 2nd-placed runner, Brent Brindle, said in an interview that I had blown up and he had closed me right down. In fact, it was me relaxing and enjoying it. I got to enjoy what may be seen as my biggest race win.'

He adds that, 'The result was especially good because I went to win, and I delivered. It was definitely the first time that I have stood there and never doubted I would win. I had done the work, I deserved it, it was mine. I was in the first three from the start, and made my move as planned on Whernside. I managed to pace it well and win that day.'

Shaun Livesey wasn't at all sporty at school and was probably not the best pupil either. He did run a bit though. 'I looked round once in a race and there was a slightly overweight lad with both hands holding up his Ron Hill tracksters. I should have quit there and then to be fair. I would go along to training and George (the club coach) had this conversation with me. "Why do you run?" "I enjoy it." "Do you have aspirations for your running?" "No, not really." "Oh good, I didn't want you thinking you might win something." He was telling me as nicely as he could. I responded to that.'

Shaun persevered. At the age of 15, at a race at Todmorden, he was suddenly in the lead over the hills. 'My initial reaction was that I was screwing myself up here. I eased up and several boys passed me. We went downhill again and came to another climb. I didn't feel I was going that hard, but it was quicker than everyone else again. I got in the lead again.' George said afterwards that he was running as quick on the hills as he was on the flat.

Soon George took him to a fell race that Harry Walker won. 'I had heard about Harry. I remember watching him and he was such a pleasant man, yet an incredibly strong runner. He became an inspiration to me in a way. It was an amateur race at the Hodder Valley Show. I think I might have been

51. Shaun Livesey with his trophy, 1986

running as a Senior but was not entered under my own name as I was too young. I realise that is very much a no-no, but I was naive then. It would be 1978 or '79. I came about 10th, and it was a short up and downer. My intro to fell running. I loved it.'

Soon after that Shaun did the Tour of Pendle which was his first ever long race. 'I think Kenny Stuart won it from Billy Bland and I was 3rd or 4th. After the race Billy said to me (and it was the first time I'd ever spoken to him), "You are a bit overweight" [laughs]. He said, "Yeah, you could probably do with losing a stone, maybe a bit more. How heavy are you?" I said, "Around nine and a half [stone]." He said, "Get a stone off and you could be quite good."'

John Wild started training Shaun. 'I made the weight loss from training harder with John. I was now doing around 70 miles a week. I am extremely good at doing what I am told, and not questioning it. Always do a mile or two more rather than a mile less. I followed his training to the letter.' The training gave him confidence. He also didn't get injured, so he could do the high mileage, doing a lot of reps which were long and fast.

Later, Nick Dinsdale took Shaun to another level when he took over as his coach. 'I got fit with John and got a good mindset, making me very competitive. My first Peaks win (1986) was when I had been training with Nick.[30] His training was so different to John's, it was very structured. The objective was to get to 100 miles a week. So, for example, I would do 35 miles, 40, 45 and then week four would be a drop to 35 and do an easy week. Then it would increase by five miles each week, with step-downs built in. I also did weights and circuit training.'

---

30 Shaun shared his training summary for the build-up to his Three Peaks win. Some detail will give an idea of how his training looked. The Three Peaks race was in week 17 of that year. Weeks 1–4 were for endurance and strength, and totalled 86, 89, 91 and 62 miles. Weeks 5–8 were also endurance, with mileages of 90, 97, 101 and 81 (note, every fourth week had reduced totals). Weeks 9–12 were for speed and included three quality sessions (one on a track) per week. Mileages were 73, 53, 64 and 56. Weeks 13–16 were 'peak' weeks (including rest), with mileages of 52, 48, 80, 85. Week 17 was race week, still clocking 62 miles, but with the satisfaction of his first Three Peaks win.

Chapter 18

FIRST WOMEN'S MULTIPLE WINNER

1987

On the changed course for 1987 Vanessa Brindle won her second Three Peaks Race, setting a new record for that version of 3-44-05. Coming in 2nd was Helene Diamantides, some 13 minutes later, with Jacky Smith not far behind. Helene comments that, 'Alison Wright persuaded me to do the Three Peaks. You have to have experience to do well in this race, which I really didn't have.'

In a profile, written by Bill Smith, Vanessa Brindle commented on the 1987 win: 'I set off feeling great and going well, but due to the heat, I realised too late that I hadn't drunk enough and slowly ground to a near-halt going up Whernside. I continued only because of the encouragement given to me by other runners, and then someone gave me a drink of Lucozade on the way up Ingleborough, for which I was extremely grateful!'

The race provided a third win for Hugh Symonds, by seven and eight minutes respectively from Brent Brindle and Bob Whitfield. Andy 'Scoffer' Schofield was already showing his good endurance potential, coming 3rd in the Junior Pen-y-Ghent Race in just under the hour. Hugh Symonds explains that the time-consuming barn work he had taken on was now done and he was back into full training. 'I was disappointed to win so easily. Was it a race or a nice run? You don't want to win by such a margin really.' His diary was again brief: '3 hours 1 second. Hot.' 'I think that victory put me off running in 1988. It seemed an empty victory, and I don't mean to give Brent Brindle a disservice here. That year I was going for the Championships races instead.'

52. *Andy 'Scoffer' Schofield ascending Pen-y-Ghent, his first time at the Three Peaks Race in 1988*

53. Vanessa Brindle leaving Ingleborough summit, 1988

1988

Vanessa Brindle had a storming run to set another new record of 3-37-16, over six minutes faster than the previous year. Again, she had a clear victory, with Ruth Pickvance coming home some way behind, with Sue Ratcliffe chasing her.

The men's entry list suggested that it would be pretty open and so it turned out. On a glorious day the lead changed hands several times as the race unfolded. By the top of Pen-y-Ghent John Reade was in the lead, which he still held at Ribblehead, although Mick Hoffe and Robin Bryson were now up with him, and Ian Ferguson starting to move through in 8th. Bryson took the lead ascending Whernside, followed by Hoffe, with Ferguson racing through to 3rd. Ferguson had assumed the leader's mantle by the Hill Inn, with Hoffe and Bryson having changed places, and were now in 2nd and 3rd places. Ferguson pulled away somewhat on the run-in to win by over 3.5 minutes (in a new record) from Hoffe, with Bryson close behind.

Talking recently, Ian Ferguson admitted that his win that year wasn't the first time he had run the race. 'I had done the race a couple of times before my win in 1988. I had walked round it before and camped on the summits several times. But I don't remember much about the race that year.'

1989

After the laying of hardcore paths on some sections of the route in the last couple of months fast times were expected, and delivered, by both the women and the men. Vanessa Brindle took advantage to record her fourth win in five years, and to set another course record, by over four minutes. Her time was 3-32-43, to 2nd-placed Ruth Pickvance's 3-42-25.

Vanessa Brindle/Peacock had a very successful career, completing a Bob Graham Round in 1985, running in the World Cup twice, and setting a couple of other records, including the Three Shires, also in 1985. Looking back, she noted that when she started running there weren't many rules. 'You just set off and did the race. There wasn't a kit check or anything, but that obviously changed.'

For training, Vanessa usually used to go out three times in the week and then would have a long run at the weekend with her husband, Tony Peacock, and his friends, usually about 15 miles. In the week she would go up to about eight miles on one of her runs. 'There wasn't any structure to my training and diet as it didn't exist, certainly not in Clayton. I did some training with the Clayton ladies, but it was mainly on my own or with my husband Tony or the Clayton men, who were always there if I needed them in races or to give me encouragement!'

Commenting on the fact that she won just one English Championship, and never won the British Championship, Vanessa explains the situation. 'I didn't want to get too involved with competing for the British Champs. Fitting in the ten races was a big commitment and I couldn't always get the time off work to race. Generally, it was 9–5 work in the hospital, but we had on-call and late shifts sometimes.'

Vanessa does admit that she isn't really one for remembering

54. Runners at the Hill Inn checkpoint

her times or any records. 'I just used to think that it was about how you were on the day. I was pleased to do what I did and enjoy it really. I would say that I enjoyed the experience and the friendship and the bond that you got with people through fell running.' She also says of the event that, 'Winning the Three Peaks Race gave me a greater satisfaction and sense of achievement than winning any other race. The demanding course, the spectator involvement, and the special history of the event all create a great sense of occasion. It's the fell equivalent of the London Marathon.'

By Ribblehead that year there was still a lead group of 15 men. Going up Whernside Shaun Livesey and Gary Devine stretched away from the others, and it was then just between the two of them. Shaun seemed to be pushing the pace, with Gary working hard to keep with him, only to lose out as Shaun strode down the long descent to the finish, with a new fastest time of 2-51-45, taking over five minutes off the record from the year before. Ian Ferguson had set that, and he came in 3rd in 1989 (also within the previous record). Having seen the winner pull away from him, Ferguson commented, 'Shaun was a cracking runner. Very powerful, very good uphill.'

Shaun adds some detail to that report. 'I was in about 14th place on the road to Ribblehead but could see runners ahead. I passed loads and caught up with Gary Devine. I said to him, "Who is in front?" He said, "Ian Holmes." I asked if he was any good (as at that point I had never come across him). He said, "He is good, but not that good." So, I decided to make a move, and managed to win. Gary was a good competitor, and I had a lot of battles with him. He was interesting with a different approach and outlook. I liked him a lot. For some reason my win in 2-51 that year got in the *Guinness Book of Records*.' Hearing Gary Devine's assessment of him, Ian Holmes commented, 'That is probably a fair assessment in 1989. Actually, I don't recall being able to be in front of Shaun and Gary that year. Often it is going up Ingleborough that the race is decided.'

1990

The race was notable for the worst mist in many years, with visibility at about 50 metres on all the summits, and one group of runners managed to lose themselves in the High Birkwith area. There was little wind and a comfortable temperature, but with wet ground underfoot. Whernside was particularly muddy and greasy. It meant that many people's times were something like ten minutes down on the previous year.

The winning woman was **Ruth Pickvance**, who was only slightly slower than her time from the previous year (which was

55. *Clayton-le-Moors winning team, 1990. L to R: Wendy Dodds, Ruth Pickvance, Eileen Woodhead*

for 2nd place), so a great run in the conditions. Underfoot it was wetter than anticipated, with Whernside being particularly heavy on the ascent and greasy on the descent. Ruth says that the race was always a favourite with her. 'This was the third of four times I ran the race. It suited me as a runner – quite fast, not overly technical and I had good endurance. This was in the early stages of my running and so I would just rock up and run it. Perhaps you need a bit of that in your early running career! And I loved it – I think it's such a classic race – not necessarily a classic *fell* race – but the three iconic peaks and the connecting of them together, the way it's so firmly rooted in Yorkshire heritage. It was so runnable, and I had a lot of running in me back then! My abiding memory from the early days is just how heavy those *Daily Mirror* bibs were - it was like running with a weighted piece of lino attached to your front!' Ruth Pickvance led the Clayton-le-Moors team home as they retained the team award, ably supported by Wendy Dodds and a delighted Eileen Woodhead, who after pulling out the year before only decided on the Sunday morning to run, to ensure that Clayton would finish a team.

Ruth Pickvance won the British Championship in 1989, and competed in many classic UK fell races, and also some early European races. She was later involved in the effort to stage Skyraces in the UK in 2008, which was probably slightly ahead of its time.

The race report notes that: 'The race soon developed into a contest between last year's winner and runner-up, Shaun Livesey and Gary Devine, who were clear of the field at Ribblehead and still together on Ingleborough. Gary broke clear on the descent to Horton to reverse last year's placings and become only the third Yorkshireman to win the Three Peaks.' Livesey was 2nd, with Ian Ferguson 3rd. Having seen Gary Devine win that day, Ian Ferguson now adds, 'Gary was also very talented. We had many a good night out with him and the Pudsey and Bramley lot.' Gary remembers it well. 'I've come to realise that it was quite an achievement and that I am proud to have won it. I can still recall most of the race, mainly because of the tussle I had with Shaun Livesey.'

56. *Ruth Pickvance, 1990*   57. *Gary Devine, 1990*

Shaun Livesey gives his personal take on how it panned out. 'It was a strange race. I had won the year before because I didn't want people to think my 1986 win was a fluke. But in 1990 I don't think my heart was really in it. My recollection is that I made a break on Whernside but missed the top, hit the wall and turned the wrong way and then went through the summit about one minute behind Gary. Coming off Whernside I had a fall. The fall came at a stile which I clicked onto with my shin. It hurt, it was a miserable day, and for a while I thought I have had enough of this. I was going to pull out. I jogged the track bit to the Hill Inn and soon came round and got going again. By this time, I felt good after easing off for a bit. And I thought I could still win it, so I took after Gary and pretty much caught him on the top of Ingleborough. It was misty, but I could see him. As we passed at the summit, we nodded at each other. So, he knew I was there. I still thought I was going to win. I didn't lose that much due to the fall. My head didn't go down either. I was where I needed to be. I chased him all the way to the finish, but he basically wanted it more than me.'

Shaun Livesey had mixed results at the Three Peaks. He did one more race there after that, when Andy Peace won (in 1994). 'I was behind Ian Holmes when we got to the Hill Inn, I was

3rd and to this day I can't explain it, but I just walked off.' But Shaun was an absolutely top runner in his prime.

Later in his career, Shaun went for physiological testing, when he was about 30. 'They did Vo2 max, lactic acid tests and heart rate, everything. The bloke looked at the stats afterwards and said to me, "How come I have not heard of you, your stats are that good?" They had just not done any fell runners.'

Shaun notes that a lot of fell runners would not call the Three Peaks a fell race. 'The Peaks was a real race, if you know what I mean. At Wasdale or Borrowdale say, you wait for much of the time for something to happen. Biding your time for the break. The Peaks was always full on. Often the break came up Whernside, with a long way to go still.'

He also reckons the Three Peaks Race is the hardest race he ever did, 'but Wasdale is the toughest race. I enjoyed the Duddons, the Borrowdales and the Ennerdales. Loved doing the races and everything about them. I enjoyed the Peaks because I could race it. The Peaks had no real route choices; you just raced it.

'One of the reasons I say that first Peaks race, in 1983, is so memorable is that I analysed my losses afterwards. The races I have won just go into memory and I would move on to thinking about my next race. I thought my 1983 race there was in a sense my best one of all. I paced it so well, and actually came through the field, for a 20-year-old it was quite a mature run. I got to Ribblehead and was alongside Jeff Norman, we were 14th and 15th, I think. He doesn't remember this conversation, but why would he? He said, "There is no point carrying on as I feel the race is over, and there is no chance of catching the leaders." As I ran on to get 3rd place, he said later, "Obviously I were wrong!" [laughs].'

In summary Shaun Livesey concludes: 'I just wanted to achieve certain levels, and also wanted to be improving. I was 42 when I did my last competitive race. It had just got a bit samey. I wish I had enjoyed long races more, as I'd have liked to have done the Three Peaks Race more. I would have liked to have gone for more wins, looking back, but wasn't that interested at the time. I did win the English Champs twice, though.'

Chapter 19

REFLECTIONS
FROM JEAN SHOTTER

Jean Shotter is currently equal second on the list of female runners who have done the Three Peaks multiple times, with 23 to Wendy Dodds' awesome 37. Jean was born in Laisterdyke (in Bradford) in 1962. As well as the 23 races, she says she has done it as a training run at least as many times. She recently reflected on her Three Peaks experience.

'My first race there was in 1989, the hardest run I'd ever done. It took me 5 hours 19 minutes, finishing 404th out of 410. For that first race I had done no specific recces, but I had walked the route a few times. I was 2nd lady and first FV40 in 2002 in 4-20, but I think my 3rd place in 3-56 in 1998 was better, though finishing in 3-56 in 1996 was only good enough for 7th place. My last race was in 2019 and my times are heading back in that direction, as I just managed to squeeze under five hours.'

Her reason for doing the race was simply being a member of the Horsforth Fellandale club, where Dave Hodgson was one of the leading people. 'He was Mr Three Peaks for some time. He introduced me to fell running and to Fellandale. The Three Peaks was a big club thing then, and nearly everyone in the club aspired to doing it. We used to train from Dave's house.'

Jean was a reasonably experienced fell runner when she first did the Three Peaks, having already done the Haworth Hobble, and a good number of other fell races. She says now that unfortunately the race she has the most complete memory of is one that she did not complete, in 2017. 'After a torn cartilage and many subsequent other injuries, I was pleased to make the start line of this race. I set off with no ambitions, other than to get round. I did OK up Pen-y-Ghent, but disaster struck on the way down. I tripped on the stoney track and fell flat on my face, bashing both knees. I picked myself up and ran stiff-legged to Ribblehead. The time I had lost lying on the ground and the slow, stiff-legged running meant I got there within seconds of the cut-off time. I decided I couldn't now make the Hill Inn cut-off so retired hurt. It was a long wait in the minibus for the last finisher for transport back to the finish field. There I put myself in the hands of the St John's Ambulance team, who must have had too many bandages as they almost mummified me.'

'A more positive memory is from 1991, being shown a better route off Whernside by one of the sports legends, Alan Heaton, avoiding that nasty stoney track almost all the way to the tractor museum (no longer there, I think). Unfortunately, that route is no longer available and the perils of the stoney track must be dealt with.'

She provided a couple of amusing asides when looking back over her Three Peaks experiences. 'I was taking part in the race one year and the pre-race announcements told us that it was Dave Scott's birthday and he was doing his 47th race (the most I think). As I went up Pen-y-Ghent I passed him and asked him, "How many is it?" He replied, "Forty-seven," to which I replied, "Bloody hell, you must have had a long paper round, I meant birthdays."'

Another time, in 2002, a colleague at Jean's work had recently started fell running, with his main sport being cycling. 'He had entered the Three Peaks Race and had previously done a few cycle races where he had been around Sarah Rowell's finish time or had beaten her. He had looked up her Three Peaks time and decided he would aim at her best, 3-15. I explained that this time was in 1991 when Sarah was a formidable athlete and it had given her an overall placing of 22nd. I suggested he should aim for a more realistic time so as to not go off too fast and blow up. On race day he set off well in front of me never to be seen again until the finish, or so I thought. The weather that year was awful, cold wet and windy, so times were generally slower, but I wasn't too surprised to see him on the shoulder of Ingleborough donning waterproof trousers. I finished six minutes ahead of him.'

Jean suggests that being selected to run for Yorkshire at the inter-counties and finishing 3rd by milliseconds to claim one of

58. Jean Shotter at the 2002 race

the bronze medals was one of her greatest achievements in the
sport. 'The inter-counties venue was the Shining Tor race. I did
also get selected to run in the inter-counties cross-country one
year, I think it was 1996, and I came 3rd. I can proudly say I got
a sentence in the *Athletics Weekly* report for that too.'

Jean puts her longevity down to luck, being able to stay injury-free and get in enough training to complete the race, except that the luck seems to have run out recently. She explains why she kept coming back to the event. 'Being a member of Fellandale in my early years competing in the event, it was in my blood. I have helped out with marshalling as well as running in the event, most notably for me on Whernside summit, for which you need to take all the clothes you own and maybe consider borrowing some. I was initially driven to get to the 15-race award, then 21 to equal the men's, then I had the second most completions behind Wendy. I never thought I could pass her, but I wanted to hang on to 2nd, but injuries and old age seem to have other ideas – I've not made the start line for some years, though I would like to get fit enough to do it as a FV60. My descending is nowhere near good enough to do well now, but getting a V60 Three Peaks win would be good!'

Jean concludes with some thoughts about the Three Peaks event itself. 'It is a great event, but it seems to have got too big in recent years for me. The organisation is still spot on and copes well with the numbers, but the route itself, I'm not sure that does. Being involved in race organisation for a long 'A' race I have a feeling for how much work goes into it. The Three Peaks themselves, however, not just the race, seem to be suffering from the race's success. The route itself seems to be swamped with walkers and runners. In my most recent races on top of the 500-plus runners there seem to be lots of groups of sponsored walkers all vying for the same space. It is particularly problematic on the descent of Whernside. Changes to the route have been for the better. It is Three Peaks Challengers that cause problems, I think. The Challenge has become like the London Marathon – a must-do thing for many people. I have heard locals say that the village of Horton has a bit of trouble with the numbers of Challengers, with inappropriate parking etc.'

Jean finishes on a positive note. 'Having said all that, some of it is probably because it has become too hard for me. Sitting on the grass after completing the race on a lovely sunny day, as it has been about 90% of the time, is the best feeling ever. If I'm lucky enough to get fit enough I will do it again.'

Chapter 20

ROWELL AND FERGUSON DOMINATE

1991

Two athletes swept the board with double men's and women's category wins in 1991 and 1992. For the 1991 race it was very different conditions, having been dry in the week beforehand. There were also further improvements to some of the footpaths. There was an emphatic win for Sarah Rowell, who took an incredible sixteen minutes off the women's record (with her 3-16-29) in her first Peaks race, helped by the path improvements, and achieved an impressive 22nd place overall. Cheryl Cook was 2nd and was also inside Vanessa Brindle's previous record. Veteran Wendy Dodds came in 3rd, for 1st Vet. Carol Greenwood came in 8th woman in her first run at the Peaks. In an interview in *The Fellrunner* back in 1987, at the age of 20, Carol had replied to a question about future ambitions that, 'she would like to have a go at some of the longer championship races, like the Three Peaks.'

In a wide-ranging interview recently, **Sarah Rowell** briefly gave the background to that first Three Peaks Race for her. 'I had come 2nd in the London Marathon in 1985, had my first leg operation in 1986, a second leg operation in 1987, then had a period of significant overtraining/under recovery, which took me out for a year while I was doing my PhD. I had moved up to Leeds and had done the first World Trophy in 1989 [coming 4th], and the Three Peaks was difficult to get into in those days as it was THE big race. At the World Trophy (at that time) we ran for under 40 minutes while the men were well over the hour. I still trained as a marathon runner and thought of myself as a marathon runner. The Three Peaks just seemed logical to do. I am pretty certain I recced it with Wendy Dodds, by going over it on a couple of days. In 1991 I also did the Haworth Hobble with Wendy, and we broke

59. *Sarah Rowell, 1991*

Veronique Marot and Angie Paine's record.'

Prior to moving to Leeds, she had lived in Eastbourne for ages so had no fells close by, but she reminds me that she was always good at running off-road. 'I trained on the Downs and could flow over roughish surfaces. My first fell race was probably Box Hill (in Surrey). Wendy said when I did the Boulsworth fell race, "Oh, you have come to do a proper fell race." The runnable fell races were where I was at my best.'

Sarah then gives a short discourse on nervousness. 'On that start line, in 1991, I certainly would not have had an expectation of the time it would take. I have a recollection of Helene Diamantides doing it one year and being nervous at the start. There were some people I was aware of there. I was naturally a nervous person on any start line. In races, I never thought about winning but thought about doing better than I had done before.'

She can remember having an ASICS drinking bottle that Joyce Smith had given her for this race. 'I think I probably had glucose tablets too, or similar, in my bumbag, as you did in those days. The main thing that worried me and would make me nervous was the bit of road leading to Ribblehead. I would have to stop and stretch out my left leg. It was cramping that took me away from road running rather than other things. Was I surprised by the winning margin? Probably.'

Sarah then turns to an entry from her training/racing diary for that year and gives a fascinating reading from it from the entry for that race:

Conditions good. Nearly too good as it was hard underfoot. I wore a pair of unstudded Walsh PBs. Felt OK, but a bit heavy-legged the whole way round. Led the whole way. 2-mile road stretch was a bit unpleasant but survived. Ate Dextrosol on the run between Pen-y-Ghent and Whernside. Probably ate too much for the amount of fluid drunk. Felt out of it and dead-legged over last couple of miles. Not sure if bonk or dehydration. Ended up 22nd after being in the top 20. Feel there is more to come, especially as I had no zip at the end.

Despite being held on a weekend between two British Championships, with some top runners missing it, the race promised fast running and possible records. Ian Ferguson and Andy Trigg stretched away from the field on the way to Ribblehead to establish a two-minute lead. Ferguson managed to gap Trigg going up Ingleborough and went on to achieve his second Three Peaks Race win, three years after his first, breaking the course record by some four minutes. To celebrate Ferguson astonished a packed crowd by performing a handspring over the finish line, which apparently he had also done when winning at Ben Lomond and the Bens of Jura. His performance is remarkable considering that two weeks before Christmas he had had an operation to remove a piece of cartilage in his knee that he damaged in that year's Three Peaks Cyclo-Cross. That was an event Ferguson had always wanted to win, and sadly never managed.

Ian Ferguson reflected on that year and explained the injury and rapid recovery. 'Andy Trigg and I got away and arrived at the Hill Inn together. I got away from him over Ingleborough. The handspring? Ah yes. I was quite good at that. I could walk on my hands, like. It was like a little party trick. I did it on the line, not after. There is a picture somewhere. I think I was that jubilant that I had won again. Why not? I couldn't do it now [laughs]. For the operation they just went in my knee and snicked off a bit of cartilage. Within two weeks of having the operation I was back running and there was no problem. It wasn't major surgery.'

60. Ian Ferguson, 1991

61. *Ian Ferguson
handsprings
across the line,
1991*

1992

There were gale force winds and heavy ground conditions for the race, although the summits were clear and there was no rain on the day. Interestingly, **Sarah Rowell** says that she feels that this Three Peaks Race win was her best performance at the race, despite it *not* being a course record. She explains. 'I would always look at my time relative to the men's winner, and ideally aim for between 108–112% of the winning men's time. While I certainly did not achieve that all the time, the percentage gap I had that year behind Fergy [*Ian Ferguson*], a great athlete, was a really good one – plus I made the top 20 overall.' Carolyn Hunter-Rowe, predominantly an ultra-runner, was 2nd, and Carol Greenwood gained more experience in the race in 3rd place.

For the record, Ferguson took 3-01-11, Sarah (impressively in 15th place, the highest ever women's position at the time) took 3-19-11, a percentage difference of

62. *Sarah Rowell setting a new record, 1992*

109%. At the time Sarah said that, 'It was everything I could have asked for. It was a great run. It was a pity about the weather. I suppose if you are always worrying about the weather though, you shouldn't be fell running, should you?'

That year Sarah was coming back and like a lot of runners was not very good at resting. At the back end of 1991 she had had her third leg operation. Sarah commented on the race itself in her diary:

My fitness was confirmed two weeks beforehand, when having a great run at the Wardle Skyline on the Saturday, followed by zipping comfortably round my standard Sunday run in 2-08, easily my fastest.

My training diary unfortunately is quite brief: 'conditions worse than last year, windy, cool and wet underfoot. Set off what felt like steadily but was quite far up the field, felt OK, strong, got passed by a few on the run to Ribblehead and 2-3 more on the climb up Whernside; me in the mid-20s but feeling strong. Pulled through going up Ingleborough and on the run to the finish, to come 15th overall and very happy with a good race.'

For those interested, Sarah says she drank two bottles of Maxim (an early energy replacement drink) and ate one Boots energy bar on the way round.

Sarah Rowell had some terrific results in the next few years. Eventually she won the Three Peaks Race four times, as well as the Wasdale, Borrowdale and Ben Nevis races. She finished 2nd in the 1992 World Mountain Running Trophy and won both the British and English Fell Running Championships in 1995 and 1996.

Sarah adds that she ran in an era when unless certain female runners were on the start line of a fell race a lot of the time she knew she should be able to win. 'Carol Greenwood, and Menna Angharad were two of the runners I knew would mean it would be a good, hard battle when racing against them. However, I still always stood on that start line being concerned about other runners; when I ran my second Three Peaks my time was 15 mins faster than anyone else's. It didn't stop me standing on the start line worrying.'

Ian Ferguson achieved his third win, almost four minutes ahead of Andy Trigg, with Dave Neill 3rd. In a look back at the race, Ferguson gave his thoughts on how the race panned out between himself and Trigg:

> From the start, Andy Trigg was the stronger, running nearly all the way up the Pen-y-Ghent climb and he had 20 yards at the summit. I managed to pass Triggy on the descent, but along the Pennine Way section my shoelace came undone and lost me 200 yards. I debated whether to chase or hang back. I decided to go for it and if I blew up at least I'd given it a go. Going through Ribblehead is always easy, due to the spectators and tannoy announcements. Once running alongside the railway viaduct and the slopes of Whernside fatigue can soon catch up.
>
> Up Whernside, running and walking, I decided he couldn't be fitter than me or else he'd have broken away. I closed the gap, and we reached Hill Inn together. Over the steep duck boards he took the lead. In my mind I was settling for second and I had a mental picture of a full set of silver salvers [*he was 3rd in 1989 and 1990*], but over the boulders he suddenly dropped 10 yards and by the summit 200 yards.
>
> We crossed on the top and I gave him some encouragement, but got a huge negative response which made me feel ACE. From there I never looked back and down Sulber Nick spectators kept asking if I was going to do a handspring over the finish line. Feeling so good, I thought – Third Time, YES![31]

Ian Ferguson recently revisited that finish with me. 'We got to the top of PYG together and ran all the way neck and neck until coming down Whernside. As to that cross-over on Ingleborough – if you look at someone and they look like they are dying it gives you a buzz, doesn't it, and they go downhill. Andy said afterwards, "Shit. Not again," because it happened just like the year before.'

Ian had active people around him when he was young, even though his mother and father weren't sporty. One of his uncles did a lot of caving and climbing. Barry Peace (Andy's dad) is also his uncle, and he was very sporty too. He then gives me a potted history of his taking up running. 'At school I played football and basketball but what started me off on the road to the life I lead now was going to Stainforth Youth Hostel on a school trip. One of the highlights of the week was that we went for a walk up Pen-y-Ghent. I was 12 and had never done anything like that. I enjoyed it and something must have clicked. At the end of the trip, we got a leaflet about Bradford YHA Club. They go

---

31 In an article entitled 'Third Time Lucky – for the Yorkshire Action Man', in the spring 2013 issue of *The Fellrunner*.

63. Ian Ferguson, 1992

walking and do outdoor activities. I went along and for five years I went youth hostelling. When I was out, I used to see runners. When I was 16, Barry Peace started doing a bit of running and he told me about Bingley Harriers. I went down there, and we entered the Copeland Chase, up in Ennerdale. I entered the short course and actually won it. I won a flask. Barry did it as well and enjoyed it, so we entered the Fellsman next. We went into the ballot and got in. Wow. We did it in 23 hours. If Bingley were going somewhere I'd go along. I then bought a Bedford van for £200. Then I met Ian Holmes at the club.'

He did carry on doing a bunch of sports for a while. 'For a while I would do anything, canoeing, climbing and that. But eventually running became my thing. I have always been better at the longer races. I enjoy being outside in the hills for a long time really. I entered the Three Peaks because it is in Yorkshire.' How many times might he have done the Three Peaks? 'I just enjoy doing it, I don't count them. I just do what I do. I reckon I could have been round it about 75 times walking, running and cycling. Pen-y-Ghent is where my ashes are going to be scattered as well. It is in my will. It is a very special place to me. I still remember that first walk up.'

Ian seems to want to underplay his running abilities in some ways. 'What I can't understand is that I don't class myself as a real runner. What I mean is I don't do cross-country and fast type running (like Andy Peace does). I seem to do better in the Lakes races where it is more rugged and up and down. I could never quite understand why I have done so well at the Three Peaks. But in a way I get to ten miles and come into my own so maybe that is why.'

He then gets all chirpy as he mentions something he is particularly proud of. 'The Three Peaks Race is the only race I can say that Ian Holmes, and we are very good mates, has never beaten my best time there. That is my claim to fame.'

Ian Ferguson finished by sharing his thoughts about the event itself. 'I think the Three Peaks will always be my favourite win, because I am a Yorkshireman. I think I might have been the first Yorkshireman to win the race actually. The thing with the Three Peaks is that I could go to work tomorrow and say I have won the Ennerdale race and folk would go, "What's that?". If I said I won the Three Peaks it would be, "Wow, how long did it take you?". Most people will have heard of the race.'

Chapter 21

EVERYBODY HURTS

1993

Things didn't always go well for the top runners, as we shall now see. After their battle the year before, **Carol Greenwood** ran in the 1993 Three Peaks Race and Sarah didn't, the report saying she was injured. Sarah is adamant she wasn't injured. 'After talking to my coach, Alan Storey, we decided the Three Peaks was off for me. I wasn't injured, but I wasn't running as well in training as I would have wanted, and I was not motivated by running around in 3-30 even if I might win. I wanted to go there and run faster than 3-16. I didn't think I could do it that year.'

It can only be described as a wet year. Carol Greenwood didn't have it all her own way and was chased hard by Ruth Pickvance and Kath Drake (whose shoes disintegrated on Pen-y-Ghent), who were 2nd and 3rd respectively. Greenwood, the slightest of athletes, had a tough time at the beck crossings, surviving a ducking at Little Dale Beck to take the win, her first of three. Dave Scott recalls the incident. 'Carol was swept off her feet just in front of me as we crossed the river at the foot of Whernside and was taken 30 yards downstream before she managed to reach the bank.'

Six years after announcing her intentions, Carol Greenwood had come back and showed her strength, to win the race on a tough racing day. Greenwood had attempted the course a couple of times before, but said after this win that, 'It was the first time I've taken it seriously.' Ruth Pickvance said after the race that she didn't expect to finish anywhere near 1st or 2nd, having just been on a two-week cycling holiday across France.

The *Huddersfield Daily Examiner* gave a vivid, and perhaps over-dramatic, account of the stream incident:

64. *Carol*
    Greenwood
    and Gavin
    Bland,
    1993

Carol [Greenwood] lost about 20 places overall in a nasty incident shortly before the start of the second climb up Whernside. Rain, almost torrential at times, had swollen the beck to a raging torrent and [she] was in the water almost up to her waist.

Suddenly, she lost her footing and was submerged. A male runner behind her plunged straight in, grabbed her by her top and bodily lifted her out on to the bank. She was soaked to the skin and contemplated pulling out but decided to soldier on and although cold and shivering, ran the remaining 12 miles to win an event which had previously eluded her in two starts.[32]

Carol Greenwood later sent her thanks to the un-named runner who had helped her in that difficult moment.

The weather was particularly bad, as Dave Hodgson noted in his race report:

---

32 In an article entitled 'Greenwood survives scare to win Three Peaks race', by Grenville Beckett, 26 April 1993.

The rain started at 6am and continued with varying intensity until the leading runners finished. Sell Gill was knee deep and Little Dale Beck was a raging torrent almost waist deep. Given these conditions, judgement of pace and what clothing to wear were of critical importance and several runners suffered from the debilitating effects of mild hypothermia during the long descent from Ingleborough to the finish. The number of retirements was, however, the lowest for three years, which must reflect credit on the fitness and experience of entrants in the event.

Not surprisingly, the winning times were generally slower. Mark Croasdale had the mortifying experience of losing a lead of five minutes between Ingleborough summit and the finish. All credit to Gavin Bland, whose strength in the closing stages enabled him to become the youngest ever winner of the Three Peaks Race.

Gavin Bland recently explained how the end of that race panned out, saying it was his luckiest win ever, which had the closest of finishes at just four seconds. 'We had gone around the course a fortnight before, three of us – me, Scoffer [*Schofield*] and Bob Whitfield. I was absolutely knackered and hanging on. I thought, "What am I doing this for?" Meanwhile, Scoff fell off a sink and he couldn't run in the race. In the race Paul Sheard was up near the front but went wrong halfway round, so Mark Roberts and I ran around with Paul Mitchell, racing as we thought for 2nd, 3rd and 4th places. We got to the last field and Mark Croasdale, who had been in the lead, lost out as he had run out of petrol coming off Ingleborough. Mark and I left Paul, who had showed us the way round, and sprint finished across that last field, and I won it.' Being reminded of the event, Scoffer said to me, without any apparent irony, 'I would have won the Three Peaks that day. I came 2nd three times and 3rd three times, but never won it.'

Mark Roberts recalls that clag and torrential rain made it difficult that day. 'Mark Croasdale was billed as the big favourite, and he totally died a death,' he says. 'There was a film of it. They played that REM song, 'Everybody Hurts', as he ran in slow motion. After that if you bonked in a race, everyone said, "Oh, I REMed." That year Gavin Bland went wrong as well on Ingleborough. He was going back towards Ribblehead and a hiker put him right and sent him back. Towards the end Gavin legged it up the last little bit of banking which I didn't know about. Then it was a sprint along the road to the finish.' Mark adds, 'Scoffer must have run it 20-odd times and he's never won it. You would think it might have suited him.'

Gavin Bland grew up on a farm in Borrowdale, and always knew he was going to go into farming. When he was young, he was diagnosed with Osgood-Schlatter's (severe knee pain experienced by some growing adolescents) and stopped doing any sport. He didn't really start again until he was aged 15–16. Gavin Bland spent a year on the professional scene before changing to the amateur code and joining Keswick AC. Gavin's best pro race results in his one year of competition were coming 2nd at Grasmere, and also at Kilnsey.

Although often competing in Junior races Gavin also showed his massive talent by competing in Senior events when he could. The farming lifestyle he chose had an effect on his training, and racing. He commented after winning the Three Peaks Race, 'I was out with the sheepdogs at 5am the next morning. I often walk 20 miles a day on the fells around the farm.' He says that if they had a good day gathering the fells there was no need to go for a run, and often he couldn't possibly face it anyway. 'We would fit the running round the gathering. I could never run well at lambing time, for a start, from the middle of April till the end of May. I was on my feet too much. They were long days. My body couldn't cope with it. I could go to a race and run but unlikely to be winning.'

Gavin Bland is fiercely proud of his achievements. He first ran internationally in the World Cup race in 1989, finishing 7th in the Junior race. In 1990 his performances were being recognised, and he was again selected for the Junior team for the World Cup race at Telfes, in Austria, where he finished in a brilliant 2nd place. Gavin admits that the Junior World Cup was a nice incentive. 'We had been nowhere, never been abroad. There was no two weeks (holiday) in Spain when you worked on a farm. For a boy from the fells it was great that I got abroad for a couple of years courtesy of the FRA.'

His 1991 season really picked up and he managed to win

65. *Gavin Bland, 1994*

some of the Lakeland classic races, finishing 2nd in the British Champs, but having the consolation of winning the English Champs title. In 1992, aged just 21, Gavin proved he could run long and short courses equally well. With victories at Borrowdale and Ben Nevis, he also won the short Butter Crags race in 12-43. This was just one example of where his proficiency at descending would serve him well, and garner him comparisons with the best descenders. In 1993 the Three Shires race was run in unsettled weather but still resulted in a new course record for Gavin.

Gavin admits to not being a brilliant climber. His stated preference was for steep, rough courses and he did better in longer races, saying Borrowdale and Ben Nevis were his favourite. In the early days he claimed he wanted to run on the roads later and wanted to beat uncle Billy's Bob Graham Round record. But his career took a different path.

In 1997 he set the present course record of 1-45-08 for the Three Shires race, and then in 1999 it all came really good for him. Setting records at the Carnethy 5 (which still stands) and the Edale Skyline race, he finally achieved his ambition of being crowned as the best fell runner in Britain, by winning the British Championships.

The enforced break from running the fells that Foot and Mouth caused in 2001 also signalled the end of a period of good running for Gavin. 'But I never really stopped running until I was over 40. I made a big effort at 40, going for the Vet Champs. For me, I have to go running every day. It is psychological. Sometimes it is too hard, but as long as I have been, it is good.' Despite some up and down form, Gavin Bland once reckoned that he had won a race every year since he started running.

1994

Sarah Rowell was back again, winning convincingly despite fading somewhat on the run-in. She finished in 34th place overall, in the slowest of her four wins – in 3-21-50. Sarah said at the time that she was running quite well that year, 'but unfortunately, I had a cough earlier in the week. I knew going up Pen-y-Ghent that it wasn't going to be my day. So, it became

66. Sarah Rowell, 1994

just a case of getting round.' Helene Diamantides and Carolyn Hunter-Rowe came in 2nd and 3rd, respectively, with future winner Jean Rawlinson in 5th. Sarah's diary for the event read:

> Weather good, but still wet and boggy underfoot. Quite a breeze. Felt OK warming up. Cough seems to have been tackled. OK early on sitting in main bunch. Once climbing Pen-y-Ghent it was a case of let's get round. Mixed feelings. At least I ran. No high on finishing, but a feeling of 'if only', given the shape I was in a couple of weeks ago.

After Gavin Bland's 1993 win a new runner came to the Three Peaks Race and left his mark in a big way, eventually setting a course record in 1996 that has never been beaten (and never will as the course changed again in 2023), and also becoming the third male athlete to win the race four or more times.

Andy Peace had a seemingly easy win in 1994, by a margin of almost four minutes, from Mark Rigby. Winners from the previous two years were 4th (Gavin Bland) and 5th (Ian Ferguson) respectively. There had been a group of 13 runners together at Ribblehead. Peace then charged up Whernside in what was reckoned to be one of the fastest ascents to that summit ever. That gave him a one-minute gap which he extended gradually all the way to the finish. He also won the 1st newcomer and 1st Yorkshire runner titles and led his Bingley Harriers to the team award.

Andy Peace's win was his first crack at the Three Peaks Race. He explains that if you ran in Bingley everyone seemed to do Burnsall and Ben Nevis, and also run the Three Peaks. You felt like you had to run the Three Peaks. 'I wasn't really aware of the history of the race then. I was aware that Fergy [Ian Ferguson] had won it a few times as I had seen him do it. To be honest I had no idea how I would get on that day because I had never run that far before.' He hadn't been doing long training runs and doesn't think he had recced it by then. Tellingly, he did do some recceing after winning.

Andy relives that race for me. 'As I recall a big group of maybe 12 of us all ran to Ribblehead, including Fergy, Scoffer,

67. L to R: Ian Ferguson, Andy Peace and Mark Rigby, 1994

and [Mark] Rigby. Whernside is a fell runners' climb, tussocky and with no set path. I got to the front and didn't really mean to get away. You climb, then there is a plateau and then you climb again. On the second climb I looked round, and I had about a 30-metre gap, and I thought well I am not pushing hard here. I just put me head down and went. I had no idea if I could hold them off. Going up to Ingleborough I couldn't see anyone behind and still felt fine. Ascents were my strength so I could hopefully go on to win. When I set the record, if you look at the descent times off Ingleborough, I ran sub-26 minutes and the guy running this year was just under 28 mins for that stretch.'

Andy Peace and Ian Holmes obviously have a strong rivalry, as Ian adds this coda to that day. 'Andy and I had done the National 12-stage relay the day before, but only on short legs. I don't think I was down to do the Three Peaks, but in the pub the night before I decided to do them both. I think Andy must have been taking it easy the day before [*laughs*].'

1995

There was a new women's winner, with Jean Rawlinson improving impressively from her 5th place the previous year, to lead her Clayton-le-Moors team to the team trophy as well. The race report noted that, 'the presence of the Army Shower Unit created a favourable impression.' Sarah Rowell turned down the chance of a fourth win, because she was focusing on the British and English Fell Championships titles and doing the Three Peaks didn't fit in with that.

Looking back on it recently, **Jean Rawlinson** recalls that she had the frame of mind to just get round and enjoy it. 'The weather was perfect and I was running up towards Pen-y-Ghent alongside another good lady runner called Kath Drake. I had never beaten Kath and she said, "Well Jean, I am going to push on now," and she left me and headed up Pen-y-Ghent. After descending and as I reached the road section towards Ribblehead Viaduct I heard them announce that the 1st lady, Kath, was just going through the checkpoint. I eventually caught up with her on the climb up Whernside and I told myself that I was going to get to the trig point before she did. I never saw any other ladies after that and continued to enjoy the run. When I was running along the last stretch I heard them announce over the loud speaker that the 1st lady, Jean Rawlinson, was just about to enter the field to finish. It was only then that I realised that I had won the ladies' race, and then running into the finish funnel my husband Barry (who had also done the race in a great time) was standing with open arms when I crossed the finish line – and we were both very emotional.'

Jean adds that she also collected a medal for first team prize for Clayton-le-Moors. 'I also have a 3rd place female medal from the Three Peaks (from 1994) but winning is much sweeter.'

Jean Rawlinson didn't start fell running until she was 40 because her husband Barry started running with her. 'We

68. *Jean Rawlinson ascending Ingleborough, 1995*

69. Andy Peace and Ian Holmes with a clear lead on Pen-y-Ghent, 1995

started entering races and got the bug for fell running and he was instrumental in helping me have faith in myself. We started doing championship races and found many of them tough, especially when the elements were against you, but enjoyed meeting people and talking after the races. I started winning my age group category and after a few years of racing I started to get a few wins under my belt, but the one race I should have won was Ben Nevis in 1994. I was 1st lady to the top, but I had a fall when descending and ended up losing it by ten seconds. Being born in Glasgow I was gutted I didn't win.'

There was a clash with a British Champs race in 1995 which affected the overall quality of the men's field, but the front of the race was still very strong. The two Bingley athletes, Andy Peace and Ian Holmes, ran through Ribblehead together and appeared to be on for a new record. Still inseparable at Whernside summit, Peace opened up a gap on the Hill Inn approach which he increased to seven minutes on Ingleborough and over ten minutes by the finish. However, perhaps through the lack of a challenge in the latter part of the race, he missed the record by just over a minute. Holmes was chased home by Paul Briscoe, who had broken his wrist during the descent from Ingleborough. Holmes agrees now that they were chasing the record. 'But I was 2nd to Andy again. He trained hard for the Three Peaks, and I would often go out with him to train on the Peaks.'

Andy Peace animatedly says, 'Holmsey was on fire, but I was not going to let him get away. I was thinking this is harsh. It was a lovely day. I expected to gap him on Whernside as I am a better climber than him and he is a better descender. The fact that I didn't drop him on Whernside had me thinking this could be a bit close. Then he dropped his bumbag on the ridge of Whernside as he was fumbling about trying to get something out of it. No way I was going to wait for him! I never saw him again after that, which was bonus really. I think the fact that he set off so hard cost us the record on that day, because I was tying up and cramping by the end.'

Chapter 22

REFLECTIONS
FROM STEVE BRECKELL

Steve Breckell's last run at the Three Peaks was in 1995. He says now that he wasn't doing the training anymore really. 'As a Vet I won a few shorter races but never won a longer one. In that 1995 race I was 18th and 2nd Vet to Bob Whitfield. I was running for Clayton Harriers by then, and we won the Vets team award as well. I did sixteen Three Peaks races and one that I didn't complete. I dropped out in 1978 in bad weather, the year Ted Pepper died. I got to the Hill Inn, and I was tired, and I was looking up Ingleborough and it was misty and very windy and cold. I just didn't fancy it. That is the only time in 17 goes at the race I have thought that way. I dropped out.'

Steve was born in Blackburn in 1951. He always enjoyed running but was not particularly good at it. He says his natural ability wasn't that evident. 'I did make the school cross-country team at senior school. I started running for Blackburn Harriers in 1968 and it was primarily a track club then. I looked up to John Calvert and Harry Walker when they joined Blackburn from Clayton Harriers. Harry was doing fell races, then I got into fell running too.' Steve didn't make the Lancashire team at cross-country, as he says they had a whole load of internationals, like Colin Robinson, Mike Freary, Ricky Wilde, Ron Hill, Mike Turner, Dave Lewis and John Calvert, who was an English Junior cross-country international.

The first fell race Steve competed in was at Pendle, as it was only about ten miles away. 'It was a real baptism of fire. It was about eight miles long in them days, starting in Roughlee village. Pretty soon we went straight up the face of Pendle. At the trig point we turned round, and it was like looking over the edge of the world. It overhangs and you can't see the downhill bit initially. Once I had finished the race I thought, "OK, I liked that." I am a bit of a masochist really.'

In the early 1970s Steve did the Fairfield Horseshoe fell race and turned his ankle coming off Fairfield and damaged his ankle bone and some ligaments. 'It was only because it was a lovely day that I didn't get into trouble. The fell rescue team had to come out. But I was hobbling back slowly. My foot and ankle had been jammed between two rocks coming from the checkpoint on Fairfield summit. After that experience I have treated rocks with the utmost respect.'

His first Three Peaks Race was in 1973, were he finished 17th, aged 22. He had done some longish runs by then but not nearly enough, he reckons. 'I was still a novice and certainly not doing that much training. I had a heavy job, as I was a plasterer by trade. My running had to revolve around that. Blackburn won the team prize that year, and I was the third counter. We also won in 1975 and 1977, when I was 6th and 8th respectively. I remember going to recce it (very slowly) with Harry Walker once, and a few others from different clubs, but it wasn't before the 1973 race. Probably before the 1975 race.'

The 1973 race started from Chapel-le-Dale, going up Ingleborough first and finishing up and down Whernside. 'I was going up that last peak and John Calvert was in front of me. He was just stood there, slumped over. I said, "Come on John," and he didn't respond. I passed him and got to the top and set off down towards the finish. It has a slight uphill for about 200 yards near the end and I was like Jim Peters at the end of his marathon, weaving from side to side.'

Steve recalls that in 1977 he was recceing the route with a teammate, and they were going over Black Moss. 'Inadvertently the teammate wandered into a bog and started sinking. I had to grab him and drag him out. It wasn't funny at the time, and he reckons I saved his life.' Steve adds that initially he had competed in 'fell running studs', and then moved to Walsh shoes which he liked, and still uses now.

In 1982 Steve had his worst ever position, of 75th, an occasion that he reflected on. 'I was reading in my diary recently, and it says I was going well to Hill Inn and got up to Ingleborough and walked and jogged back to the finish. That is all it says.' Interestingly, he says that the worst he has ever felt was towards the end of the 1984 race, when he finished 3rd – the best position he ever achieved in the race. He explains that apparent anomaly.

'I was in a big group with Bob Ashworth going across to Ribblehead. Just before the road I said to him, "Are we going too fast?" He replied, "We might be, and I am dropping back." When we got to Ribblehead Viaduct I think I was 3rd. Somehow, I made it into 2nd place, because Shaun Livesey later passed me coming off Ingleborough. I believe he must have stopped at the Hill Inn, for refreshments or something, so I must have taken him there. He must have picked it up as he sailed past me about halfway down from Ingleborough summit. I remember him saying to me, "Come on, Steve." I just thought it was very good of him, but I just wanted him to go away. I could have laid down to have a sleep, I was feeling that bad. I did manage to get to the finish and was about a minute behind Shaun. Maybe he was feeling the same as me by the end. I was disappointed with that result because at the British Championship race beforehand at Black Coombe I had beaten [*the Three Peaks winner that day*] Hugh Symonds in finishing 3rd. Again, in the race after that I beat him at the Northern Counties 14-mile British Championship fell race from Honister Pass slate quarry, finishing 3rd again (to Kenny Stuart and Jon Broxap, the same as at Black Coombe). I actually won the Lancashire fell running title in that race, which was a big but pleasant surprise. Before the Three Peaks John Calvert said to me, "You could win this." I thought it was a possibility, but it was not to be. I think the '70s and '80s era was when there were masses of top runners all running in the major race, probably the best standard overall there has ever been.'

Steve points out that the only fell season he concentrated on trying to get a good position in the Fell Runner of Year was 1984. 'I had some good finishes, but there were loads of championship races in them days. I missed some towards the end, as I got a back injury which cost me a number of points. But I won Rivington Pike that year, which was another big surprise.'

70. *Steve Breckell ascending Ingleborough in 1984*

He reckons his greatest achievement on the fells was getting an England vest in 1984, to run in Bergamo in Italy. 'Sadly, it didn't go that well. It was shortly after my bad back and I had missed some training. The team was Kenny Stuart (who won), Jon Broxap, Hugh Symonds, Dave Cartridge, Malcolm Patterson and myself.' Steve Breckell certainly mixed it with the best in an era when it was packed with hugely talented runners.

Finally, Steve Breckell comments that the Three Peaks Race always has a good atmosphere and there is a camaraderie among the runners. 'It was a good day out, unless you got it wrong. I have had a few health problems over the past few years, but I hope I might be able to do a few more fell races. I do the odd parkrun though at the moment.'

Chapter 23

TWO SUPERB RECORDS

1996

Sarah Rowell achieved her fourth win in six years, with a second course record. She thus matched Vanessa Brindle as a four-time winner, and it was Vanessa whom she beat into 2nd place that day by a staggering 19 minutes, shaving 12 seconds off her own record from 1991. Sarah again finished high up the field, this time in 20th position.

Not being a watch-wearer in races, she was told by spectators at Ribblehead that she was one minute down on the pace for the record. This didn't faze her though, as she had suffered badly after Ingleborough in 1991, and this time was feeling strong.

Ever analytical, she said afterwards: 'I knew when I heard the time it was going to be close. With the conditions being as they were, the record was always on my mind. I found I was losing ground on the climbs and regaining it afterwards. Maybe I didn't do enough hill work. I'm sure the record can come down a lot further than this. Maybe I'm just not the person to do it. Who knows?'

Sarah was always tough on herself, and as noted, she judged her performances

71. Sarah Rowell with the ladies trophy

on her 'percentage of male winner' metric, not by her position in the women's field. Of course, it didn't always go that well, statistically at least. 'For the 1996 Three Peaks I was way out of it (by percentage value it was 118%), despite setting the then record. I always aspired to run 3-10 for that race, which of course I never did. But when I look at all the splits and how far behind the men's record the women's should have been, that was what I ideally was aiming for. Victoria Wilkinson has proved that a woman can run it that fast, and that's great. Her time is where the women's record should be and where I always said I should be.'

Some athletes have prepared so well that they *expect* to win when they race. Fell icon Billy Bland had that in his armoury and rivals would be going to the start line thinking they were running for 2nd place. Sarah Rowell says now that she had that expectation – to an extent. 'A lot of my self-belief came from good training. Then what I wasn't able to always do was take that self-belief and use it as well as I could have done.' She gives an example from 1996, perhaps part explaining her not getting the time she felt capable of. 'I can remember going out doing a loop I used from Leeds, for which I had a best time ever of 2 hours 8 minutes [*training for the 1992 Three Peaks*]. I went out one day and ran 2 hours 6 minutes. At that point I should have had the confidence to say, "You know you are in really good nick, you are two to three weeks out from the Three Peaks, you don't need to keep pushing." My training, in particular that long run, showed I was in good shape and should have backed off more rather than ending up going into the race tired.'

This year also saw a stunning men's new course record, set by Andy Peace (alongside Sarah Rowell's for the women). The fact that both these records were set when underfoot conditions were firm just emphasised what effect that, and the weather, can have. Time for a slight statistical diversion here.[33]

---

33 In the 14 years from 1983, when the course had some changes, course records were set in eight of the years, and ALWAYS in both male and female categories. The weather and underfoot conditions were noted in the reports as good in four of the years, neutral in three others, and only bad in 1983 (but that year automatically had new records due to the changes). In the other six years NO records were set in either the male or female categories, whilst admittedly the weather varied during those years. In summary it seems that some years were very conducive to running fast, as demonstrated by the list of records.

72. *Andy Peace, 1996*

Andy Peace set off as though he was aiming to do some damage to his cousin Ian Ferguson's course record from five years previously. Peace recalls that the year before Ian Ferguson had called out, "You'll never beat my record!", which of course just added to his determination to do so this year. By Ribblehead he had a two-minute lead over the chasers: Mark Roberts, Paul Sheard and Colin Donnelly. Peace powered on to win by over eight minutes. Peace's brother Martin ran well to take the first newcomer prize in 6th place in his first race there, and helped Bingley win the team title.

Delighted with the result, Andy said afterwards that, 'Nobody was prepared to push it up Pen-y-Ghent, so I just went for it. It was always my aim to go for the record and I thought if I blow it, I blow it. Even so I felt confident I could do it. The hat-trick is a great feeling. I used to watch my dad running it many years ago [*he was a top-20 finisher*] and I never thought I'd get round, never mind win it!' The record he set that day, of 2-46-03, has never been beaten. In fact, no one has run under 2-50 since.

Andy Peace quietly mentions that he can recall the splits from that record time from the top of his head: '28.5 on Pen-y-Ghent, 72 something to Ribblehead, 1-40 on Whernside, 1-55 at the Hill Inn, 2-20 at Ingleborough, and 2-46 at the finish'. He then gives a full resumé of his approach and how it had gone. 'I knew I was going well and was in good shape. I was in my late 20s and confident. I stood on the start line and Mark Roberts had the times on his wrist to run 2-52. I said to him, "Well you are not going to win then, are you?" [laughs]. I had run in the National 12-stage the day before and we had won it. I had run a short leg and I was a bit disappointed in my time really. We had a massive lead and subconsciously I was probably taking it a bit easy and didn't push like I could have done. Holmsey ran faster than me by 15 seconds at those relays and I would expect to beat him. We had a great team, possibly our best ever, and I wanted to be part of that. I don't think I had an after-effect on the Sunday. I remember setting off on the Three Peaks thinking it wasn't a mega strong field that year. I was definitely going for the record, that was my plan. I could tell it wasn't fast enough early on, people were chatting away with each other! I thought this won't get me the record, so I just buggered off and nobody came with me, and I ran the whole thing on my own.'

Mark Roberts finished 2nd that day and chuckles, 'But who remembers who finishes 2nd!' He says he kept expecting to see Andy coming back to him. 'Andy was going for it. Over each hill I kept thinking, he can't keep that pace up. I had all my times written on my hand to run a time under 2-55. I think I ran 2-54 in the end. It was good weather, and I probably ran it in road shoes, I don't know. The race doesn't start till the viaduct. Most people

73. Mark Roberts, 1996

tried to chill until there. If you are going to go for the record, then you have to push it. I think he was determined to go for it that day. His cousin (Ian Ferguson) had the record from five years before, and he wanted to beat that.'

Andy Peace was the first person to manage the double of winning both the Three Peaks fell and cyclo-cross races – twice, in 1995 and 1996. 'I had won the cyclo-cross in September 1995 between my two fell wins. I was lucky in the cyclo-cross as it was in between two eras. There was Tim Gould and Co. before, who were pro bike riders, and I was just a fell runner messing about really. There was a little gap with no pros, and I nipped in and got a couple of wins. Then Jebby took over the cyclo-cross event.' Even more noteworthy is the fact that Andy Peace didn't enter the Three Peaks Race for another seven years yet came back to win in 2004 for the fourth time. This gap of eight years is the longest ever between wins by a male or female athlete at the event.

Andy Peace was born in Keighley. Although he is equally proficient at both sports, running came before cycling in his life. 'My dad was a member of Bingley Harriers, and I went to do a local fell race – the Eldwick Gala race. I didn't want to go really. My twin brother was going, so we both went, and I think I won a prize. Then I joined Bingley and it escalated from there. It wasn't serious though till I left school. My brother was a better runner than I was right up to soon after leaving school. There were a few lads coming through at the same time and we had a really good Junior team. We won the Junior cross-country team prize. We all moved into the Seniors doing more cross-country than fell racing, with the odd track and road efforts. I soon realised I wasn't a track runner. My dad did the Three Peaks Cyclo-Cross, coming 2nd in the mid-1980s, which I went to watch. I think he did the Three Peaks Fell Race too, but I don't recall how he did, but do remember watching him. My dad used to take me running a bit but didn't pressure me at all.'

Andy says his training was mostly track and cross-country style, doing what others in the club, like Colin Moore, were doing. 'I wasn't training for the fells at all. We won the Northern cross-country title 11 years on the trot and won the National a good few times. It was a fight to get in the team.'

Prior to 2004 Andy had started doing duathlon events, and he did some long duathlons, till he got bored. 2004 was the 50th anniversary of the race and he decided to do it again but wasn't really expecting to win. 'I had trained hard, mind, but hadn't run any fell races yet in that year. On the day, I felt alright. I may have had the fastest ascents on all three hills, but Simon Booth caught me on the descent of Whernside and we ran through the Hill Inn together. I got away from him up Ingleborough and I don't think he pegged that much back on me. I was in trouble by the end. The last two or three miles I was proper struggling.'

No one has beaten Andy's 2-46 time from 1996. Andy reckons Mark Lauenstein might have done a better time in 2016 if conditions had been better. 'He ran round in full body cover and there was snow and ice on the summits. If anyone would have beaten my time it would have been him. He was a very good runner, no doubt about it.'

Andy declares that his wins at the Three Peaks Race are definitely up there as top achievements for him. 'I have done other stuff too that I am very happy with, like top 10 in World Mountain champs, top 10 in the World Duathlon, and 4th at Sierre-Zinal. It may not have been so big at the time, but as I've got older, and the Three Peaks record has stood the test of time, I have kind of grown to appreciate it even more. The record has gone now with the newly extended course in 2023. That is a shame really.'

Andy Peace reckons that the Three Peaks Race is part of fell running history. 'It is a hard race, and it is a race people want to win. If you don't respect it, it will bite you on the backside. Just because it isn't mega rough and there is no navigation to do, it doesn't mean to say it is easy.'

1997

There were ideal conditions for running, and it was a first repeat victory for 1993 winner Carol Greenwood. She showed a return to winning form after the birth of daughter Katie, some 12 months

74. *Carol Greenwood, 1997*

earlier. Carol also became the first female Bingley Harrier to win the coveted title. Runner-up Vanessa Brindle couldn't add to her four victories, despite her best efforts, with fellow veteran Karen Slater taking 3rd place. Wendy Dodds became the first woman to achieve 15 race completions, a commendable achievement in this the 19th edition that women had been able to run in.

Meanwhile a drama was taking place, as a helicopter paid for by a charity that grants wishes for dying children was diverted to airlift an injured runner. It was carrying a terminally ill teenager, so she could watch her mum [Karen Slater] run, as the *Yorkshire Evening Post* reported:

A runner in the men's section slipped and badly sprained his ankle. With the weather threatening to close in and the man's temperature falling, race organisers called in the Mountain Rescue Team. By chance the charity helicopter was passing overhead, and the pilot changed his plans to airlift the runner to safety.

Event organiser Dave Hodgson admitted: 'It made for an eventful day. By the time the message was received the runner's body temperature had already dipped. To have got the Mountain Rescue Team out would have taken an hour or more so we were extremely grateful.'

Charlotte Slater said: 'It was absolutely fantastic. The helicopter picked me up near our house and mum and dad waved to me from the ground. At about 1-30pm the message came over the radio to say a runner was injured so we landed to pick him up.'

Being reminded of the event, Barry Slater (Charlotte's father), who was running in the race with Karen, added this poignant coda to the story: 'It was a foggy start, and it was touch and go whether the helicopter would be able to fly. Fortunately, Roger the pilot was Force's trained! In the race Karen and I had just started descending off Pen-y-Ghent when the clouds parted, and we heard the helicopter soaring above. I had to stop whilst I sobbed, unable to see through the tears. Charlotte sadly passed away in October that year, but it was a beautiful day and memory I'll cherish forever.'

Bingley's Ian Holmes set out hard and led to the top of Pen-y-Ghent, over a minute up on Paul Sheard, Gary Oldfield, Mark Horrocks and Paul Briscoe. Running close to Andy Peace's record pace from the year before, he had a six-minute lead by Ribblehead. After the race he commented, 'when I got to the Hill Inn I glanced at my watch and realised I was bang on schedule. Andy had told me that I needed to go through the Hill Inn in 1-57 or 1-58, so from then on I thought I could give it a go.'

Feeling the effects of his pace as he climbed Ingleborough he had to ease off and finished over eight minutes clear of the previous year's 3rd-placer Paul Sheard. Despite missing the record, the time Holmes did that day was not beaten for another ten years.

Ian Holmes recalled that race when we chatted recently. 'It wasn't the strongest field, and I thought this might be my chance to win the Three Peaks. I was on course for the record early on, up to the Hill Inn, but I started slowing going up Ingleborough. By the top I was four minutes off Andy Peace's schedule. He was the only person who would have caused me any concern that day, and he wasn't doing it. I thought I could ease off and save something for the Champs race in a week's time. I think I could have run at least two minutes faster that day. Unfortunately, I slipped past Fergie's time – so he has a faster time than me! [*By 47 seconds*] He [*Ian Ferguson*] still reminds me of that whenever he can.'

Ian Holmes's father was more of a track runner, as the 800m and the mile were his distances, often on grass tracks. He retired from racing when he was just 19, not even out of the Juniors. Ian loved playing rugby when he was young, from 11 to 17 years of age. 'I also went diving as well (in a swimming pool) and I did something to my back. I suffered for almost a year with that. I did cross-country as a kid, but off no training. I was good enough to medal in the Bradford area cross-country champs.' His first fell race was a BOFRA race locally. Ian had a brother who was 18 months older than him, so he used to go along and do races as well. 'My dad would take us. When I was about 19, I was friends with Ian Ferguson and he got me into running races again. It was probably his love of the Three Peaks that got me thinking about it. I knew he'd won the Three Peaks and I thought I will have some of that as well. I think I ran the Three Peaks first in 1987.'

75. Ian Holmes descending Pen-y-Ghent, 1997

Ian Holmes thought he was training quite hard until he read Ron Hill's two autobiographies. 'He went from being a fairly average runner and turned himself into one of the best runners in the world. He was the definition of dedication to training. Ron Hill had a cold shower for 30-odd years because he thought it did him good, and then later on found it was a load of bollox!' Ian still trains every day, getting up early and going for a run. He says it is hard in winter though these days, when it is cold and raining, but he still does it. He also adds that he never practises descents. 'You don't run downhill hard unless you have to! Where I live it is hilly, not big hills, but plenty to do.'

Ian has also dabbled in cyclo-cross racing more recently. 'I was close at v40 to winning my age group in the Three Peaks Cyclo-Cross but had a few mechanicals that day. Then I nearly won the v50 when I got to that category but just missed that too.'

He puts his longevity down to being quite lucky with injuries. He did have a knee injury in his late 40s and struggled for two years with that. 'I was going to have an operation but fortunately I didn't, as Rob Jebb's mum (who is a physio) got me back running again. You have your aches and pains as you get older, don't you? I am doing around 40 miles a week these days. If I get carried away and try to do more something will always flare up. Back in the day it would be at least 80 miles per week.'

Reviewing his own career, Ian Holmes says he is proud of his Championships wins, 'but Simon Bailey has won the English more than me. One of the reasons I wanted to win four British Champs was because Colin Donnelly had not won four! I had to do four. Colin was unlucky on his fourth one. If he had won four, then maybe I would have gone for five. The most pleasing was the first time I won Snowdon which was quite special, because so many come out to watch the race and it is such an atmosphere, particularly on the corner by the Victoria Hotel. They even cheer on the English runners. I only just beat Mark Croasdale that year. I only got away really on Victoria Terrace. I stopped him getting his hat-trick as well.'

He adds that he has few ambitions really. 'I make it up as I go along now. I just choose things I want to do. I hadn't won a race for about 12 months, till I found one I could win the other week – the Pendle Clough race.'

We finished with Ian giving his thoughts on the Three Peaks Race itself. 'I came back when I was a v50 some ten years after 2007. I didn't do it for a while as it clashed with my favourite race, which is Coniston. Sometimes it was on the same day or sometimes the day after. If I had to choose, I would do the Coniston race. I probably did Three Peaks around ten times though.' For the record Ian Holmes was 1st v50 in both 2017 and 2019, finishing in 26th and 15th places respectively.

Finally, Ian Holmes proudly said that coming from Yorkshire it means a lot to him. 'I did enjoy it and I didn't enjoy it, if you get what I mean. It was always a really hard race. You could never relax on it, or slow down. It is a classic race over three mountains but was never a real favourite for me. They are long descents and long climbs, something over 1500 feet each time, which you don't get in the Lakes as there is a lot of ridge running with short sharp drops and rises. If you are a Yorkshireman and a fell runner you have to win the Three Peaks really.'

Chapter 24

TWO GOOD MARKS

1998

Conditions were very different, with the ground underfoot being described as a mud bath. This didn't hinder Carol Greenwood though, as she won in a time 23 seconds faster than the year before. She was delighted to claim her third win in six years. She placed 41st overall in conditions she said were the worst she had ever faced in an event. 'I am happy with my run, especially considering the conditions,' she said at the time. 'I just ran my own race, picking off men on the climbs.' Vanessa Brindle was 2nd again, with Jean Shotter showing good form to come home in 3rd.

Carol Greenwood has a wide range of running achievements, many of them achieved under her maiden name of Haigh. Carol has one claim to fame that no other woman has achieved. That was international selection at fell, road, cross-country and track. 'I ran for England on the track in Ireland and I got a GB vest to go to the Commonwealth Games on the track, but sadly got a stress fracture just beforehand.' One unusual international Carol ran in was the (winning) Ekiden Relay team in 1984, in Japan. The photo of her in the event appears to show that it was snowing. 'I was running for Great Britain in the relay and as I was doing the last leg it started snowing, which you can see in the photographs,' she confirms.

Carol won the World Mountain Running Trophy back in 1986, in Morbegno. She had further success abroad, finishing 3rd at the 1993 World Trophy, and 2nd at the 1997 European Mountain Running Trophy, and ran twice at the World Cross Country Championships. Greenwood won the first English Fell Running Championships in 1986. The middle of her running career was affected by sciatica, but she returned to prominence in the early 1990s, winning at Ben Nevis. She had a remarkable run of 38 consecutive victories in 1993, when she repeated her

76. *Carol Greenwood at Sulber Nick, 1998*

77. *Mark Roberts refuelling, 1998*

English Championships success. One of her wins that year was at the Snowdon Race, where she set a record time of 1-12-48.

Mark Roberts had a long-held ambition to win the Three Peaks Race, and he achieved it in style in 1998. Talking after the event, Roberts commented on being favourite to win. 'I'm chuffed to bits. It's not easy when everyone makes you out to be the favourite. What do you do? Do you go off hard and risk blowing up or do you hang back and see what happens? To be honest I found it really hard today. The conditions were really bad, and I've felt better than that when I've finished 2nd. I know Mark Horrocks felt it too and I only got away near the end because I was perhaps a bit stronger than him. Scoffer (Schofield) had a brilliant run as well to finish 3rd, his best ever in this race.'

Having a cold on a day that saw all four seasons of weather hit the area – snow, hail, rain and sunshine – didn't help Roberts, who described how muddy it was. Schofield and Horrocks pushed the pace up Whernside with Roberts trailing them. But he managed to

78. *Mark Roberts, 1998*

shake them off in the final stages to win by just 11 seconds. The fact that several top fell runners chose to run the Knockdhu Classic race, in Northern Ireland, the day before, should take nothing away from Mark Roberts' tactically supreme run at the Peaks.

Mark Roberts acknowledges that as a multiple champion he had the favourite's tag. He had won the British and English Fell Champs the year before. Having been 2nd, 3rd and 5th in the British Champs he really wanted to win it, so didn't run the Three Peaks in 1997. 'But in 1998 I was ill all week. I thought it was my chance, so I ran anyway. I remember running with Scoffer and Mark Horrocks and thinking I am hanging on here – that was my tactics! With a couple of miles to go I was still with Mark. I just managed to shake him off in the end. His partner had said to me please let him win! No chance. "Tactically supreme run". I'll take that! We celebrated afterwards, as always.'

Mark Roberts was born in Kendal in 1962. He began running when he started secondary school, after always being interested in football before that. His father was a football manager, and Mark played a lot of football when he was younger. At cross-country he usually came in the first two or three and one of the lad's parents came up and asked if he wanted to join Kendal AC, to help their son out who was a really good runner and wanted some teammates. His first fell race was when he was about 12. 'I think I did either the Grasmere Sports or the Ambleside Sports, or maybe ran at Coniston. But I did a lot of cross-country and track racing earlier on. I was County Champion at 800m, 1500m, 5000m and steeplechase. I represented England at steeplechase in my early 20s, when we had some good steeplechasers.'

Fell running was always there though, and he says he came more onto the fells after his track career. His 1997 British Champs win was a tie with Ian Holmes. 'I think it was the first time it was reduced from six races to four. It was always going to be close. I went to Ireland to recce the course for the last race and went over on my ankle, so I couldn't do the race. All my Borrowdale teammates didn't go over, and they could have sorted Holmsey out, but it was an easy run for him in the end. I was more than happy to share it with him.'

In fact, Mark won a fantastic treble in 1997. As well as the British Champs, he won the English Champs and the Inter-Counties Fell Race. 'I don't think anyone else has done that in one season. The inter-counties was a tough race at Buttermere Sailbeck. That treble is probably my most pleasing achievement.'

Mark also ran well internationally. 'After winning the Champs in 1997, myself, Ian Holmes and Mark Rigby got invited out to Borneo for the Mount Kinabalu race. It was billed as a big thing. The Brits are coming! We ended up finishing 1st, 2nd and 3rd (the order being: Ian, Mark, myself). It was a brilliant trip, and a really tough course. I also finished 9th in the European Championships in 1998 in Sestriere, which was probably my best international performance.'

Mark reflected on the Three Peaks, its status and how to run it. 'The Three Peaks Race has its own place in history. A brilliant event, a one-off really. There is nothing like it. It is not really an 'A' category fell race, as there is a lot of cross-country in it. But it is one that a lot of people want to win, as are the Ben Nevis race and the Snowdon race. I thought with my track and cross-country background, and with having good speed, that it would help in the Three Peaks. If you push too hard on the fast bits, then you are going to struggle. Some of the sections have eroded (e.g. coming off Whernside) and are rougher than they used to be – which contributes to slower times.'

Mark Roberts concludes with another impressive statistic. 'I won the v60s category at the English Fell Champs last year. I think I am the only person that has won every category at the English Champs: Senior, v40, v45, v50, v55, and now v60. So Holmsey has got to keep going a bit longer yet [*laughs*]!'

1999

There was an outstanding women's performance by race newcomer Angela Mudge. Reaching Ingleborough in a stunning 9th place, she finished 11th overall, the highest ever placing for a woman. Sarah Rowell came in 2nd, her 1996 race record remaining intact.

Angela Mudge says now that she approached the race like a real novice. 'I didn't recce the course beforehand. I had no car, and it was a long way from home, so I just hoped I started at the right pace and could keep going. I remember being surprised at the amount of running between Pen-y-Ghent and Whernside. It had been pretty wet leading into the race, so the ground was really boggy between those two peaks, which kept me happy. Disappointingly, it is now a made path. My favourite section will always be the steep climb up Whernside, and I have always enjoyed walking up a steep climb and overtaking the men (although not anymore). It was a very lonely experience coming off Ingleborough, as the field was very spread out, and I wasn't sure if I was on the right track.' Mudge has won the British Fell Running Championships five times and has a mighty list of race victories both in the UK and abroad.

Sarah Rowell's diary entry gives a comprehensive review of the race:

79. *Angela*
    Mudge,
    1999

Conditions wettish underfoot. Sunny breeze from the east. Felt good on first climb with Angela pulling ahead. Really good across the flat bit and was 30 seconds down on Angela plus big group of men by time I hit the track. Did I then try too hard? Who knows except had real problems on the road. Stopped to stretch leg out. Took till top of Whernside to recover. After that had lost too much time on Angela and some of the men I would normally have beaten. Faster than Angela off Ingleborough but she was faster than me on pretty much the rest, particularly the run to Ribblehead. Top of PYG she was 32nd and I was 33rd. By Ribblehead she was a minute ahead of me.

There was another new men's winner, in **Mark Croasdale**. In 2nd and 3rd for the second year in a row were Mark Horrocks and Scoffer Schofield. Graham Schofield (not related) won the Veterans' award in an excellent 7th place. Mark Croasdale had unfinished business with the event, as he had blown up spectacularly when leading in 1993 and he came back six years later for redemption.

The 1999 race was the only other time Mark ran the Three Peaks. When I interviewed him recently, he confirmed that he was always going back to do it again, it was just a matter of when. 'At that time, I was doing the internationals still, and a bit of road racing. The Three Peaks didn't quite fit in for six years. It got to 1999 and I thought, right let's do this. Conditions were better and I was very cautious and didn't take the lead. My thought was, "Just win the race." I had no interest in times, records or anything else. I remember going up Whernside and Mark Horrocks was ahead of me, which was fine, only by about 40 seconds. I caught him over the top and just kept a short distance ahead, maybe a minute ahead coming off Ingleborough. The gap was big enough for the run-in. Even then I was cautiously thinking – just win the race.'

Mark Croasdale grew up in Lancashire and could see Ingleborough every day. He knew people who ran the Three Peaks, but not much about it when he was growing up. He was a reasonable runner at school, at county standard, but mostly played football and messed around a lot, like most lads. Mark joined the Royal Marines at 16 years old and spent nine months

80. *Mark Croasdale, 1999*

at the Commando Training Centre Royal Marines (CTCRM) doing his basic training, before joining 42 Cdo RM. He went to the Falklands War at 17 and spent time in Norway training, as 42 Cdo was also an Arctic Warfare Unit.

Mark says he stumbled into the Marines' ski team, having won their cross-country champs and started skiing by then. He explains that they had a good biathlon team and within a couple of seasons he was on the Nordic Cross-country Ski team. 'I also competed for Great Britain for the cross-country team. Then training got more serious, and fell running became part of the summer training that we would do. Then I thought maybe I could do a couple of local races, like Wray Caton Moor. This would have been 1986. In 1987 I started to do more fell running. It was just good endurance training really. The Three Peaks came a few years later when I started being more serious and thought about having a go at the international stuff as well.' He got to a high standard as a skier and went to the Olympics for the 1992 Winter Games, in Albertville (France), and also went to two World Championships (for skiing) in 1989 and 1991. 'In 1987 I became a full-time athlete which was a good thing and a bad thing, because I was 22 and had over-trained really. I was with a group of athletes who had been training for three to four years, and I did not have the endurance to deal with that level of training. Come the winter I was worn out.'

In 1992, after the Olympics, Mark left the Marines and had effectively finished with skiing. 'I had a problem with a shoulder injury which had dislocated a number of times. I made the England team for the Mountain Running Champs

81. Mark Croasdale, 1999

in 1990, and again in 1991/92 and so there was an overlap in training and sports around that time, but by the Three Peaks Race in 1993 it was only running for me.'

By the 1990s Mark had done the Ingleborough race, and still holds the record for that race (from 1991) and had done the Pen-y-Ghent race, so knew quite a lot more about the Peaks, and to him it seemed time to give it a go. Looking back to 1993 he gives his memories of the race. 'It was my first time in the race. But I had been going there and doing a couple of peaks as training. My wife would come up in the car with me and drop me off somewhere and I would do two hills and then be picked up again. I had recced it all separately. I was comfortable with doing the race.'

Mark had won both the English and British Fell Championships in 1993, but says he was probably running at his best on the fells in 1991 when he was preparing for the Olympics (skiing) because he set some good course records. There is one that still stands to this day, that for the Ingleborough race. 'I was running so much faster and had good endurance from my skiing. In 1991 I won Langdale and then the Butter Crags race the following day. Short ones like Butter Crags didn't really suit me. I needed to climb really well to get a gap to hold on the descent there. I also started doing some road running in 1993. Up to two hours in a race I could go hard. Three hours, like the Three Peaks, was tougher. I didn't quite get it, if you know what I mean. I needed to be able to hold on a bit better.'

Going into the 1993 Three Peaks Race was the longest race Mark Croasdale had ever done. He gives his perspective on that day and how wrong it all went for him. 'I was in really great nick though. Prior to the Three Peaks I'd won Criffel Hill, a British Championship race that year, and set the course record which still stands. I won Kentmere in 1993 which I believe was a good time on that course of 1-25-18. I'd also run a sub-64-minute half marathon at York in my build-up. On Three Peaks race day the weather was pretty rubbish, and I probably didn't give the distance the credit it was due. Maybe I went off a bit too fast. I felt good for 2.5 hours. Going up Ingleborough I felt good, but then just totally blew coming off Ingleborough. I was about four or five minutes ahead and even though it was downhill once you go, you go. I was slurring my words even! It was my error. I should have been more cautious. Gavin Bland and Mark Horrocks caught me in the bottom field. I was very frustrated. I had been racing the lads and had been beating them quite regularly.'

Mark had a fine record of successes across his career. He set several course records which have disappeared due to course changes, including Hutton Roof, Clougha Pike, and Wray Caton Moor. 'The Man v Horse was also a race that I ran numerous times, winning it six times individually (once when I'd only been back from the Iraq War 2003 for only a few months), and ten times with a relay team. The closest I came to beating the horse was 80 seconds when only one horse beat me. I did hold the record for the course, but again I think the course has changed and so there's a new record.'

In an interview in 1991 he said his ambitions on the domestic fell running scene were: 'To win the British and English individual titles, and also win Ben Nevis and the Three Peaks. Just once each will do nicely!' As noted, he achieved both fell championship wins in 1993, and won the Three Peaks Race in 1999. He did not, however, succeed at the Ben Nevis race, but did win the prestigious Snowdon race twice, in 1991 and 1992.

He comments on that missing win: 'I did the Ben once, in 1992, and was leading at the summit and feeling quite comfortable. I knew the better descenders might catch me on the descent. Often the date for the Ben race didn't fit in with other things I was doing. This year it did. I tripped and fell in the Red Burn. I landed on my back and was lucky not to injure myself seriously. It knocked the stuffing out of me, and I started walking down. I jogged the bottom bit and finished 6th. I should have won that day. Even if anyone caught me, I was confident of taking them on the road at the end. I never went back again.'

Looking back over his whole career now he muses that his fell running period had quite a short span really. It was from 1987 to 1995, as he had moved on to the roads by then. As for highlights he says, 'well, certainly being the first person to win

British and English Fell Champs in 1993, after coming close in 1991, whilst still skiing. The Three Peaks win sits alongside that though. Then running for England was fantastic. In 1992 we had a team that won the World Trophy Short course. Martin Jones won, Robin Bergstand was 3rd and I was 9th, and Craig Roberts 14th. That was a great result.'

Mark reveals how good he was at the marathon at one point in our discussion. 'My marathon time would have been good enough for Commonwealth qualification, but it was just at the wrong time. I did my 2-16 in 2000, so it wasn't good enough for the Olympics. I was 5th or 6th British runner in the London Marathon (the trial) so was not going to be selected. I was selected for the World Cup (marathon) once but couldn't go because I got ill.'

He concludes that winning the Three Peaks Race is right up there for him. 'I would have been very frustrated if I hadn't won it. It sits up there amongst the classic races. I had run a 2-17 marathon the year before that. It is a fast course, but it is also a tough course. You certainly shouldn't underestimate it, and maybe I did that the first time. It is an iconic race though.'

For many years Mark Croasdale has been doing team management for the international teams, from the first time in 2005 in New Zealand right up till now. 'Being involved with the GB and England Mountain Running Teams has been fantastic. It has been great to give something back to the sport having run on the teams in the '90s. There have been many highlights, as our teams have always been very successful and that's down to the quality of the athletes we have had and the support they've been given by the likes of Sarah Rowell, Anne Buckley and Angela Mudge over numerous years. To see the sport evolve to what it is now is brilliant. Going to Thailand in 2022 for the World Championships, now a combination of mountain and trail running, to a country that's never put on this type of competition was great to see. The fact that we could take a team of 44 athletes and staff was superb and to take home nine medals was the icing on the cake. It is great to be involved and see the athletes do well.'

Chapter 25

RUNNING FOR THE TEAM

2000

The Three Peaks Race was the second race in both the British and English Championships in 2000, and duly attracted a high-quality field, on a really hot day. Glossopdale's Sally Newman took the win in 66th place overall. Newman was 2nd behind Sarah Rowell at Pen-y-Ghent but soon found herself in the lead as Rowell dropped out on the moorland section to Ribblehead. Vanessa Brindle gained yet another 2nd place, and also took the v40 prize.

Sarah Rowell says now that she had a lot going on personally at this time, which wasn't helping and on the day meant her normal focus was not there. She was also doing a five-day adventure race, the Adrenaline Rush, later that month in a team of four in Ireland. Her diary notes:

> I started the Three Peaks, and I had my ankle strapped up. Warmed up. Mind on anything but the race, ankle, you name it. Really strong going up PYG and down but put off by the number of people who seemed to go past me. Ankle was OK but brain had gone so I stopped.

She says that was the last time she entered the Three Peaks. In her words, it was very much a case of, 'if I didn't think I was going to run the time I felt I should be able to do, then I most certainly wouldn't do it.'

Sarah Rowell signs off our chat by saying the Three Peaks is a brilliant event, and explains why. 'I'm both proud and frustrated because I do think my first Three Peaks was brilliant, the second was brilliant, third was struggling with a cold, and fourth I should have backed off training before the event. The biggest frustration, bizarrely, is my fastest one (1996). That is because when given what Andy [Peace] did, I should have been faster still.' She argues with herself about whether it really does meet the criteria for a proper fell race, and says, 'by the true definition of a fell race, maybe it once was, but not now. When I ran there were still a few places where there was route choice, now other than the line off Ingleborough I do not think there is any. It is still an exceptionally hard race because there is no recovery. Some fell races give you recovery periods. The Three Peaks is just hard from the start. It is more like a marathon with three hills in it. It needs a broad skillset to do well. Andy was good at it because he had the hill strength, and the flat speed.'

Overall, Simon Booth was always in contention in what was one of the hottest race days there had been. The Pen-y-Ghent checkpoint was reached in 28-00 by a quartet of Alan Bowness, Ian Holmes, Rob Jebb and Simon Booth. The same four passed through Ribblehead close together, with Holmes now leading, and continued over Whernside as a group. On the climb of Ingleborough, Booth and Holmes were neck and neck, but Booth edged clear to win by just over a minute. Jim Davies and Mark Roberts had moved through to take 3rd and 4th, with Rob Jebb close behind in 5th place and Alan Bowness in 6th. Mark Roberts adds a coda to that moving through. 'Jim Davies and I took turns getting cramp going over the stiles on the way back from Ingleborough. That part is notorious.'

Simon Booth claimed when I interviewed him recently that he had only entered the Three Peaks in 2000 because it was an English Champs race, and he was running for the team. It was the first time he had run the race. He adds: 'For some reason I never in my wildest dreams thought that it was a race I could win. I guess I'd formed an opinion based on views from others, in particular descriptions of it being a road race from some of the Cumbrian fell running community.'

It was a race he was not looking forward to, a race he had never recced, or even put foot on any part of the course before. 'I remember the pace being a little uncomfortable up to the top part of Pen-y-Ghent and I had just started to lose some distance before the top, but then being surprised how easily I regained it on the turn. After that the pace was good, but comfortable, to Ribblehead and then I was pleased to be able to walk up Whernside but not lose much distance. On the descent to the Hill Inn, it was easy to regain it again and at that point it was just me and Ian [Holmes]. As we headed towards Ingleborough I was enjoying the [limestone] pavement and I was thinking, "Wow, I'm going to be 2nd at the Three Peaks!" As we started climbing, Ian was pulling away but not too much and as we neared the top, I think I was reducing the lead again, so it didn't take long to catch him again, and of course then my thoughts were about winning. At the time my legs were always good for the last descent no matter how much I struggled on climbs. I don't recall needing to put any effort in and I think I just drifted away to a decent lead. I can't remember now whether Ian was cramping or suffering somehow, but my only concern was how well the last few fields to the finish would be flagged. We had a good team and were chasing the championships. It was so unexpected to win, and I loved it. But I would have been happy with 2nd place if Ian had beaten me. My plans to go straight home had changed and I stayed and enjoyed some beer at the pub.'

Ian Holmes recalls that he and Simon Booth had a good lead coming to the Hill Inn. 'Simon stopped at the bottom to get some food or drink and I just carried on. He caught me and we went to the top together. I didn't want to wait any longer so picked the pace up and when it got to the flatter terrain, I could feel it coming on to a bonk. Then he ran away from me.'

2001
Sadly, there was no Three Peaks Race in 2001 due to the outbreak of Foot-and-Mouth, which decimated the sporting calendar that year.

2002
There had been good weather before the race in 2002, but there was overnight rain and bad conditions on the day. In these difficult conditions Tracey Brindley took the race by the scruff of the neck. She ran strongly throughout to secure a win in a highly commendable 30th place overall, well clear of Jean Shotter,

who was also the 1st Vet. Tracey Brindley went on to have some excellent results both in the UK and on the international scene. In 2004, she was both British fell running champion and Scottish hill running champion. She won the individual bronze and a team gold medal at the World Mountain Running Trophy in Girdwood, Alaska, in 2003, and improved her individual result to come 2nd at the 2005 World Trophy, which was held in Wellington, New Zealand. She won the w35 women's race at the World Masters Mountain Running Championships in 2007 and finished 2nd in the mountain race at the Commonwealth Mountain and Ultradistance Running Championships in 2011.

A trio of men took charge early on in 2002. From Pen-y-Ghent to Whernside, Simon Booth, Scoffer Schofield and Gary Wilkinson were setting the pace together, with a small group not far behind. Booth pulled clear descending Whernside and increased his lead to come in a comfortable winner, but well outside the course record. Scoffer and Gary Wilkinson held on for 2nd and 3rd places. The race's safety organisation was tested by the higher than usual number of mild cases of hypothermia, and one severe case.

Simon Booth reflected recently on that second win. 'I was back to defend the title after there being no race in 2001, due to Foot-and-Mouth. It wasn't a championship race and to be honest I expected to win quite comfortably. The persistent rain meant I wasn't keen to go off from the start and spend three hours on my own, but instead ran with the lead group. I remember getting cold and starting to struggle quite badly going up Whernside. I was losing interest and started to think about the option of dropping out at the Hill Inn. After Whernside I remember being very keen to get off the hill for a bit more shelter and in doing so took the lead and started to open a gap. I was pleased to reach the Hill Inn and was in a bit of a dilemma as I was still extremely cold. The enthusiasm from the supporters made me appreciate my position, so I put on my waterproof top and pants and gloves and balaclava. I thought I'd just carry on a bit longer and see how it goes until Scoffer catches me. I started to feel better on the steeper stairs section and at the top the rain stopped and

82. *Simon Booth, 2004*

gaps in the cloud started to show. The descent went reasonably comfortably, and I warmed up but finished with all the kit still on. It was a bit of a strange feeling winning that one.'

Simon Booth admits that football was the sport he enjoyed most in the early days. Running was something he was good at, but he didn't really do any running training. As he got older others started to beat him – they *were* training. Because he was getting beaten (and didn't enjoy that), he says it was easy to stop the running when he was around 15. He also comments that events were very few and far between for him at the time. 'I did cross-country at school and got put forward for the Allerdale trials, but never took it seriously. My dad started running when I was running at school, I think. He would be doing more running than I was.'

Simon then goes on to tell an amazing story about doing a marathon at the age of 13. 'At that time the Cockermouth marathon allowed kids and because it was a "marathon" it was somehow exciting. I can't recall if my dad was doing marathons then or what, but obviously we became aware of it, and were quite keen to do it. I did no specific training though.'

Simon explains how a move to Cumbria changed life for him. 'My dad encouraged me when I was young, but I suffered quite badly with asthma. That was the reason we moved up to Cumbria when I was about five or six, for the better air. It was probably more an excuse for him to move actually! He would take me out walking up the mountains. That was where I got my basic fitness from and where I learned the technique for downhill running. Later on, I lost interest in all sports. When I was 17, he could see I was lazing around, so he challenged me to run the Skiddaw fell race. I didn't think I would need to train to beat him. It was rather different though, being much longer than anything I had run by then (except for the marathon). It was way harder than the marathon.'

Simon's father had said he'd beat Simon, and he did. 'It was a hot day and I expected to be able to comfortably beat my dad. I set off OK but was soon getting overtaken. Oldies were overtaking me downhill and I was walking bits and stopping to sit in the stream. It did make me aware of the need to train if I wanted to do this stuff.' Simon got back to running again when he was at college, aged 18, when his asthma was noticeably getting worse. He obviously became a very good runner eventually.

Simon ran very well, but inconsistently, between 1989 and 1997, winning a lot of races but never really fulfilling his potential in the championship races. He thinks now that 1995 was his best year in that period. 'I then focused my training and racing around the championship races and my best years were 1998–2004 with the exception of 2003 when I was recovering from a foot injury, which held me back all year.' He was double British Fell Champion in 2002 and 2005. 'In 2005 I was definitely not as good, struggling particularly on the short races but also taking longer to recover. I did really well to win the championship but to be honest maybe competition was not as high that year.'

The foot injury occurred in the Kinabalu race in October 2002 when he was wearing road shoes, which he thought was sensible for that course. 'But I slipped off one rock and then bent my big toe right back on itself on another rock. I limped down, holding my foot differently and then I sprained my ankle pretty badly. My whole foot swelled up and my big toe didn't really recover. I probably gave up hope that it was ever going to be right again. I could run uphill fine, but downhill on rough ground was awkward. In about the August of the next year it kind of came right again. I was still very fit and was doing a lot of cycling at the time, but my skill is in the downhills and without that I wasn't the same athlete. I think people thought I was just making excuses. By then I loved running and didn't want to stop. It wasn't so much the races, I just loved running up and down mountains as fast as I could. I still do.'

In an earlier interview Simon was quoted as saying there were two races that he wishes he'd won: Ben Nevis (he was 2nd four times), and Kinabalu (he was 2nd in 1999). He explains. 'I think it is because they are two of my favourites and I didn't win them. If I hadn't won any of Borrowdale or Wasdale or Ennerdale or Langdale or Duddon or Great Lakes or Buttermere Horseshoe, I would have wished I'd won them!' He says he should have won Ben Nevis one year, when his old favourite shoes fell apart. 'It was 2002 and I was British champion, and I was really fit for once and not suffering from hay fever, which I often do in September. Walsh had changed the material in their shoes that year. It was a more plasticky material, much harder than previously. I didn't get on with that style. So, I used a pair of my old ones out of the cupboard. The glue must have been going because I got to the top OK and as soon as I turned to come down the shoes started coming to bits. Within a kilometre they were both flapping. I ended up slowing down, but getting through the stream above Red Burn I took them off for the grassy section and carried on barefoot. At the bottom of the grassy section, on rejoining the main path, I got a shoe off Jebby (who was spectating). He is a size ten and I am size eight. I think I finished with one of his shoes and a shoelace tied round my feet to keep my other sole on. But I still finished 2nd and I think about a minute behind Andy Peace. I reckon I would have caught him on that descent if it weren't for the shoe disaster, though not wanting to take anything away from him.' He adds jokingly, 'maybe I'll win it one day!'

Simon Booth has also done a fair amount of international mountain running throughout his career. 'It was great to represent Great Britain and England abroad at Kinabalu and Alaska, but it was also good getting support from Salomon to do the World Skyrunner series in from 2005. I have always loved travelling and it's great to explore new places by running. Holidays have often been based around races, but they are very much part of holiday plans and not so much of a running career. Highlights can often be the adventure or encounters in the pre-breakfast run or a day alone in the peaks.'

He continues. 'Out of all the races Zegama and Kinabalu were very special to me. Most people probably know what to expect at Zegama these days, but back in 2005 it just seemed crazy that mountain running could be that popular with spectators. They pat you on the back and rattle cowbells in your ears. Looking up to the peaks the whole skyline is covered in people. It is a very popular event. I was 2nd to Jebby.'

Asked what his career highlight was, I was expecting Simon to say winning Borrowdale 12 times. But no. He suggested something else, then listed several highlights. 'I think my career highlight was being British champion. It was a secret (distant and unrealistic) goal for a lot of years. Also getting international vests representing Great Britain (initially at Kinabalu) and England were major achievements. Twelve wins at Borrowdale is a proud achievement especially since the race always attracts a great field. Generally, I only did the other Lakeland longs when they were championship races, as I was put off by the lack of competition (the reason the Lakeland classics was introduced which has made a massive difference). The Great Lakes is possibly my favourite race, due to the amount of climb and rough terrain in a relatively short distance – and I would have loved to have raced it at my best (I was 40 for the first one in 2008). Other highlights are doing the Mount Kinabalu race (six times), but also winning the La Plagne 6000D race three years in a row and then getting myself a centre spread in *L'Equipe* magazine.'

As we shall see, Simon ran the Three Peaks again in 2004, but had not wanted to defend his title in 2003 thanks to the aforementioned foot injury which affected him from October 2002 until August 2003. He hasn't done the Three Peaks since then, as he says he probably has never really reached the same levels of fitness after 2004.

Simon Booth concludes that he has never really stopped running but has done very little in recent years. Until 2023 he had not raced for five years. 'I had bad cramps and thought I'd pack up racing. We had a family quite late, and I have three girls now. One of them last year started getting into fell running. She said she wanted to do the Junior races and expected me to do the Senior races. It was a shock to the system, but I am enjoying it. I am winning the v50s generally. I still enjoy the competition. My ambition is to keep up with my daughter as long as I can.'

Chapter 26

THE RACE ORGANISER

Current race organiser, Paul Dennison, reflects on the task of organising the Three Peaks Race:

In 2000, I had the honour to be nominated as the chairman of the race organisation, and since then it has been a great pleasure and challenge to hold this position for the last 23 years.

The first challenge I encountered in this role was the cancellation of the event due to Foot and Mouth Disease in 2001. The restrictions enforced in the countryside to stop the spread of the disease meant that the race could not go ahead. The second challenge was in 2020 when the whole world stood still due to the Coronavirus. Determined not to miss a second year due to the pandemic we moved the event from April 2021 to the October.

I had first become involved with the Three Peaks Race in 1975. I was a member of the 9th Airedale Venture Scouts and was asked by Dave Hodgson, who was a Scout Instructor [*as well as being heavily involved in the race*] at the time, to come and marshal on the summits. That year I was on the top of Pen-y-Ghent and had such a good time that I have been involved ever since. I have also been a member of Horsforth Fellandale athletic club and more recently Baildon Runners.

After the tragic events that happened with the death of Ted Pepper in 1978, new safety measures were put in place, such as the tag system which was introduced to keep track of where the runners were out on the course. At this point I left marshalling on the summits to become involved at race control, overseeing the retirements from the race. This led me on to the position I still love and hold today, as after about three years helping at race control, I moved on to the race director's job.

In 1989 I nearly missed the race due to my eldest daughter being born at 5.20am that morning. This was, fortunately for me, when the race was still held on a Sunday and a lot smaller

*83.   Paul Dennison,
race directing*

event to what it is today, so I managed to nip home from Airedale to Burley in Wharfdale, have a quick shower and make it to Horton in Ribblesdale for the start, with an hour to spare.

All my family have always been involved with the race. My wife used to oversee registration and the finishing funnel, my eldest daughter is joint checkpoint leader at Ribblehead and ensures the SPORTident system keeps working there, and my youngest daughter assists with registration. She helps me at race control overseeing the retirements.

The usual challenges faced each year are in the form of all the weather-related conditions imaginable, injuries to competitors and emergency call-outs. Fortunately, these are not regular occurrences, but do emphasise the trust that is instilled in me to make the right decisions at the right time.

The race began to evolve and grow when Dave Hodgson won us the opportunity to host the World Mountain Running Association's race in 2008. Myself and three other long-standing members of the committee were invited to Interlaken in Switzerland to experience their 2007 event, and we left with the realisation that we had to raise our game considerably. So, in 2008 we took the decision to move the race to a Saturday, so we could create a race village vibe with stalls, food, a bar and entertainment to encourage competitors to stay after the event and celebrate their achievements. Ever since then the race has grown in numbers and popularity.

I have loved every minute of my time involved in the race, and it is all made possible due to its amazing and committed committee who will continue to take the race forwards into the future.

Chapter 27

LIKE FATHER LIKE SON

2003

For this year the event organisers chose to dispense with the traditional ring and tag system, which had always worked well, and use electronic tagging for the runners. The new system had the added benefit of producing comprehensive results quickly. There had been weeks of fine weather, but overnight rain softened the ground somewhat. It was a time of lower entries for the race, as 235 started and 205 finished.

There was good running to be had, as the weather on the day was kind. Beverley Whitfield (Clayton) pulled clear of the women's field on the run across to Ribblehead. Chasing hard was Helen Sedgwick, pro racer Tommy Sedgwick's daughter. Whitfield increased her lead over Ingleborough, to beat Sedgwick by over six minutes, with a winning time of 3-56-40. Whitfield, at 23 years, was the youngest competitor in the race.

The main field was soon in line going up the track to Pen-y-Ghent, and a group of five had established themselves at the front of the race by the first summit. On the long run to Ribblehead and up Whernside that leading group was reduced to four: David Walker, Scoffer Schofield, Matthew Whitfield and Jason Helmsley. David Walker stretched ahead over Whernside and had over five minutes lead going over Ingleborough. He extended his lead slightly to the finish, by which time it was well over six minutes. The race report notes: 'He was understandably emotional at the finish, no doubt overcome at winning a classic race to join an elite band of Three Peaks Race winners, and emulating his father, Harry Walker, who won the race three times in 1978, 1979 and 1981.' Jason Helmsley was 2nd with Scoffer another four minutes back in 3rd.

On the same occasion that I interviewed Harry Walker for this book, **David Walker** came over for a chat too. He lives just

84. Harry Walker and David Walker, 2003

over the road from Harry. He says now that he 'hadn't recced the Peaks that year, but had probably done it ten times in all, with training and racing.' He knew the course well. He adds, 'I had also done loads of stuff in the Lakes and in Scotland. It all just worked out that day I won. I really reined it in a couple of weeks beforehand, and I just felt good on the day.'

Reflecting on his life, David Walker notes that running was just there when he was growing up. 'I wasn't especially talented. I just kept grinding at it. I tried really hard when I was 14/15 and got to a reasonable standard.' He admits with a slight chuckle that the story of his running career was overdoing it. 'I didn't do as much in my late teens. I then got back into it when I was 21. I often did too much and had a lot of injuries. I got it right for two or three years leading up to when I won the Peaks. Six months after that I had a big injury and never really got back to it.'

He agrees that it was just natural that he would follow his dad into fell running. 'I think my first fell race was Black Lane Ends, which Mum and Dad organised at the time,' he recalls. 'I was probably far too young to have done it really.' David mostly trained on his own. Later Denis Quinlan gave him a bit of advice. Quinlan had a group on a Tuesday night at Bingley, and Walker used to go to that. He says he was probably about 21 when he first ran the Peaks. 'A rule of thumb was that we used to do about ten miles a day, a bit less on a Friday and a bit more on a Sunday. I tried running twice a day and had mixed success with that. It got me really fit but I was knackered a lot of the time. By the time I won I was nearly 26, but hadn't done the race every year. I'd maybe done it three times by then.'

David then reflected on his win, giving some more detail of his approach. 'Everyone was saying Matt Whitfield was going to win, whom I had known since we were kids. I waited for him at the bottom of Pen-y-Ghent and we ran together. He slowed down and let Scoffer catch us up. The three of us ran to Ribblehead together. I could tell on the road that Scoffer was weakening a bit, so we dropped him there. Starting up Whernside and I could tell Matt was going. So, do I carry on at this speed or ease up and run with it, as it was still a long way to go? I thought bugger it and just went. It was perhaps a bit gung-ho and maybe a bit reckless, but it paid off. I was generally better at going up. That season I found a rough descent of about 100 metres, and I used to do it every morning before work. Jog up and throw myself down several times. That year I was really running well downhill, helped by that training. Earlier I used to lose a lot of time on downhills. I have done some of the same training runs since I was 15 and am still doing them now at 40. On Boulsworth generally.'

David Walker concludes our chat by saying it was a strong ambition for him to win the Peaks. 'It suited me, and my father had won it. It is tough but not too technical. I was really pleased with that result. Very happy to have done it. As much as anything

I was happy that it had all worked out. That result was the best of my career really. Injury eventually stopped me from racing.'

As an added bonus a message was sent to David Walker's son William, and he joined in the conversation. Harry's lounge was now crammed with top fell runners, as John Calvert was there as well. William Walker is part of an up-and-coming generation of young fell runners. He gives a brief resumé of his running:

'I started running at primary school. One of our teachers used to take us out on a Friday after school. I had always wanted to be a runner. I remember going to Wasdale Head with my dad and grandad in a van, and we went up Lingmell to watch Dad running. Even at that age I just enjoyed being in the environment, in the Dales and the Lakes. Fell running has that as an added bonus. I am currently in the u19s. When I am 18, I will be able to run anything. This year I have had my best performance in the Junior Champs, coming 2nd. I certainly have an ambition to run the Three Peaks Race. I am doing double-figure distance runs now and will build up in the next couple of years. I do a flat speed session on a Tuesday with other members of Clayton-le-Moors. I can run in the Three Peaks when I am 18. I definitely want to keep running. I am currently doing my A levels and then will be going to university, probably, but not sure where yet.' [*Dave, who is a builder, interjects – either that or he will have to come and work with me.*]

William Walker just might be a third-generation winner of the Three Peaks Race at some point in the future. I for one will be watching with interest.

Chapter 28

LONG RACES: HATE THEM

2004

This was the 50th anniversary of the Three Peaks Race and it was run on a boiling hot day. In an article in *The Fellrunner*, Graham Breeze reported on an analysis of aspects of the entry numbers, part of which is included here:

> For environmental reasons there is a limit on race entries and although the Association accepted 625 entries it was known that no-shows on race day would reduce actual numbers to an acceptable level. In common with other long fell races the Three Peaks Race has recently suffered from a relative decline in entries, although not to the same extent as Wasdale and Ennerdale.
>
> The massive entry for the 50th race was clearly untypical but the fact that over 600 runners applied can only be welcomed. Analysis of the 625 who entered (of which 508 started and 407 finished) also provides some encouragement in the category make up of competitors compared with 2003, when there were 291 pre-entries. For 2004:
>
> - Ladies rose to 12.5% from 10%, which is the highest ever proportion of the field
> - Newcomers rose to 38% from 22%
> - The number of runners under 25 rose from 2 in 2003 to 16, mostly male, including one 20 year old.
>
> Nevertheless, despite the encouraging numbers of younger entries, the average age of male entries was 44 years and 39 for ladies.[34]

The race typically has a dropout rate of 20–25%, which is pretty high, and is an indication of how tough an event it is. Graham also noted: 'As the driver of one of the pickup vans drolly observed, "You don't get much conversation on the way back to Horton from the runners who have retired."'

---

34 'And The Sun Shone: The 50th Three Peaks Race: 25th April 2004', June 2004, *The Fellrunner*.

While many entrants may have been concentrating on 'getting round', there was some excellent racing at the head of the women's field. The race report noted that: 'Andrea Priestley (Ilkley) at Ribblehead was over 3 minutes ahead of the 2003 English and British Champion Louise Sharp (Keswick), who was

85. *Dave Hodgson and Danny Hughes, 2008*

competing in the event for the first time. But by the top of Whernside Louise was 2 minutes ahead of Andrea, who dropped out at the Hill Inn.' Louise went on to win in 3-39-49 (57th overall) almost 14 minutes ahead of Sharon Taylor who was a further five minutes ahead of Sue Becconsall. That made it eight different winners in the past nine years for the women. Future winner Helen Sedgwick was in 6th place.

Louise Sharp (now Lou Osborn) grew up in Cheshire and had never heard of fell running when she was young. She competed in every sport possible at school and was always put in the 1500m in competitions as nobody else would do it. She used to go to the Lake District on walking holidays with her family. When she was 14, one of her PE teachers put a sign-up sheet on his door asking if anyone wanted to go on a climbing trip to the Alps. She signed up and was the only girl from her year. She spent the next three years visiting crags around Staffordshire, Derbyshire and North Wales and decided that this was the direction that she wanted to go in her life. She says, 'I still absolutely love climbing, but now I get a bit freaked out and am happy for (my partner) Corny to lead everything.'

Lou studied Outdoor Education at Charlotte Mason College (Ambleside) and started running regularly in her first year at college to keep fit. 'By the time I left college in 1994, I had become less obsessed with climbing and had started to take part in a variety of other sports – mountain biking, kayaking, sailing.

86. *Lou Sharp, 2004*

I moved to Keswick when I left college but didn't dare join the local running club, thinking I would never be able to keep up. I learnt what routes they would do on training evenings and would run the same route but in the opposite direction!'

Lou says she honestly can't remember what led to her competing in her first fell race. 'I don't remember much about it other than it was right at the bottom of Langdale, up a very steep climb to a summit below Crinkle Crags and straight back down to the finish. Gunson Knott was the race, in 1994, and it doesn't take place any longer. I was absolutely rubbish but it was good fun!'

The next race she did was at Dale Head, and she does remember a bit more about this one. 'On the way back down, I descended past the tarn and the mist came down and I had no idea where I was. I must have gone off route as I heard someone shouting, "Follow me." The friendly runner was Chris Knox from Keswick AC, who waited for me, showed me down the descent all the way to the finish and is someone I class as a very good friend now. Chris told the Keswick Ladies that I could run, and I was then asked to run at a relay event for the club. There I was paired with Carolyn Charlton on leg two of the Hodgson Relays. Everyone was so friendly and supportive.'

In 2002, Lou gained her first GB vest, running in a Grand Prix event at Grabs, in Switzerland. She is a three times British Fell Champion (2002, 2003 and 2016, also coming 2nd in 2017 and 2022), and English Champion twice (2003 and 2004, with a 2nd in 2016). This suggests a sort of double career, spanning the two decades. Lou says now that she thinks 2016 was probably her best year. 'I worked so hard and was that much older at 44.'

She explains that there wasn't a big dip in her career really, adding that, 'I never had a break from racing, just some years I didn't do the championship races, and some years I was just really slow! I had a pretty big operation in 2018 and had about a year out from racing then and was quite ill with pleurisy in 2012, so had about six months out then.'

In an interview, in the February 2004 *Fellrunner*, she said: 'Long races: I hate them. They take too long, and I get knackered'. The Three Peaks was an English Championships

87. *The marshals, police and mountain rescue. All keeping fell runners safe, 2004*

race that year and Lou duly entered. Talking about it now, she confirms her previous view. 'Yep, I have never really enjoyed long races, but unfortunately I seem to do well at them so if there are two in a championship, I normally get my best results from them, so have to do both of them.'

By 2004 Lou knew the course well and had recced all of it in various sections, but never all in one go. She looked back on that day and reflected how it had panned out. 'I had great battles with Andrea Priestley in those years. We were very similar runners, both really strong uphill then not as strong relatively on the descents. I knew she was ahead of me at Ribblehead as she had gone out of sight. I pushed on up Whernside and from memory it was misty. I had no idea I had overtaken her, I didn't see her and thought I was coming in for 2nd place at the finish. I tried really hard to catch her going up Ingleborough but didn't catch her and just thought she must be going really well! [*Andrea had dropped out at Hill Inn*]. There was no big celebration from me, but I was really chuffed to get my name on the plaque, which used to be up on the wall in the pub.'

88. *The commentary van at the finish, 2004*

Lou notes that she did run the Three Peaks again, in 2008. 'I did a much slower time. I also got really bad cramp coming off Ingleborough – I was in so much pain! It's a race I want to do again but will have to train properly for it, so I don't get cramp again.' For the record, Lou finished as 18th woman that year, when it was the World Long Distance Championships, in a time of 3-56-57.

The 2004 win by Andy Peace was described in some detail by Graham Breeze in the article in *The Fellrunner*, a slightly edited-down version of which follows.

In addition to celebrating its 50th Anniversary, the race also determined the Yorkshire Championships and was a counter for the English Championship. Not surprisingly the start line was packed with past winners.

It was a past winner that won again but delightfully it was Andy Peace (Bingley). Andy who won in 1994/5/6 but had not entered since, set off at a storming pace, despite the heat. Chasing Ian Holmes (1997 winner), by the top of Pen-y-Ghent he was already 22 seconds ahead of his clubmate, followed by Rob Jebb (Bingley) and the Borrowdale pair, Simon Booth (2000/2002 winner) and Mark Roberts (1998 winner).

Andy never lost the lead and although Simon closed up with him on Whernside to show just a 3 second deficit at the Hill Inn, Peace eventually won in 2-55-46 with Booth finishing in 2-56-38. Holmes was well adrift, and Roberts over 4 minutes back on him. Rob Jebb dropped out at an early stage with a hamstring problem.

With a 100% record of wins from his previous entries Andy had more than most to lose in reputation and had trained for the race. Commentators had observed his superb form earlier in the

89. Andy Peace, 2004

year and this victory, after a seven-year gap, suggests that had he continued to enter the event the record six consecutive wins of Jeff Norman may have been eclipsed long ago.

Graham Breeze also noted that the use of SPORTident's timing technology at the event allowed splits for all runners. The race naturally falls into six sections, three 'ups' and three 'downs'. Andy Peace showed where his strength was, by being fastest on all three of the climbs.

Andy Peace claims that Simon Booth had been favourite to win that year and get his treble. Simon responds now: 'It is a fair reflection to say I was favourite because that is what I thought. I heard a good few people saying that Andy was the favourite which kind of got me more motivated. I was thinking Andy was a has-been! [*He laughs at this, as Andy is younger than him*]. But he certainly reminded me of his class that day.'

It was again a championship race and Simon was very fit, well trained and confident of his chances of winning. 'I was extra

90. *L to R: Stan Bradshaw, Andy Peace, Alf Case, 2004*

motivated because the 2003 season had been so disappointing, but also because I was so pleased the toe injury had recovered. I realised I had to make the most of these opportunities.' He had even been and recced the whole route. 'I think I had gone a bit OTT in my training the week before because everything had just felt so good, and all my training times were fast. On Wednesday night I had already been out for a training run and noticed there was a 10k race on that evening, so I did that and won it on a very hot night. The 10k race was in Cockermouth where I lived at the time. I think it was called the Lambfoot Loop. I often did road races in the week. I like racing Wed-Sat-Wed-Sat, it was something I always did. The problem was I had done hard hill reps on the Tuesday. I got cramps in the Three Peaks so perhaps I shouldn't have done all that in the week before the Peaks. As the race started, I soon forgot about the problems and felt really good until Ribblehead. Then climbing Whernside my calves started cramping. I hung on thinking I could catch up on the descent of Ingleborough but even that didn't feel great this time, and sadly I couldn't get back anywhere near Andy. I have to say I was disappointed with 2nd on that occasion.'

Ian Holmes adds his take on that race. 'I think that year [*2004*] was Andy Peace's best run there really. Nobody had him down to win that one. Simon Booth may have been the favourite to win having won in 2000 and 2002. But Andy knew how to run the Three Peaks by then.'

Chapter 29

JEBB TAKES OVER

2005

Fine weather greeted the runners, and Yorkshire athletes took charge of the women's event. V40 runner Sally Malir (Ilkley) gained a slight lead over young Amy Green (Keighley) by the summit of Pen-y-Ghent and went on to win by almost two minutes, with Liz Tomes of Keighley in 3rd. Wendy Dodds dominated the v50 category.

Talking with me recently, **Sally Malir** apologised for not being able to add much detail to that report. 'I can't believe that I can't remember much about the day. All I can remember is that I loved the run from Pen-y-Ghent to Ribblehead and found the descent down from Ingleborough to the finish really hard, trying not to trip over lots of limestone knobbles and with lots of stiles to climb.'

Sally Malir was always active when she was young. She explained how she got into fell running. 'I loved riding my bike, climbing trees, making dens and generally playing outside. At primary school sports day I always easily won the cross-country race and ran well when I was at high school. I always wanted to run more but didn't really know how to get into it. I wasn't one of the 'in' girls who got picked for everything at school. I tried a little bit of running at university, but not regularly. When I finished university and had my first teaching job (in the early 1990s) I joined a gym and one day tried to run there. It was about half a mile from my house, and I struggled! I persevered and slowly it became easier. In 1992 I raced a few triathlons and did quite well, then in 1993 I joined the Fellandale club as I loved running off road and was persuaded to do some fell racing. In 1994 our ladies' team won the British and English Champs.'

Sally was running the Three Peaks in 2005 because she was a member of Fellandale and so it was a natural thing to do. She

91. Sally Malir at the Hill Inn, 2011

had helped set out the course and marshalled many times before she entered the race for the first time in 1997. 'Having raced the course a couple of times before I won it, and also helped out setting up and marshalling before that, I was familiar with the event by the time I won it.'

Having run for the first time in 1997, Sally came back in 2004 but was outside the top ten, then won in 2005. She says she raced again in 2011, and definitely another time, but is not sure when. 'I love the Three Peaks Race, being from Yorkshire racing these three tall mountains in the county is an amazing thing to do. It's an iconic race which requires fast running as well as having good ascending and descending skills.'

Sally decided to have a go at a road marathon the year after winning The Peaks and went for Barcelona as her first marathon, in which she recorded a time of 3-12. 'I was always chasing sub-3 hours which I did do at Blackpool in 2009, with a time of 2-58-23, only to be told two weeks later that it was 400 metres short. I did London Marathon a few times, my best result was 3-06-48 in 2009, but I'm most proud of my London result as a V50 – 3-07-36 which gave me 4th in my age category. This was my last marathon.'

Sally Malir is still competing a bit and is proud to have earned two Masters England vests, one for 10k and one for the half marathon. 'I'm trying to overcome a few niggles at the moment and hope to get back to more racing.'

She is also coaching some young athletes, as she explained. 'I started off helping out my eldest daughter Georgia with a little bit of coaching then branched out and now coach a group of girls from a variety of clubs. I enjoy this role and try to be more of a mentor than strictly a coach. I organise talks and visiting athletes for the group and try to provide a fun environment for them to train hard in. A few of the athletes have had success and got into teams for cross-country and mountain running.'

A new men's champion was crowned at the 2005 race. Rob Jebb triumphed, after several earlier attempts, with his first of four wins in the next few years. The race report notes that, 'the course was dry and the weather on race day mainly sunshine,

92. Rob Jebb takes a swift drink

but a cool breeze on the higher slopes, made this a perfect day for a long race.' Having been a Championship race, and the 50th anniversary, the year before, it wouldn't have been a surprise to see a reduced field, but 340 finished (after 407 in 2004) – with 160 being new to the race.

Rob Jebb was keen to join the list of the winners of this prestigious race and set off determined for it to be his year. He never lost the lead and won comfortably by over ten minutes from Scoffer Schofield, with John Hunt (Cumbria Fell Runners) in 3rd. Unfortunately, there was an accident noted in the race report, 'when a runner having retired from the race was struck by a motor-cyclist and suffered severe injuries.'

Recently chatting with Rob Jebb, he mentioned his tactics and also reflected on his dominance that year. It came across to me as supreme confidence, rather than arrogance. 'Winning by ten minutes? I was good then! At the Three Peaks Race it is good to be out at the front. The route is not hard to follow so you run at a pace you want and not at someone else's pace. You are doing what you want to do. If you have a gap like I'd got, then it doesn't matter where the others are, does it? No need to look over your shoulder. Anyway, there is nothing you can do about anyone else, is there? Someone once told me: "The guy in 2nd is suffering more than you are." I always believed that. They would have gone with you if they were good enough.'

2006

In the women's event Jo Smith (Calder Valley) held a comfortable lead on Pen-y-Ghent and kept it until Ingleborough. She suffered from there onwards, and was overtaken by the eventual winner, Helen Sedgwick (Ilkley), and 2nd-placer Kate Davison (Dark Peak). Helen (Ilsley as it is now) comments on how she saw it. 'Jo set off really fast and I let her go because she was running way quicker than me. She got well away from me, and I recall having a good climb up Whernside and thinking that I was making ground on her. Maybe there was a chance that I could catch her. I knew she was the only woman in front of me, as my dad had told me at Ribblehead. Going up Ingleborough I was just feeling stronger and stronger, and I began to think I might be able to win. I think I passed her just before the top of Ingleborough. My sister was on the top and she ran the first bit off Ingleborough with me. I remember feeling good and thinking I could do this, even though there was still a long way to go. Don't look back, just keep going, I was saying to myself. To win was the biggest shock of my life.'

Helen Sedgwick/Ilsley was born in 1976, in Kendal. Her father is Tommy Sedgwick, who was one of the top professional fell runners at the time. She says now that the family spent most

93. *Helen Sedgwick with her father Tommy, 2006*

weekends watching him race. 'My older sister Judith started running before me. She had natural speed, whereas I was the chubby one! Judith was quite keen. I decided to start running because I didn't like being chubby and as we were going to the races anyway, I decided to have a go. I was about 12.' The Kendal Winter League and the BOFRA races were where she started out. She thinks her first race was a Kendal Winter League race (which her father helped set up). 'I can't remember much about it, other than it was hard. I remember feeling very pleased with myself for getting round. There weren't so many girls running back then. I was towards the back to start with and then there was a group of three or four of us that were running every week.'

Helen ran through her teenage years but didn't join a club until after she'd completed her nursing degree in Leeds. She joined Ilkley Harriers and started doing the English and British championship races with the women's team. 'I had a few wins and won a few trophies. The Kendal Winter League events were proper fell races, and they still go on now. It was a very encouraging environment for young people. My first race was likely to have been in The Lake District. Grasmere and Ambleside were the ones we wanted to do well at. Grasmere was the pinnacle of my dad's year every year.'

She went to university and decided she wanted to do the Great North Run and the London Marathon, and duly did them. 'Pete Shields, one of the coaches at Ilkley, suggested I have a go at the Three Peaks Race. I didn't know much about it prior to that – despite growing up looking at Ingleborough every single day from our window. So, it wasn't a race I'd always wanted to do. I'd been up Ingleborough several times but had no idea where the race went. I don't think I'd been up Whernside or Pen-y-Ghent prior to my first Three Peaks attempt. I didn't recce it at all. It was the longest fell race I'd ever done by a long way. It was in the early 2000s. I think I finished 13th in that first attempt, which I was thrilled with as it was off no proper training. I think I have done it five times in all. My dad was always very supportive, and I would see him at Ribblehead.'

Helen Ilsley's Three Peaks win in 2006 was in the year she got married and she had trained hard for the event. She says she wasn't expecting to win it, and that was never in her wildest imaginings. 'Getting married that June I changed my name, but it felt like the biggest honour to win the Three Peaks with my maiden name (Sedgwick). It was very special, particularly with my dad being there. Sadly, my mum couldn't be there though.'

When Helen had children, she took quite a time out of running. She also had pelvis issues and was advised to stop running, probably missing six or seven years competitively altogether. 'I missed it so badly, so I did a bit of swimming and bought a bike, after my third child was born. I was desperate to compete again. I didn't think it should be running, so decided to have a go at triathlon. I read Louise Minchin's book (*Dare to Tri*) and I was inspired. I wanted to see if I could get on the GB age group team. I qualified in my first race in Leeds in 2019, for the World Champs in Edmonton, Canada, for 2020. Then Covid struck and the event got rolled over for two years. Finally, I got my chance to race last year in Abu Dhabi. Age grouping is a fantastic way of keeping up your sport and do it with people of

94. Rob Jebb, 2006

your age. Fell running is still where my heart is though.'

Helen concluded by saying the Three Peaks Race was definitely the highlight of her running career. 'The Three Peaks is to me well up there, but I am not sure about other people. There are so many races now. The Three Peaks feels to be an iconic race still, and it holds a lot of personal values too. It is close to where I grew up, it is special to me because I won it.'

Early in 2006 Rob Jebb had won the Three Peaks Cyclo-Cross Race and was going for a double in the same year at that year's fell race. Dry weather produced good conditions underfoot and it was forecast to be good on the day. John Heneghan stayed with Rob Jebb this time for much of the race but started to lose touch over Whernside. Jebb pulled away to win by over six minutes from Heneghan, with Lloyd Taggart (Dark Peak) closing in for 3rd, in his first attempt at the race.

Chapter 30

NO SPECIFIC TRAINING

2007

Some of the best ever conditions greeted the runners in the race in 2007. For the women, Mary Wilkinson made a last-minute decision to run, which paid off handsomely. She won in the fastest women's time since 1999, leading Bingley to the women's team prize, over favourites Ilkley. Wilkinson's clubmate, Sharon Taylor, was a full six minutes behind, with the previous year's winner, Helen Sedgwick/Ilsley, back in 5th place, in 3-49-05. Helen adds, 'It was a much better field in 2007 than the year before, when there was a Champs race the week afterwards and people may have saved themselves for that race. I may have been a bit lucky in 2006 with who was there (or not). But I wasn't disappointed to come 5th with the field as it was in 2007.'

Mary Wilkinson wasn't really into running but was just extremely sporty when she was a youngster, as she recalls: 'I was at the Langcliffe Gala, playing football for the boys' primary school team and saw the Fell Race advertised and begged my mum to let me run it. I was immediately hooked ... on the feeling of winning!' She went on to win the BOFRA Girls Championships title in 1991.

'During my BOFRA era it was very much local champion Roger Gibson who was the biggest influence on encouraging me to race. I was good friends with his daughter, and he used to take me to a lot of the races. Their whole family would go and make a day of it. My parents were also very supportive, but neither were particularly sporty, so it was very much supporting me do what I wanted to do and never pushing me towards a particular thing or any pressure to be successful, which I think was hugely positive.'

Mary had difficult choices to make. 'Running was definitely low down my list of sporting priorities, especially as I moved up to high school. Netball and hockey were my first loves, and I was lucky to enjoy quite a lot of success and experience a lot through them. Running was something I did because the school needed people to do it and I was fit enough to get round! It was only when I moved on to university that I returned to running as my relationship with team sports dwindled. Running was something I could do anytime, anywhere and fit around the social and academic demands of university.'

Having studied Sport Science at Loughborough university, Mary Wilkinson's original aim was to be a PE teacher. But when she got into the study, she found that it was the practical and academic side that she enjoyed the most. 'This led me to study for a master's in Sports Medicine at Glasgow University and a return to Loughborough to complete a PhD in Psychophysiology. Subsequently, I have worked in Sports Nutrition Development as well as website work at a local Outdoor Store, which are job choices to support my choice of lifestyle rather than a career.' She envisages that she will return to sports science, or some related research, in the future.

Although she has run on pretty much every surface, her main success has been on the mountains. 'Up and down courses were my favourite, as I was a far better descender than climber. I never really got into fell racing that required navigation, as I prefer the focus to be purely physical. I loved mountain running especially for the places it takes you both in this country and abroad. The tranquillity, beauty and isolation. I have been lucky enough to experience a huge range of countries (30+) through the sport. However, I also loved road racing and I definitely didn't get a chance to do enough. Two very different environments to train and compete in, but both were close in terms of a favourite. I was never really a huge fan of cross-country, I loved the concept but my running style as a toe runner was never very conducive to the soft, muddy conditions.'

Returning to running at university coincided with Mary recovering from an eating disorder that she says was triggered (in hindsight) by a need for control following her brother's death in a car crash in 2018. 'In contrast to what many people perceive, and is often the case, running was actually something that helped mc recover from this rather than being a driver for "wanting to be skinny". When I started running, I had no intention of racing. It was purely something I was doing for myself. But as a naturally very competitive person it wasn't long before the seeds of competing were sown. I was working in a running store in Glasgow in 2004 while studying for my master's, and the store had a team running in the Edinburgh Marathon Relay. The day before one of them dropped out and they asked if I'd step in. I did and ran the first 10km leg, but when I got to the hand over point for some reason I asked if I could carry on! I did and finished the whole marathon in about 2 hours 50 minutes. I'd never run more than 90 minutes before and with that performance I started to realise that actually I was alright at running.'

With her previous roots in the fell running scene it was these races that she then turned to, albeit still very tentatively. 'I was based in Aberystwyth in 2005 and joined a brilliant training group under the guidance of Dic Evans, and it was him who encouraged me to have a go at the trail race for the 2005 European Mountain Running Championships, as it was held on Snowdon not far away. To win that race, qualify for the GB team and then head out to the Championships in Austria was a whirlwind and something I'd never planned or dreamed of.'

Mary had no plans to race the Three Peaks in 2007, so had done no specific training. She still rarely ran for longer than 90 minutes and there was certainly no recceing of the course. 'I know the area as it's very local to me and did occasionally run on the peaks individually. 2007 had been a bit of a disaster running-wise. I'd suffered my first major injury the year before, following a big fall in the Snowdon Race and I'd struggled to get back to any sort of form and my enjoyment was pretty low. I ran the famous Bunny Run on Tuesday evening and Dave Woodhead knew I was struggling for motivation and enthusiasm. He said I should run the Three Peaks at the weekend. I just laughed: firstly, because it seemed ridiculous, and secondly, because it was pre-entry and full. He then rang me on the Thursday night and said a Bingley runner had dropped out and I should take

95. *Mary Wilkinson heading for the finish, 2007*

96. Mary Wilkinson raises the trophy aloft, 2007

their entry (you could swap within a team at the time). I have no idea why, but having slept on it on the Friday, I said why not. So, literally the day beforehand I decided I'd run. A quick kit list shop and I was all set.'

Mary says she actually doesn't have a lot of memories of the day. 'It was perfect weather, dry and warm, and I remember starting off very conservatively up Pen-y-Ghent and then really enjoying the run across to Ribblehead. Climbing the face of Whernside I remember Victoria Wilkinson and her father being there and handing me a bottle and telling me I was leading, which I couldn't believe. At the Hill Inn Lee Athersmith had just retired ahead of me and handed me his Lucozade (I was really unorganised without any fuel strategy!). My best memory was descending Ingleborough across the limestone pavement still feeling great and knowing I was actually going to finish.

Winning was just a bonus and totally unexpected. A clearer memory is walking down our land in Long Preston that evening and looking up the valley to the Three Peaks and being unable to believe that I'd actually run them all in three and a half hours.'

Mary Wilkinson would have loved to have run more Three Peaks races, but because she was forced to stop running in 2014 with an injury her focus was very much on the shorter races and the event never fitted in. 'It never really crossed my mind to do the Fell Championships. Maybe if I'd been able to run as I got older, I may have taken them on, but I guess I'll never know.'

She explains that the injury happened after she ran in the World Championships in Italy on the Sunday. She went for a run the next morning with the team before they flew home and had to cut it short because her foot was a bit painful. 'That was pretty much the last time I ran. Despite seeing many specialists and seeking lots of different opinions, even going down alternative routes, I haven't been able to find a cause of the problem. But basically, after a few minutes running my foot becomes hypersensitive, then almost numb, but painful at the same time (I know it is contradictory, but it's really hard to describe) and subsequently the whole leg doesn't function properly and I can't run. It's probably neural, but where and exactly what is a mystery.'

Fighting to get back running was a very long, painful and hard journey for her, mentally as much as physically. All she wanted to do was run. 'My whole life revolved around running. Virtually all my friends were runners. So having it taken away was hard. Harder still was dealing with the rollercoaster of raised and dashed hopes of finding an answer to the problem time and time again. It wasn't until I accepted that I probably wasn't going to run again (in 2017) that I could move on. When I made that decision the relief and weight off my shoulders was immense. But I still needed something to fill the void of pushing myself physically and ultimately competitively. That's where cycling comes in and I feel very lucky to have found another sport that I can be competitive in and have found some success.'

The cycling highlight for her she says has to be winning the Lancaster round of the British Cycling National Series last year.

'I never thought I'd stand on the top step of a national series race and to do it on the race closest to home was extra special. Although frustrating, taking five silver medals at the National Hill Climb Championships is something I'm very proud of, because to be so consistent across a variety of climbs and time isn't easy.'

Mary Wilkinson concludes our chat with her thoughts about the Three Peaks as an event. 'It has a special place in a lot of people's hearts and for me as a local race it does too. I'm very pleased I made the decision to run it when I did, otherwise I might never have got to do so and that would have been a big regret. The winners of the race are a who's who of fell running and that itself shows how highly it is held by so many as a race. The Three Peaks win is definitely a highlight for me, as well as my three consecutive Snowdon Mountain Race wins. Internationally my highlight would probably be the 2012 European Mountain Running Championships in Denizli-Pamukkale, Turkey, where I was 4th and although initially disappointed to just miss the podium it had been a long journey to the start line after an injury-plagued few years.'

Rob Jebb completed a hat-trick of wins, with the fastest time since Andy Peace's record in 1996. There was an excellent run by Simon Barnby, an 18-year-old Sedbergh School boy, who went with the leaders on Pen-y-Ghent, and managed to hold on for 8th place, to win the First Newcomer Trophy. The group split up and Rob Jebb showed his strength by opening up a gap of four minutes by the Ingleborough summit. His time at the finish was just three minutes ahead of John Heneghan, who had over eight minutes on 1st Vet Ian Holmes, who comments: 'I was with Rob all the way up Pen-y-Ghent and across to Ribblehead, but he left me going up Whernside. John Heneghan caught us later on and I had to let him go. Once I had won [in 1997] I was quite happy not to go back for a while, and this was ten years since that win.'

Rob Jebb recalls how well he ran that day, how the race progressed and explains why it was such a fast time [and eventually the best time he achieved]. 'In the 2005 and 2006

97. *Rob Jebb heading for the finish, 2007*

races you weren't allowed to run under the railway and into the finish. You had to run round, so it was about 800 metres or so further then. That would be worth at least three minutes on your time. Ian Holmes was first to Ribblehead, with me about 20 metres behind him. Then I pushed on from there. I always thought the race didn't start till Ribblehead. You need to get there as relaxed and comfortable as you can. A lot of people get that wrong and go too fast too soon. You still have about 12 miles (and two mountains) to go, with hardly any flat running. I think the competition was probably better in the 2007 race. I was pushed more, which also accounts for the fast time. I think it was a nice day for running too. I remember wearing Nike road shoes instead of fell shoes. If someone is pushing the pace, then it makes the race faster. If it was me leading from the gun I might not go as fast as when someone else is making me work for it. You have to judge whether the pace is going to come back and bite you, haven't you? Go with it if you think you are going to win. If you give them too much of a gap it can be game over.'

Talking about his Yorkshire roots, Rob says that his father influenced him and encouraged him to take to the fells. Jebb Senior used to run the Three Peaks Race and reached a very good standard, winning the Fellsman for instance. Rob started running at the age of nine, although he says he wasn't any good in the early days. At 17 he started improving and started doing Senior races at that age. But he didn't win his first race until he was 21. He has had a long and very successful career since then, both locally and internationally. As well as dominating the Three Peaks Race at his best he is also capable on shorter courses, having won the Grasmere Guides race nine times. He says he is not the best descender and is a better climber. 'I am not the best at any one particular thing, but I am jack of all trades and master of none. Someone like Simon Booth, who is a fantastic long-distance runner, would never win Grasmere. I am not as fast as some on short ones, but I am good overall.'

Rob first did the Three Peaks Race in 2000, because it was part of the English Fell Running Championships. 'I had done lots of other long races by then, including Wasdale and Ennerdale. It was just up the road from me. I think it being called the marathon with mountains might have put me off doing it. Just ran round behind the leading three or four the whole way really (and came 5th). I got well under three hours and was happy with that. I may have had in my head that I wasn't that good on the flat, yet it turned out I was in fact, when I got the hang of it. I was good at fast races like Fairfield or Kentmere, which are run at a faster pace.'

Rob Jebb took up cyclo-cross to supplement his running and has become one of the finest exponents of the sport, a rare ability to reach the top of two different, but similar, tough sports. He was recently awarded the Charles Arthur Rhodes Memorial Award in 2022, in recognition of his winning the Three Peaks Cyclo-Cross an incredible 13 times over 23 years. The citation notes that: 'Every cyclo-cross rider with Yorkshire blood aspires to ride the 3 Peaks and Rob made his debut whilst still a Junior in 1992. In 1997 he finished a creditable 3rd before climbing to 2nd the following year; then in 2000 he achieved the top spot.' So, in the year Rob first ran in the Three Peaks Race he won the Three Peaks Cyclo-Cross for the first time, after a handful of attempts at that event.

Rob acknowledges that he has done the cyclo-cross a good few times when he has not won, as well as winning 13 times, which is the most anyone has achieved. 'Me and Andy Peace are the only people to have won both the running and the cycling version, which is pretty cool. I was sort of learning the ropes for the first ten years or so. I have also had a few out injured.' Rob once said to me that the explanation for his success and longevity is because that he is the best. He qualified that recently with a comparison between his cycling and his running. 'I do well [at cyclo-cross] because I can run up hill with a bike on my shoulder and still get on it and ride well after that. I have not deteriorated at cycling as much as I have with running. Cyclo-cross does suit me. Some of the early cyclo-cross wins have been quite easy, but 2022 was very close, but I am 47 now. I do wonder if that pisses off my rivals, who might be in their early 20s. It would me. I would probably have given up if it happened to me. The 2023

98. *The Yorkshire clean sweep, 2007. L to R: John Heneghan, Rob Jebb, Ian Holmes*

race is in a month's time and I am sure they will be after me. I should really stop while I am at the top, but you keep going, don't you?' His build-up to the Three Peaks Cyclo-Cross in 2023 includes running fell races at Sedbergh Hills (a Championship race), Grasmere and Ben Nevis. So no let up for him.

He then says that he has no idea how many times he has done the Three Peaks Fell Race. 'Not loads but maybe 10 or 12 times now. I have not won again since 2009 though. I think I will do it again in 2024.' Finally, he admits that he has never really liked the race. 'Even though I won it I have found it a bit too fast. Along with the Ben Nevis Race it is one of THE races to win though. I still like racing so I will keep turning up at races. I am finding it frustrating that I might not be at the sharp end now. At least my shoulder has recovered well now.'

Chapter 31

TAKING ON THE WORLDS

2008

The World Long Distance Mountain Running Challenge was awarded to the Three Peaks for the 2008 season. Hosting the World Mountain Running Association event (the fourth year of the Challenge) was a huge reward for the Three Peaks Race Association. There were around 90 overseas entries competing against the top British fell runners. As it was also a counter in the English Championships that year there were a record number of starters. The weather even played along.

Dave Hodgson gives the background to the Challenge being awarded to the Three Peaks. 'I approached the World Mountain Running Association about us possibly hosting the event. I knew Danny Hughes (chair of WMRA). Because I had been England team manager, I also knew the ropes. I asked Danny if he would let me have an application form. I cleared it with the Race Committee and sent it off, but he wasn't very optimistic about the application.' But they got it and organised a brilliant event.

Because of the number of overseas entries received the course was flagged throughout. The organisers also had to provide accommodation for Elite overseas runners and drug-testing facilities. Despite, or because of, the novelty of using online entries for the first time the number of entries allocated to UK runners was filled within 36 hours, and soon the committee agreed they could safely increase the number of entries. In the end 756 athletes started, a number that has only been exceeded six times since then.

On the women's side much was expected from **Anna Pichrtova**, from the Czech Republic, who had won the World Mountain Running Trophy in Ovronnaz (Switzerland) the previous year. She had also been shooting for a place in the marathon in the 2008 Olympic Games, but she had had a back

99. *Anna Pichrtova with her clearly marked drinks bottles, 2008*

and pelvis injury which stopped her achieving the qualifying time (in 2007) to be considered. Her extensive *palmarès* included multiple Mount Kinabalu and Mount Washington wins. She had already been European Mountain Running Champion in 2004 and 2006, and had two WMRA Grand Prix wins. Despite her international experience Pichrtova surprisingly had not heard of the Three Peaks but was persuaded to run by her long-time physiotherapist Denise Park, in part to check if she was over her injury.

Having recced parts of the course Pichrtova chose to run in road shoes, saying she was doing it as training. However, she had viewed only the stony paths and might have chosen differently if she had seen the whole course. In the race she was surprised to find wet ground between Pen-y-Ghent and Ribblehead and said afterwards that her choice of footwear, 'held me back when I felt I could have been running faster but I was just very uncertain underfoot.' Interviewed by Graham Breeze for *Fellrunner* magazine, she added that she, 'felt good climbing Pen-y-Ghent and felt increasingly confident throughout the event and so just ran a steady pace.'[35] That steady pace took her to a new course

---

35 'Three Peaks: two winners', summer 2008, *The Fellrunner*.

100. Anna Pichrtova, 2008

record of 3-14-43, taking 1-46 off Sarah Rowell's time from 1996.

It might have been expected that Pichrtova's main challenge would come from the other international runners, but she seemed to know otherwise, saying that, 'Angela Mudge was a serious competitor, although you always have to run your own race.' As the race unfolded, Anna Pichrtova took the lead over Pen-y-Ghent, having an eight-second lead over Anita Haakenstad at the summit. By the Ribblehead checkpoint she had opened a clear lead over Angela Mudge, with Haakenstad having dropped out due to an existing leg injury which had flared up. By Whernside summit Angela, with the women's fastest climb, pulled a little time back on Anna with Angela Bateup (Australia) and Anna Frost (New Zealand) about five minutes behind. By Ingleborough Anna Frost had caught Angela Bateup only to lose out to her on the descent. Anna Pichrtrova had led from the start and had coped well with the terrain in the end to win comfortably, in 32nd place overall. After Pichrtova, Mudge, Bateup and Frost finished in that order, the next in were Sharon Taylor and then Rukhylada and Danilova, who were two thirds of the winning ParsRussia team, along with 10th-placed Nechunaeva. In *Athletics Weekly* Pichrtova explained how she raced. 'What I always plan to do is not race against the competition. I just go as I feel. I didn't have any tactics whatsoever. We girls know each other and I was trying to go steady and then push maybe the last descent.'

In a post-race interview, reported in *The Fellrunner*, Pichrtova acknowledged that Mudge ran well over the rougher stuff, and that she had run hard up and off Ingleborough, but 'on the descent fell on a rock and injured my ribs.' Having spoken with Mudge after finishing, Pichrtova said that 'Angela didn't think it wet at all', and laughingly recalled that she had arrived at the stream on the way up Whernside, 'asked the marshal where the crossing was, and he said, "Here!". I wasn't expecting a bridge but was expecting at least a proper crossing place!' Pichrtova planned to try for the Olympic marathon qualifying time a few weeks later. She explained why. 'I just love running! Mountains are my passion, and the marathons provide my income and provide me with testing challenges.' The £1,000+ that she won at the Three Peaks is a huge amount for an English fell race, but insignificant compared to the $20,000 she had won in a marathon. She ran the Ottawa Marathon a few weeks later and had her heel clipped and fell badly. She got up and finished painfully in 2-39, just two minutes outside the Olympic qualifying time. Such are the vagaries of being a professional runner.

This was the only other time Angela Mudge ran the Three Peaks, after her win in 1999. She said she was content with her performance. 'I was happy with it. I race Anna regularly in the Alps and I knew that I was going to have to have a flier and Anna to have a stinker to be anywhere near her.' She added that she felt dehydrated coming off Pen-y-Ghent having not taken on enough fluid before the race.

On the day, the men's race didn't pan out as might have been expected, partly because a good few runners paced the event wrongly. As the race developed Billy Burns led to the summit of Pen-y-Ghent. By Ribblehead Jethro Lennox was chasing Mitja Kosevelj, with Burns not far behind. Lennox descended well from Whernside to lead with Kosevelj close behind as Tom Owens started to move through the field. Potential or past winners Billy Burns, Andy Peace, Rob Jebb and Rob Hope were gathered in a following group.

Jethro Lennox, from Glasgow club Shettleston Harriers, extended his lead when ascending Ingleborough. He had been able to be the front runner on a course that he really didn't know, as it was the World Long Distance challenge and was fully marked. But he didn't have an easy ride once in the lead, as he explained post-race to Graham Breeze. 'I knew of Mitja Kosevelj (Slovenia) who was behind me at the Hill Inn, and I train with Tom Owens, who was then lying 3rd. Obviously, I was wondering how they were both feeling, and on the climb up to Ingleborough Hugh Symonds told me that Mitja was looking tired, but Tom was looking strong, so I started to worry more about Tom than Mitja. Tom then suddenly appeared behind me!'

Owens was indeed closing Lennox down, pulling a gap of over two minutes down to just 37 seconds at the race end.

Kosevelj eventually came in four minutes down on Lennox. Owens passed Kosevelj and was reckoned to have posted the fastest recorded descent time on the tricky run-in from Ingleborough to the finish. Lennox commented at the time that, 'People on the hills let me know what was happening behind me, and my coach, Malcolm Patterson, was also a great help. I owe him a lot.' A recent chat with Jethro Lennox illustrated his career and approach to training and racing.

Jethro Lennox recalls that his father was a pretty good runner. 'He did 2-36 for marathon and did the odd fell race too. I used to do a bit of running with him, although I loved any sports really. I remember finishing 11th in the Lanarkshire Schools cross-country champs when I was 11 or 12. In that race I could see the leaders, and that was probably the highlight of my Junior career. I had one side of my body slightly bigger than the other, making one leg an inch longer than the other. It is called hemihypertrophy. They put U-shaped nails in the growth points in the left knee and that stunts the growth. It was quite a revolutionary operation at the time. They were in for about three or four years, coming out when I was 17. I couldn't run for ages, but I did a lot of physiotherapy, which gave me good strength and condition when I was young.'

Jethro went to Oxford Brookes University to study cartography and joined the local running club, Headington Road Runners. When he moved to London, he joined Ealing Middlesex and Southall AC. 'Then eventually I moved back up to Scotland in 2001 and got a job at HarperCollins and joined Shettleston and that was when my running started to really improve in my mid-20s. I realised that if I trained a bit harder, I might be able to start winning some races. I started doing more hill races in Scotland, which I had always known I wanted to do.'

By 2008 Jethro had some great results, had run in the short World Trophy in New Zealand, and also on another three occasions. 'Even though it was also the World Long Distance Champs, I really thought of the Three Peaks that year as just a quality British Champs race, as there wasn't the same profile as the short World Trophy races, in terms of the international field.

101. Jethro Lennox, 2008

I thought, even though it is longer, it is in Britain, and I had better do it. I was quite relaxed because the Trophy races had been bigger and more pressured.'

Jethro Lennox had done no recces of the Peaks and had only been walking a few times in Yorkshire. 'That year I was concentrating on the British Champs. I wanted to medal, if not win, at the British Champs. The Peaks was a week or two after a Champs race in Ireland, so I did it because I thought I was fit enough. It was the one year that they had to mark the course the whole way, so I could just follow the markers.'

On the start line he definitely thought he could be in the top two of the British athletes. 'In Ireland it had been a long race (at Mourne) and I was winning with about 200 metres to go. I fell in a bog and Rob Hope ran round me and won! Even so that race gave me confidence as I knew I could have won it. I said to myself I am going to show them at the Peaks. It was probably a little more stacked than the Irish race had been.'

Kosevelj previously had World Trophy Junior wins and top-three places in the World Trophy Senior race. Jethro recalls that it started pretty fast. 'Up Pen-y-Ghent I wasn't even in the top 20 and then I remember getting on the road and was running quicker than everyone else and caught up with Ian Holmes and had a chat with him. Suddenly I was in the lead group. Mitja Kosevelj was a bit ahead, and maybe Rob Jebb. I had trained with Tom Owens by this time, and I think I may have been a bit stronger than him at this time, so I wasn't that worried about him. Going up Ingleborough I didn't know he was still so close to me. When we crossed up at the summit, I thought, "OK, that is Tom." All I thought was just think of this as a Scottish race and you know you can beat him. Mentally that really helped me. On the descent he may have been catching up to me, but I had done enough to win. I couldn't believe it when I crossed the line. Without doubt the highlight of my running career. Having a Saltire in my bag wasn't really pre-planned, as some suggested. I was quite often running team things for the club – which is what I really liked about running. The Scottish flag was for team events. When I realised that I had it in my bag I got it out to celebrate winning, and a one-two for Scotland as well.'

Interestingly, Jethro Lennox did a road marathon in 2009 because of the carrot of possible Commonwealth Games selection. He explains. 'I like to challenge myself. My coach, Malcolm Patterson, was supportive of me doing marathons and hills in the same period, but it is probably not the ideal way of going about it. I am happy that I did that though. The marathon training was actually one of the reasons I ended up winning the Three Peaks. A good marathon runner with hill experience should do well in that race. The Commonwealth qualifying time was 2-18. The London Marathon wasn't especially about qualifying. I was out of range, at 2-24, but close and I don't regret it. I think that the people who do well at the Peaks are those that do hill races well and have great endurance and speed (which marathons can give you).'

Summing up his achievements, Jethro noted that he was 2nd in British Champs twice and that it had been a big ambition of his to win those champs at least once. 'I have won the Scottish Championships four times, which no one else has done. I am really glad I did that. I was capable of winning the British but never quite got it right. The short races can let me down a bit. I also never won a British Championships race either. Far too many seconds, and I fell over in the lead in that Irish race.'

He still trains five or six times a week and tries to race once a month. 'I also run a Junior hill runners' group at the club. That is about enjoyment for them though really. I enjoy my running, but I don't think I am ever going to win the Peaks again. I couldn't commit to the training level required. The Peaks was definitely a highlight of my running career, along with the London Marathon, and getting 3rd in the Scottish National cross-country champs. Just because it is such a traditional grass-roots event.'

Shortly after our conversation Jethro came back with more on what it takes to win the Three Peaks. 'I was 9th in the race in 2016. Hence me not thinking I'll ever do it again, as every time I do it I get slower and finish further back. I don't remember much about 2016 apart from it being a fairly painful experience. I think the reason I feel I could never win it again is the amount of training I had to do to win it that time in 2008. Some folks (like Joe Symonds, for instance) excel on a few months of intensive training. It took me several years to get to that level.'

As noted, Malcolm Patterson was coaching Jethro Lennox at the time of his World Champs win at the Peaks in 2008. Malcolm's thoughts on his advice to Jethro that day give an interesting perspective. 'We were keeping it quite low-key. I certainly can't remember that we'd discussed the possibility of him winning. Though he was clearly racing well and had high hopes of a medal at least in the British and Scottish Champs that year. Instead, we just focused on the detail of the Three Peaks and the best tactics to deploy. My view is that the Three Peaks is quite close in nature to a road marathon, just with three hills in between the flat fast bits. The key similarity being that "anything can happen in the last half hour" (what I call the Stingray effect – for fans of 1960s kids' TV). In other words, you have to remain strong for the long hard fast run in to the finish off Ingleborough. Also, the usual advice about not overcooking it in the early stages is perhaps more important than ever in the Three Peaks because you have the fast section between the top of Pen-y-Ghent and the foot of Whernside. I told Jethro I wanted to see him tucked in a bit behind the leader going through Ribblehead, and definitely not pushing the pace out in front. Whilst I told him not to be overawed by any foreign runners doing the race because it was the World Champs, I told him to absorb the added pressure that the razzamatazz surrounding the race added and not be carried away by it. The race was after all the same race and the way you ran it should be no different to normal.' Pretty effective advice it was too.

Tom Owens also recently reflected on the event. 'I started off really conservatively and with lots of respect having learnt a lot when I struggled in 2006. The field was stacked and started fast. I just couldn't go that fast either! It meant that I paced it really well, and was overtaking legends of the sport and getting faster. A great feeling. I descended well back then. I rocked into 3rd position and was really surprised to pass Mitja from Slovenia lower on Ingleborough. I was more surprised to get a

102. Jethro Lennox and Anna Pichrtova with their trophies, 2008

glimpse of Jethro towards the end. I really started pushing on the Ingleborough descent. I was really surprised to finish 2nd in that field. It was beautifully free running, with no expectations. I was delighted for buddy Jethro too – World Champ. It was a fun journey on the train back to Glasgow!'

Mitja Kosevelj, in 3rd, was the only international runner to make the top ten, and the remainder of those top finishers were the cream of the fell running scene at the time. They were from 4th to 10th: Rob Jebb, Rob Hope, Ricky Lightfoot, Karl Gray, Billy Burns, Joe Symonds and Andy Peace. Some field.

Rob Jebb was more than six minutes slower than his own time the year before, and at the time described his performance as an 'off day'. He then added, 'I was happy to get 4th, because I felt terrible. I had cramp after I'd been running for less than an hour. It's a shame because I wanted to run well because it is such a good event.' Jebb adds now that he had come into the race with a hat-trick of wins and a fast time, but it was won in a time a few minutes slower than he had run (2-53 to his 2-51). 'I think I had been a bit ill and had thus rushed the training a bit. A few of the foreign runners set off really fast and so I went faster than I wanted to. A lot faster, to keep with them. I suffered and Jethro Lennox didn't get carried away and pulled through later on to win. He had run it more sensibly, and I was disappointed in my run for 4th. Most of the foreign runners had got it wrong and then blew up. It was a strange day, loads of people dropped out.'

This was the first time that Ricky Lightfoot had run the Three Peaks, and he later became a double winner. He notes that it was the first year he started racing in Europe. 'I had heard of Three Peaks Race before that through Rob Jebb, I think. I wanted to do it and it happened to be the Worlds. As a rookie I was feeling my way in the race and seeing what it was like in such a strong field. I ran as hard as I could. I am sure I was running in a pair of road shoes, and it was pretty muddy. I gave it a good go though.'

Dave Hodgson reported that: 'The feedback from overseas athletes was full of praise for the friendly way they were received, and I must thank Settle Harriers for all the help they gave in transporting and entertaining them. The WMRA also seem to be well satisfied with our staging of a World Championship event.' It attracted almost 100 overseas entries from 21 countries.

Chapter 32

THE THREE PEAKS RACE AND US

David and Barbara Weatherhead share their perspective on the race:

In 2008, the event was proposed as the World Long Distance Mountain Running Challenge and a small recce party comprising Dave Hodgson, Paul Dennison, Duncan Morrison and I attended the previous year's Jungfrau Marathon in Switzerland, which was the World Long Distance Mountain Running Challenge for 2007.[36] We were amazed at the huge organisational scale and cost of their event, and it made us realise that we couldn't match their promotion but resolved that we would do our utmost to put on the best we could! We did and it was a great success and marked a step change in the Three Peaks Race format which has continued to this day.

I first ran the Three Peaks Race in 1977 at the age of 32 after joining Bingley Harriers in 1975 and then completed the race 12 times up to 1990, along with many other classic events. My best time in the Peaks was a minute over three hours. My father was a starter in 1961 and I well remember standing in the field at the Hill Inn watching the competitors set off up into the mists of Ingleborough!

In the early 1980s I became more curious about the Three Peaks Race. I remember it had a special significance at the club with a history of members competing in the event and a reputation as one of the toughest fell races at that time! Out of interest, I attended an AGM held in the bar area at the Crown

---

36 The TPRA had bid for the 2007 World Long Distance Challenge in the autumn of 2005, but were bidding against the Jungfrau Marathon, which is one of the top Alpine races. The Three Peaks lost out, but the WMRA were so impressed with their bid that they awarded the 2008 event to the Three Peaks.

Hotel in Horton in Ribblesdale and was cajoled into marshalling on Whernside summit.

As time went by, my interest in the fell running scene became more serious and after attending a Fell Runners Association (FRA) meeting, probably in the late 1980s, I became more involved as a Committee Member and Club Representative, later being asked to be an England Team Selector. In those early days I volunteered to take responsibility for collating results and reports for *The Fellrunner* magazine, which I have done ever since. About this time Barbara Carney/Weatherhead also joined the FRA committee and took on the role of Treasurer in 1989 and also helped with the results and reports and now does the bulk of this work.

On behalf of Bingley Harriers & AC as part of a small group, Barbara and I organised the British Relay Championships in 1991 and 2011, based at Kettlewell on both occasions, and also the FRA Presentation Evening in Skipton in 2016. Due to our long-standing involvement with the FRA, we were pleased to recently receive Honorary membership of the Association. Barbara was a fell runner competing regularly and became the first female president of Bingley Harriers in 1994, serving a three-year term.

In my early days on the Three Peaks Race Association committee, I volunteered to take on the recruitment of marshals for race day which I did for about 30 years and which evolved into an almost full-time job as race day approached with all the administration work required. This important role has now been very ably undertaken by Martin Bullock since 2017. My responsibility now is ordering and hiring equipment as required, and general work as needed. Barbara served as secretary for the Association a few years ago and is still a committee member.

I have been president for the last four years and continue to enjoy the challenge of the event organisation and camaraderie of the organising committee. It is a good team, promoting one of the best fell/trail events in the calendar. Barbara and I, although not competing, have maintained a continued interest in fell running – supporting the FRA, Three Peaks Race Association, Bingley

103. *TPRA committee members Martin Bullock and David Weatherhead*

Harriers and also assisting with other events when we can.

Competition from other events, Covid and other outdoor activities has had an effect on entries in recent years and it is a challenge matching the needs of the race with the local communities, landowners, tenants and environmental considerations. Arguably, the race is not now a fell race in traditional terms and is perhaps considered more of a tough trail race. Nevertheless, it is still a hard event needing stamina and speed to beat the cut-off times. The previous list of winners is a 'Who's Who' of fell running, the aspiration to join that list is still strong amongst fell runners.

Chapter 33

LUPTON REPEATS

2009

After the change for the Worlds the year before, the event was again held on the Saturday and continued to do so from then on. Dry underfoot conditions were ideal and a bright, mainly sunny day was marred only by a breeze which was strong on the higher parts of the course.

Anna Lupton won the women's race in a time of 3-36-31 and finished 42nd overall. Hazel Robinson was a bit back in 2nd place but with a respectable time of 3-53-24. By the summit of Pen-y-Ghent, Anna Lupton had started to make her mark in the women's race, being already comfortably ahead of Helen Berry. On the long run across to Ribblehead, Emma Barclay (v40), moved in to 2nd place behind Lupton, with Berry dropping to 3rd. At the summit of Whernside, the places remained the same.

At the top of Ingleborough, Anna remained well clear, but a battle was developing behind between Emma Barclay, Hazel Robinson and Helen Berry, in that order, all within a minute and a half of each other. Barclay also maintained her lead in the Vets category, staying comfortably ahead of Nicky Spinks and Lynne Clough.

On the descent to the finish Anna strode out to win, with the fast finish from Hazel enabling her to take 2nd place from Emma (1st Vet), with Helen 4th. Nicky and Lynne finished 2nd and 3rd for the Vets. Anna comments: 'My time wasn't great that first time I won, but it was respectable, and I was chuffed to bits as I'd never run that far and was just hoping to finish.'

For the 55th race Rob Jebb was back to winning form, securing his fourth win in five years. The race report gives the details:

> By the summit of Pen-y-Ghent, Rob Jebb was already ahead, with v40 Andy Peace not far behind. On the long run across to Ribblehead, Ricky Lightfoot gained second place with Karl Gray not far behind. By the summit of Whernside, the leading men's places

104. Anna Lupton on Ingleborough

remained the same. Andy Peace retaining the leading place in the v40 category with John Hunt a few minutes behind.

With a fast descent to the Hill Inn checkpoint, and the course starting to bite with the steep ascent of Ingleborough, anything could happen. By Ingleborough summit, Rob had opened up a wider gap on Ricky, with Karl a couple of minutes behind and these three drawing away from the rest. The descent to the finish was unlikely to upset these positions and, sure enough, Rob, Ricky and Karl finished in that order.

Reviewing his second attempt at the race, Lightfoot comments, 'I don't think I was really in contention that year. Rob was such a strong climber, and I was still trying to find my way in races. Rob pulled away but he never gained a lot, and I knew I was on for 2nd.'

Rob Jebb gives a very moving account of the build-up to the race and the different emotions it involved. 'I remember it so well. I wasn't going to do the race. Sharon was pregnant and

105. *Rob Jebb at Sulber Nick, 2009*

I hadn't done very much training. Millie was born and she was extremely poorly and was in hospital in Lancaster for a couple of weeks. I hadn't run for a bit and after a while I thought I needed to get running again, so I ran on the canal towpath in Lancaster. One day I was running from there, and I could see Ingleborough, and I suddenly thought I am going to do the Peaks race at the end of the month. Being from Yorkshire I probably never thought about being able to see Ingleborough from Lancashire. But there it was. I was feeling helpless about Millie, as they were not optimistic about her at the hospital, so I was looking for a distraction. Sharon said fine, do it. Millie came out of hospital in time, and I ran, although I was not as fit as I might have been. I just ran like mad, for Millie in a way, and I won the race. I must have been really focused, and the emotion carried me through. In the end Millie was fine, and just look at her now – giving it some on the fells. I will be cheering her on at the Three Peaks one day, hopefully.'

106. Rob Jebb with his 4-week-old daughter Millie, 2009

2010

There were over 700 starters on the day. The race report notes that: 'As the day approached the weather pattern changed to give a very warm and sunny day, with very hard dry ground, which augured well for a fast race. George Kirby addressed the massed competitors at the start and announced, with sadness, the recent deaths of Stan Bradshaw, aged 97 and Peter Dugdale, aged 76. Stan was one of a small group of Clayton-le-Moors Harriers who organised the first Three Peaks Race in 1954.' Stan finished 2nd that day, as we have seen. Stan continued to take part in the race until 1980 when he recorded his 23rd finish. He was a past president and a life vice-president of the Three Peaks Race Association. Peter Dugdale was also a member of Clayton-le-Moors and won the 1957 race.

Anna Lupton repeated her win from the previous year, finishing an excellent 22nd overall. On Pen-y-Ghent the women were being led by Victoria Wilkinson, over two minutes ahead of Anna Lupton. Across to Ribblehead, Victoria maintained a comfortable lead on Anna, with Jo Waites and veteran Lyn Clough (v40) just starting to lose contact. By the summit of Whernside the leading positions remained unchanged. However, Lyn had made up ground to have a slight advantage over Jo. Anna passed Victoria at the bottom of the steep climb going up Ingleborough, to have about a minute's advantage on the final

107. Anna Lupton, 2010

summit and extended this lead by the finish to seven minutes. Victoria Wilkinson says now that, 'Anna passed me, and I said, "Go on, keep going, I am done." I had totally blown-up.'

Anna says her 2010 run was clearly much better than the year before as she was more confident. 'I'm pretty sure this is the year the entry list contained Vic Wilkinson, Mary Wilkinson, Natalie White and some other top-notchers, so I was aiming for the top five. In the end I think Mary and Nat didn't start and I managed to overtake Vic on the steep hands-on-knees ascent of Ingleborough. Vic just bonked a bit, as I think she'd not done much long stuff before, always being so damn fast (obviously she's since become a master of long stuff – and clearly it was me that taught her [*laughs*]). I just remember going steady as far as Ribblehead then the race (in my mind) started from there. I love descending and I do remember making a lot of ground on the long run from Ingleborough summit to the finish.'

Radcliffe/Black Combe runner Anna Lupton had finished 18th in the Three Peaks Race in her first attempt in 2008, when it was the World Champs event, and had a very successful season on the fells that year, with several fell race wins during the year. She claims she wasn't

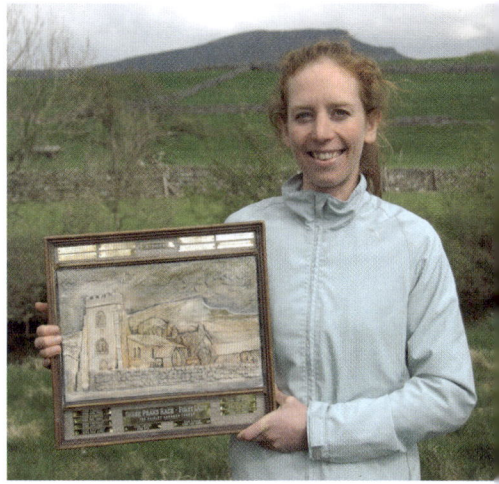

108. Anna Lupton

very fit then. 'It was just before I started a bike tour. I think I'd done the Three Peaks Race for the first time a couple of years before that and am pretty sure I've done it five times. I set off on my bike tour at the start of May 2008, so it must have been a week or two after doing the Three Peaks. My aim was to ride from my home in Manchester and cross Europe and I got to Croatia then got claw-hand from the long hours on the bike and it was 35 degrees in the shade, and I decided not to ride south to Greece but west to do some races in the Alps instead.'

Anna Lupton was born in Bury, Greater Manchester. She recalls that she did everything at school: running, swimming, netball, hockey, football, tennis. 'I loved running the cross-country league races for the club in the winter, shivering in our vests, and I did 800m on the track for Bury AC as a Junior, but I wasn't very confident and basically used to jog the first lap then sprint the second! We used to do a lot of hill walking – my grandparents lived in Ulverston, and we basically spent every school holiday there, tramping about.'

Anna was with Bury AC as a Junior, because her older brother and sister ran for them. Then she joined Radcliffe when she briefly came back home after university in her early 20s (to her parents, who live in Prestwich). 'They were such a fab, friendly club. After that I moved and travelled loads for the next ten years, so I trained with other clubs but stuck with Radcliffe as I never knew where I was going to settle. I finally settled in the South Lakes in 2011 when I was in my early 30s and joined Black Combe, who I'm still with.'

When Anna joined Radcliffe AC she tried fell running. 'Two blokes there (Hi, Mick and Brian!) kept badgering me to do a fell race. I finally gave in and did one somewhere near Halifax, probably around 2004. All I remember is running up onto a moor and there were windmills, then loving running the downhill – we won the female team prize, got a bottle of wine each and I was hooked!' Her intro to mountain running (as in racing abroad) came with the cycle tour in 2008. Grossglockner was her first race there, and she absolutely loved it. 'I started representing England at the World Long Distance in 2009. I did the World Long every year for the next six years, racing in Austria, Slovenia, Switzerland, the Czech Republic and twice in Colorado. Winning the Three Peaks in 2009 shook my thinking up. I might be OK at this running lark.'

So, is she a fell runner or a mountain runner? 'I have no idea. A bit of both, I suppose. Though I've probably done more mountain races in the Alps than fell races in the UK, as I spent every summer there from 2008 to 2019. I'm not ashamed to say I prefer racing in the hot sun on firm ground than flailing round in tussocks in a gale. Mark swears at me when we're fell running as I'm always asking why we're not on the bloody trod when he's dragging me over his 'best lines'! I've got to say, though, I do love a good scree run. I've won Wasdale in a good time, so can't be too much of a softie trail runner, I suppose.'

Anna says she doesn't really subscribe to the best/favourite race or course idea. 'It's been a long continuum of challenges and contentment. It's a way of life. Winning the Three Peaks in 2009 was a surprise as I didn't really realise how fit I'd got in the Alps the previous year. Winning again in 2010 was great, I felt very much at home on the course, had a real affection for the race then and still do (although the day I was 2nd in 2015 when it poured down from start to finish lessened my affection!). Coming 5th at Pikes Peak, running for GB, in 2010 is a great memory. To push hard at a race finish at 4,300 metres altitude is unique and I had no idea what my body would do (thankfully it behaved.) To be honest though, that first year of racing in the Alps in 2008 is hard to beat – it was a total revelation to me, winning enough prize money to just keep doing it and put off coming home and getting a job – it was amazing. I didn't think I could win international races, but the months of cycling had got me fit. I raced every weekend and in between was pretty much a recluse just cycling to the next race living in my tent – the simplicity and sense of purpose was wonderful.'

Anna Lupton concludes our discussion by declaring that there's something very special about the Three Peaks but that it's hard to define. 'It's just three not terribly big hills plonked in Yorkshire with a bit of trail running in between. It's the history, the number of years it's been going, the great runners who have done it. I like the conciseness of the three tops, it splits the course up nicely into sections that are manageable. Running into the finish field and hearing your name on the loudspeaker being announced as the winner is memorable, to say the least.'

Only seconds separated the leading men on Pen-y-Ghent in 2010, with Chris Birchall just being 1st there. On the long run off Pen-y-Ghent and across to Ribblehead, Morgan Donnelly started to gain a lead on 2nd man, veteran John Brown (v40), with Pete Vale and Chris Birchall a couple of minutes behind. At the summit of Whernside the men's leading positions remained unchanged. With a fast descent to the Hill Inn checkpoint and a sharp climb to achieve the summit of Ingleborough, sometimes changes happened, but on this occasion the first four men's positions remained the same at the summit and right on to the finish. Morgan Donnelly (Borrowdale) won by just over four minutes, in 3-02-34.

The summer 2010 issue of *The Fellrunner* carried the following note, commenting on some work being done by the Yorkshire Dales National Park Authority: 'You may have noticed that 50p of each entry fee for this year's race was donated by the Three Peaks Race Association to The Friends of the Three Peaks to support this conservation work. Many of the runners will have appreciated the improvements already achieved

109. Morgan Donnelly heading for the win, 2010

on the route in the 1st year of the project. There is still a vast amount of work to do. The descent of Whernside on the flagged race route was excruciating duc to the extreme erosion. We all cursed as we looked across at the lovely green track we used to follow. However, lovely green tracks soon gather top water and become eroded gullies. All the runners showed due respect to the organisers and kept to the taped route. The future of the race depends on this kind of co-operation.'[37]

---

37 In an article entitled 'Friends of the Three Peaks', by Andrew Hinde of Settle Harriers.

Chapter 34

SECOND SON

2011

Five former women's winners started the race, after there had been three weeks of sunny weather before the event, but on the day it was sunny and cool in the valley, with gale force winds on the summits. It was to be a new face that stood on the top step of the podium. New Zealander Anna Frost took an early lead on Pen-y-Ghent which she gradually increased. Coming off Whernside, though, Helen Fines (Calder Valley) started to catch her. Climbing Ingleborough, Frost re-affirmed her position and was three minutes up at the summit and finished in 3-30-00. Fines was 2nd four minutes later, with Fiona Maxwell (Shettleston) 3rd.

Anna Frost is probably better known as a trail and ultra runner but had first run in the World Mountain Running Championships in 2004, coming 4th. She became an Inov-8 athlete immediately after that, before moving to Salomon in 2009. Later she had to deal with having a hormonal imbalance that resulted in various problems, such as stress fractures and bone pain. She has subsequently tried to raise awareness of the condition, which is Female Athlete Triad (FAT) – a state of imbalance between diet equilibrium, hormone regulation and bone density.

The 2011 race had a result that could have been a repeat of the 2008 result, with a mirrored reversal of the positions, with Tom Owens beating Jethro Lennox on this occasion. However, a fall for Lennox on the descent of Ingleborough spoilt that symmetry. The weather was sunny, with a cool wind down in the valley at Horton-in-Ribblesdale and challenging gale force gusts on the tops.

A record number of 765 starters set off from a full entry list of 999, which included five former men's race winners. In an impressive start the top seven in the men's race reached the

110. *Anna Frost, 2011*

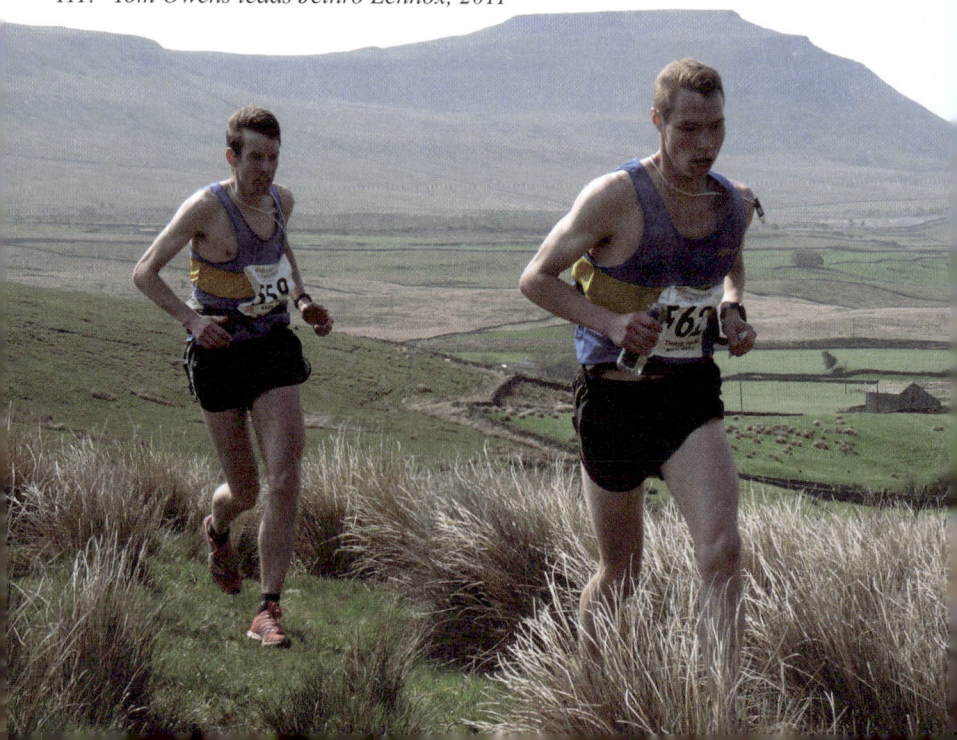
111. *Tom Owens leads Jethro Lennox, 2011*

summit of Pen-y-Ghent in 30 minutes. Then, as usual, the race for Ribblehead was on. Owens and Lennox were the first through that checkpoint, separated by only two seconds. As they started the climb up Whernside they were just over a minute ahead of the chasing pair of Robbie Simpson and Ben Abdelnoor. The leaders looked to be working together to combat the gale force winds.

Only two seconds separated them at the Whernside checkpoint, and they were still together as they came into the Hill Inn, having opened up a two-minute lead on Simpson and Abdelnoor. The climb up Ingleborough saw Owens take over a minute lead on Lennox, who was starting to feel the pressure. On Ingleborough summit Simpson was only 22 seconds behind Lennox and everything was gearing up for a great race to the finish in Horton. It proved to be very close with nine runners home within 15 minutes of the winner. The first three all finished in under three hours, but were well outside Andy Peace's race record of 2-46-03. Owens finished in 2-53-34, 2-41 ahead of Robbie Simpson (Deeside Runners), with Ben Abdelnoor (Ambleside AC) 3rd in 2-59-37. Lennox, who beat Owens by 37 seconds in the 2008 Three Peaks, was 4th in 3-00-29. The winning time was the fastest for four years.

Jethro Lennox admits he wasn't as fit that year as he had been when he won in 2008. 'To do well at the Peaks you have got to be really on top of your game. It was a nasty fall that I had on the descent, and I can't say for sure that I would have won. I probably got a bit tired in the race this time and thus the fall late on. I hadn't paced it as well this time. You need to get the fitness, the pacing and all the elements right to win, and it wasn't the case that year.' Lennox was running well though that year as he was 4th in the World Long in Slovenia (and 3rd Scot, behind Tom Owens and Robbie Simpson), a race Mitje Kosevelj won.

Race instigator, Fred Bagley, was invited to present the trophies after the race. However, he got more than he bargained for, as Tom Owens offered him the winner's trophy to look after for a year, as Bagley never took home a trophy for winning the first event, in 1954, as the first trophy was presented four years

112. Tom Owens and Fred Bagley, 2011

later after the event grew in popularity. *Athletics Weekly* reported on Tom's gesture:

> The 29-year-old Shettleston Harrier said: 'It was a privilege to meet Fred Bagley, who is such an important figure in the history of fell running. It is right that he should have the trophy to look after for me. I am proud and very happy to ask him to hold it on my behalf.' A delighted Mr Bagley said: 'I will cherish the trophy and show it to my children, grandchildren and great grandchildren. It feels so good to be able to hold it after so many years.'[38]

Race Director Paul Dennison said after the event: 'The fell runners and their supporters gave Mr Bagley a tremendous reception at the prize presentation and we were delighted that Tom Owens made such a wonderful gesture. It was a perfect end to a perfect day.'

Tom Owens grew up in London and tells me it was mainly football early on for him. He was a goalkeeper until going to

---

38 In an article entitled 'Trophy is awarded 57 years late', in *Athletics Weekly*, 5 May 2011.

university. 'I also had phases of getting very immersed into racket sports. Football remained the constant though, and I started playing in midfield at university – I loved the running around.'

He got into the London Marathon in 2003 through the ballot when in his second year at university and started to do some regular running a few times a week with the cross-country club whilst playing football. 'I followed a *Runners World* online training schedule for a sub-3 marathon and just got under in 2-57, with a massive bonk at 20 miles and a fair bit of walking!'

He adds, 'I met Andy Symonds in my final year at uni, and he took me under his wing and taught me a lot about running and training. Andy encouraged a group of us to do the Snowdon race in 2004 and then with Joe (his brother) we did the Grisedale fell race. I couldn't believe such an amazing sport existed. I'd bonked hard in every race but loved the intensity, exhilaration, excitement and exploring aspect of it.'

Tom Owens had been trying out some British and English championships fell races, local hill races and some classic races in 2006 after returning to the UK (from a post-university year travelling and working abroad). 'I tried lots of new fell races including the Three Peaks in 2006. I loved getting lots of different experiences but wasn't really fussed about championships. I ran the Peaks as an unattached runner in 2006 and hadn't really done any long races in the UK beforehand (but a few in New Zealand in 2005). There was a fastish start to the race on a really hot day. I totally bonked after Whernside and lost the skin off the soles of both feet with blisters. I can't remember my finish time, but I was destroyed. A really good lesson.'

Joining the Salomon team in 2008, Tom mostly competed in Mountain X races for a while. 'One was a six-day adventure race around the Mont Blanc area, in teams of three (Andy Symonds, Ben Bardsey and myself). There were big stages each day, usually big days mountaineering, climbing, rafting, mountain biking with a discrete running race each evening. It was really global, competitive and suited runners. It was a bit of a gamble taking me, as I was so inexperienced, but I think a good Three

Peaks run in 2008 (when it was the Worlds) helped.'

Tom adds that Salomon have always recognised the Three Peaks as a UK classic race. 'They have encouraged and supported athletes to do the Peaks, although I never felt pressured to do it. They sponsored it for a few years, which was ace as they got a few internationals over – Rickcy Gates, Emily Forsberg, Mira Rae and the awesome Marc Lauenstein.'

In 2009 Tom Owens was 2nd in the British Fell Champs. 'I think I was only semi-focused on it, in that I did enough races to count. But I was still much more interested in new experiences and locations, and in doing as much as possible.'

In autumn 2009, he had Achilles tendonitis and realised he had been doing too much. He had to take about seven months off from running. He lists a catalogue of injuries he has had over the years. 'That injury definitely kept me more local in 2009, after all the new experiences and adventure races in 2008. I could still cycle and walk so carried on with my ecology survey work. I then had peroneal ankle surgery in 2013 and late 2020, where ruptured sections of peroneal longus tendon are cut out and transferred onto healthier peroneal brevis tendon. Both have led to lengthy post-surgery static periods and slow recoveries – getting strength, balance and confidence takes many months (especially after the 2020 surgery where the damaged tendon length was much greater). Confidence on rough terrain is the toughest to regain. I've had lots of other foot/ankle injuries relating to my very strange, super high arched feet.'

By 2011 Tom was back running. He was motivated to exploring internationally again, and did some Skyraces. He also ran the Three Peaks that year, noted above, as he recalls. 'I was fit but still not massively confident. In the race I ran with training buddy Jethro [Lennox] to the base of Ingleborough and felt comfortable. It was reassuring and brilliant to run with Jethro. He started to slow and I still felt good. I pushed on midway up Ingleborough. It was a really strange feeling to be ahead of my idol, Jethro. He was always the strong and fast one (especially going uphill). He was capable of pushing himself to collapse point and is still running brilliantly.'

113. Tom Owens and Jethro Lennox locked in battle, 2011

He adds more on training with Jethro Lennox. 'When I moved to Glasgow I fell into training with Malcolm Patterson, Jethro and the Shettleston running crew. Malcolm took the weekly hill rep sessions in various Glasgow parks and low hills in the summer. He still does and they are booming. We trained together and travelled as a group to races. Malcolm has been a fabulous mentor throughout the years. Although I've never had a coach as such, prescribing sessions. I've always gone by feelings, a degree of trial and error and following some basic principles.'

Tom returned to the Three Peaks in 2012, although he really struggled with heavy legged feelings and niggles. He later found out that he was very iron deficient. He came close to winning the race in 2014, 2016 and 2017, before winning his second time in 2018, seven years after his first.

Summing up his career so far, he says, 'I love the UK fell/hill running scene, but it is also hugely exciting to run all over the world. Running has opened a lot of opportunities for a London lad late to running. I've been incredibly lucky. It's been some ride!' He then lists some highlights of his international days, including, 'I guess twice being 2nd in the World Long Course (the Three Peaks 2008 and Podbrdo in Slovenia in 2011). They were special. Twice 4th at the World Long Trail (Annecy 2015 and 2016 at Podbrdo again). Second place in the Zegama sky race in May 2011 was a bit of a turning point for confidence. It was nip and tuck with Kilian [Jornet] for a long time and I thought I had him with just 2–3km to go and pushed on, only to cramp up and get overtaken on the last wee hill. I lost out by 30 seconds or so in the end. I never got that close again. I was 4th in the UTMB in 2019. That was a bit different – an introduction to the 100-mile race scene. That race definitely gets a lot of hype.'

He does reveal that he struggles to sleep before a lot of races he travels to. 'Sometimes I don't sleep one or sometimes even two nights before a big race – especially when sharing a room with other runners. I get in a cycle of not sleeping which is mega frustrating. It sometimes feels like I'm chucking all that great training away and it has probably negatively impacted quite a few big races.'

Tom Owens concludes our chat by saying that to him the Three Peaks Race is a classic with a wonderful history. 'It tests everything – fast running, cross-country and fell. It is a great early season focus and the training sets you up well for the rest of the year. It is so tough. It humbles every runner – and your race can quickly unravel. There is no hiding. It's big for a UK fell race, with up to 1,000 runners, but still has a small grass-roots feel, but with great organisation. It is exciting to race – as positions usually change a fair bit. I don't like to repeat the same events year after year, but I've been drawn back to the Peaks several times (more than any other race). I also like the fact that you can get there by train (to Horton), especially as I have been without a car for most of my life.'

Malcolm Patterson commented on his coach/athlete relationship with Tom Owens. 'It would be a stretch to say I was coaching him, as Tom wasn't really interested in that sort of relationship. It just didn't seem to work for him, he would listen to advice and ideas but wanted to work out the detail of training and racing himself. More importantly, perhaps, was the fact that he reacted badly to any hint of pressure on him to perform well in a particular race. I think "peaking" was something of a swear word to Tom! He had a tendency to over race and to race everything hard. Injuries eventually took their toll, but in his younger days he could usually cope with this regime. Tom was blessed with natural talent and speed, and he was a stylish runner.'

Patterson adds that he doesn't remember what they talked about before the race in 2011, but he does recall thinking it would be no surprise at all if Owens won. 'He'd already almost done it in 2008, after all. Just as long as there wasn't a slip! In the event, he dominated the race, leading from Ribblehead onwards, with Jethro in tow until Tom was able to drop him going up Ingleborough and secure a well-deserved victory. It was a celebratory prize-giving, with the Scots dominating the men's race. Topped off by Tom's lovely gesture in giving the trophy back to the man who had just presented it, Fred Bagley.'

2012

Two top international ultra-runners were entered, with those in the know expecting them to figure highly. On the men's side Rickey Gates was over from San Francisco for a crack at the race, and for the women Sweden's Emelie Forsberg was very much up for her first experience of UK fell running. As we shall see, they had mixed results in a field that included some of the UK's top exponents of the kind of running that the Three Peaks requires. After days of heavy rain, Saturday was dry, but there was a bitterly cold easterly wind and the temperature barely lifted above three degrees on the summits. The 745 starters from an entry of 1,000 found themselves battling against showers of sleet. The gathering storm had destroyed the two main marquees in the start field.

Sarah O'Neill (Hunters Bog Trotters) won the women's race comfortably in 3-28-46. O'Neill's time at the Pen-y-Gent summit was 20 seconds ahead of 2nd-placed woman Emelie Forsberg (Salomon International) who finished 2nd in 3-43-52. Forsberg was a biology student in Tromso (Sweden) at the time and had sat an exam the week beforehand. Forsberg was further behind at Ribblehead and O'Neill was 4-38 up on her on Whernside and reached Ingleborough 12 minutes ahead of Forsberg, who was running the Peaks for the first time. In 3rd place was the Welsh international fell runner Sarah Ridgway, in 3-45-51.

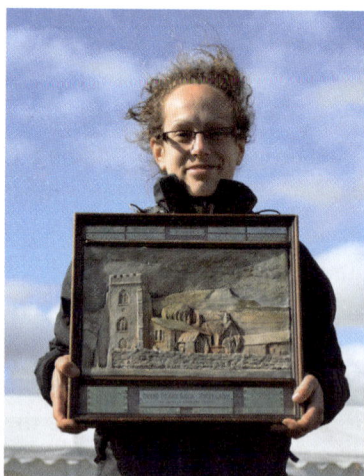

114. Sarah O'Neill, 2012

In her own blog, **Emelie Forsberg** described the race and the Salomon presence there. 'It is a real English fell/cross competition and I understand it is a prestigious race for all trail- and fell-loving people in England. After my exam last Friday (which exceeded

115. Sprint finish between Emelie Forsberg and Craig Stansfield, 2012

116. *Wendy Dodds, winner of the w60 trophy, 2012*

expectations! Phew!) I met up with Rickey Gates (from the USA) and Salomon ambassador for the UK, Matt Ward, so we continued the journey up to where the competition takes place. It was super nice to meet all the runners again. The team from Salomon were: Tom Owens, Ricky Lightfoot, Rickey Gates, Andy Symonds and myself. As is customary, we drank a lot of tea and ate loads of scones. I was given a thorough description of the competition and the atmosphere was top notch!'

She then described how it went. 'As always, I'm totally pumped when I'm on the starting line. I'm jumping and bouncing and can't wait to get going. Getting ready for the first climb, I had a good pace that felt sustainable. I assumed I was 1st lady, but 200 metres before the top a small, small lady jumps me. I thought I would be stressed but felt that I had a chance in the downhill run. I picked up several minutes there. But, after that downhill run, there is a straight stretch in mud, over fields and rocks. Here she ran around me, light as a piece of paper. I felt that I had to focus on how I know I can run. So, then I just focused on making the race as pleasant and smart as possible.'

On Whernside she says she met with a wall. 'Arms and legs were needed to get up. Then a technical steep downhill run, with lots of rock and lots of mud. I liked that! I was still 2nd lady but had no idea how far behind the others were. At Ingleborough I felt fresh, had eaten a gel, drunk lots of water and my legs felt OK. Then I started playing with the idea that I might be able to run into 2nd place. Imagine if I could! Up and down the last mountain. Everything felt good. Nice trails there and a little drier than so far had been. Six kilometres to the finish line. At 4km before the finish I felt really heavy. I was out of energy and 4km is quite a lot. But it worked. I came 2nd. Wow. All in all,

117. The leaders early on, 2012

I'm satisfied that I was able to stay together the whole distance, I was careful about eating and drinking and, above all, I had a great time.'

On a windy day it was another new face on the winner's podium for the men, Joe Symonds from Hunters Bog Trotters. A men's and women's double for the club.

Joe Symonds was following in the footsteps of his father Hugh, and he and Tom Owens and Ricky Lightfoot were prominent throughout the race. But by the finish things had changed. Joe Symonds came home in 2-55-58, and 2nd and 3rd places went to two runners running the race for the first time. Carl Bell (Howgill Harriers) was 2nd and Rob Baker (Dark Peak Fell Runners) finished 3rd – both well inside three hours. Showing the strength in depth of the field, Ricky Lightfoot was 4th, with Karl Gray 5th (and 1st Vet), Andrew Davies 6th, Rob Jebb 7th and Tom Owens 8th.

Ricky Lightfoot was a Salomon athlete by then, and he

118. Joe Symonds, 2012

confirms that as a sponsor they pretty much let you race what you wanted. There were incentives for finishing on the podium though, which that year he just missed out on.

Rickey Gates hadn't fared so well on his debut in the UK. Starting off in the lead group, he started to feel the effects of a calf/hamstring injury, which had been worrying him all winter, and even a shoe change wasn't enough to relieve the pain forcing him to drop out of the race after about ten miles. He did say afterwards that it was still a wonderful experience.

119. Joe Symonds with the trophy, 2012

One anonymous runner, quoted in the race report, perhaps best summed up the race and why they keep coming back. 'What brings me back to run this race each year? The nervous apprehension as the announcer counts down to start time. The spectators whose cheers can lift a weary and footsore runner through a bad patch. And, of course, the finish, with the field in sight from half a mile away and the tannoy announcing your arrival on the final run in. It is always a grand day out and it is in Yorkshire.'

Chapter 35

I WANTED TO
EXPERIENCE IT

2013

After two days of hail and heavy rain, which left the start area deep in mud, the mountain tops had a thin covering of fresh snow early on race day. But by the 10am start the snow was gone. The women's race was won by Three Peaks first-timer Jasmin Paris (Carnethy Hill Running Club) in 3-33-04, who finished 42nd overall. Paris caught and passed Oihana Kortazar Aranzeta, a Spanish member of the Salomon International Team, on the descent from Swine Tail off Ingleborough summit.

Aranzeta had led the women over Pen-y-Ghent and Whernside and stayed ahead up the steep face of the last of the Three Peaks. Paris commented post-race: 'When I descended from Whernside to the Hill Inn checkpoint that was when I first saw her. From there, as we ascended Ingleborough, I was maybe 30 metres behind her. Everybody kept shouting she is just in front of you, you can catch her, but I said I can't. I had been trying all the way up Ingleborough.' She did catch her though. Aranzeta finished 2nd, in a time of 3-36-29, but was later taken to Airedale General Hospital in Keighley, West Yorkshire, with a suspected broken arm after taking a tumble during the race. In 3rd was Helen Bonsor, of Carnethy, in 3-39-07, and 4th Jill Mykura, sealing the team prize for Carnethy with a score of eight points.

Jasmin Paris started running after leaving University in 2008. After a move to Edinburgh in 2010 she took her running more seriously. In 2011 she won the Scottish Long Classics at her first attempt and repeated the win in 2012. She won the 2012 Lakeland Classics Trophy, with all her races run on sight (except the Three Shires). She has only run the Three Peaks once, but

120. Jill Mykura, 2013

when I asked if she felt she had the ability to run much faster there on a better day, she replied, 'Yes, I have thought about it, and likely will do it again at some point, I just keep getting sidetracked by other projects!'

Jasmin also gave a detailed breakdown of her slightly unorthodox approach to the race that day, saying she doesn't remember recceing the race beforehand, but had walked parts of the route with the Open Air Club when she was at university in Liverpool. 'For the race, my partner Konrad and I travelled down together, and I dropped him off at the *Fellsman* race registration on the Friday night before staying in a hostel somewhere close to the Three Peaks start. I can't recall why now, but I remember taking my sleeping bag outside halfway through the night and sleeping under the stars, instead of the dorm room, which was lovely. On the day of the race, I remember being nervous before the start, and glad when we were away and running. Compared to most of the races I liked to do, the Three Peaks was quite fast and runnable, especially the first half. But I had been told by a friend (Dave Ward, Pennine) before the race that it would get better on the climb up Whernside, and he was right, after that it

121. The winning Carnethy team, 2013. L to R: Jill Mykura, Jasmin Paris, Helen Bonsor

felt a lot more like a fell race.'

She spotted the leading female runner (Aranzeta) somewhere on the descent from Whernside but couldn't make up any ground on the following climb. 'The summit of Ingleborough has a bit of an out-and-back where one can see the competitors in front, and I realised there that she wasn't that far ahead, especially as she seemed to move more slowly than me on the more technical terrain. I pushed hard on the descent, and it wasn't long before I caught her (I am not sure if her fall was before or after this point). I continued to push hard, to build up as much of a lead as I could before the running became less technical again, since the earlier and flatter sections of the race seemed to have favoured her running style over mine, and I felt she would have the upper hand on more runnable ground. I was expecting her to catch me until the very last moment, so it was a real thrill when I reached the finishing field and looked over my shoulder to discover she was nowhere to be seen. After the race I think I washed my legs in the river, and once the prize-giving was over, I drove to the *Fellsman* route, and climbed onto the tops above Wharfedale to cheer the front runners through, before going to the finish line to see them finish. I slept in the hall there that night, along with

Konrad and the other *Fellsman* finishers, then we all had a big breakfast the next day before driving home.'

Asked what attracted her to the Three Peaks Race and thus encouraged her to run it that year, Jasmin replied: 'The Three Peaks is such an iconic race in the history of fell running, that I wanted to experience it for myself. Besides that, I think it was a selection race that year for the World Long Distance Mountain Running Championships in Poland, which I was eager to qualify for.'

Jasmin also says she thinks the Three Peaks is a great test of running ability, since it does require speed as well as climbing ability, and for the later sections also skill over rougher terrain. 'The race attracts an interesting mix of runners – road, trail and fell. Personally, I found it quite fun moving through the field in the second half, as all the fast road runners suddenly came up against the real climbs! That said, the Three Peaks Race isn't what I would class as a pure fell race, in the way that Wasdale or Ennerdale are – there's too much road and fast running, as well as too many people.'

Since 2013 Jasmin has gone from strength to strength, with some amazing results, only some of which are possible to mention here. She won the Scottish Hill Running Championships in 2014 and 2015, and in 2015 and 2018 she won the British Fell Running Championships. In 2015 she a set new record for the *Fellsman*, and in 2016 completed the Ramsay Round in 16-13, which was then the fastest time by anyone for the round, since beaten by Es Tresidder. In 2016 she was 6th at the UTMB, her first 100-miler, and the same year she won the Skyrunner World Series.

Jasmin Paris became well known outside the confines of the sport when she set a new race record in January 2019 in the Spine Race along the Pennine Way, finishing the 268 miles (431.3km) in 83 hours 12 minutes and 23 seconds. Becoming the first woman to win the event overall, she surpassed the previous record of 95 hours 17 minutes set by Eoin Keith in 2016 and the previous female record of 109 hours 54 minutes achieved by Carol Morgan in 2017.

122. Carl Bell leads from Joe Symonds and Tofol Castanyer, 2013

Joe Symonds chalked up his second successive win of the Three Peaks Race in 2013. Symonds gave his take on how the race panned out soon afterwards: 'We were quick from the start. I knew we would be because Carl Bell was there and that's his approach to racing. No matter how long the race may be, he will go off hard, so I knew I had to set off quickly. We shared the lead until about halfway up Pen-y-Ghent and then Carl and the Spaniard, Tofol Castanyer, dropped back a bit and I found myself on my own. It was a long, lonely run from there on.' Symonds finished in 2-54-39, Bell (in his second attempt at the event) hung in there for 2nd, with Karl Gray just six seconds behind him, and Rob Jebb coming home in 4th. Salomon runner Castanyer had slipped to 9th.

Speaking after the event of his hat-trick hopes, Joe said: 'I would love to. It is an addictive race. There is something about it. I will be back with a clear intent. I love this race. It is very close to where I grew up, and these are iconic mountains. I was brought up in Sedbergh, which is just round the corner, so I know these mountains, especially Whernside. You can run up Whernside from home, through Dent. It is kind of on the edge of the land of my upbringing, so I will definitely be back.' He also reckoned the revised route over Whitber, to avoid the boggy section through Black Dubb Moss, was a joy to run.

I caught up with Joe at the same time that I interviewed his father Hugh, and we chatted through the relationship they both have with the Three Peaks Race. First off, he apologised that, unlike his father, he had no diaries to refer to and would be relying on memory.

Joe Symonds started running the fells in the mid-1990s, competing in the well-established Junior Fell Championships series. 'I was definitely not the best runner at school, maybe fourth best [*he chuckles*]. The short Junior fell races suited me though. I could run up hill quickly and hold my own going down. I started as an under-15, I think. Most people I ran against haven't carried on running though. I remember going to races and watching the prize-givings. Sometimes Dad was there and sometimes he wasn't [*laughs at the recollection of the time Hugh was in the pub instead of the prize-giving*].' More often Hugh would finish a race, be handed the three kids and his wife Pauline would go off for her own run.

Joe says he doesn't have any recollection of watching the Three Peaks Race. 'I was aware that the Three Peaks was a thing. For some reason my running ambitions were focused on the Championship and International races, particularly as a Junior. Pete Bland used to take Junior teams to events like the Black Forest Teenager Games (in Germany). They were very short races, about eight minutes long, after travelling all that way in a minibus. I missed a connection once and had to travel to the venue on my own, at the age of about 14, including a taxi for the last ten miles or so. Hitting the Seniors is quite hard though. It took me a while to break through.'

In 2005 Joe first went to the Worlds as a Senior, in Wellington, in New Zealand. He was 22 years old. He was fourth in the Worlds in 2007, missing out on 3rd place in a sprint. Then in 2008 Joe ran his first Three Peaks Race. He remembers being marked as a Novice in the programme. He was doing it because it was the WMRA World Long Distance Mountain Running Championships race. 'I felt it might be too long for me, as I was used to 10–12k fell races mostly. It was definitely a stretch for me. I wasn't thinking I could win it. The race went off far too quickly, and some of the favourites blew up big time. I remember running off Ingleborough with Lloyd Taggart and seeing him take an atrocious trip and landing flat on his face with blood everywhere. He just said, "Keep going, Joe."' His father Hugh recalls, 'It was very competitive. We watched on Ingleborough.'

In the 2009 race Joe Symonds suffered badly from sore legs and retired at the Hill Inn. 'It seems like a cop out, looking back,' he says quietly now. He did not race the event in either 2010 or 2011, but then had back-to-back wins in 2012 and 2013.

Joe explains that both those victories had a context of him having completely separate objectives for the year. 'For the first year I was trying to win the FRA British Championships. The Three Peaks happened to be in a gap between races. I was fit so I thought I could do the Peaks, as it was two weeks after one Champs race and two weeks before the next. The 2013 victory was two weeks after I had run the Rotterdam marathon, where I was going for 2-19 as a qualifier for the Commonwealth Championships. I got 2-20, and never got another chance.'

For 2012 he says he hadn't done much recceing really. 'I probably did two recces of the course in my life. I was living in Inverness both times that I won it. Recceing is to find out how to run the course really. For Whernside you need to be familiar with it to have the confidence to go for it, however big a hill it looks.' Hugh chips in at this point. 'There is a good line off Ingleborough where you can avoid a lot of the rocks. It is a grassy run, but you have got to know where it is as you won't find it by accident.'

Joe and Hugh Symonds briefly discussed aspects of recceing the Three Peaks. Hugh: 'I remember taking my sons Joe and Andrew and dropping them off at Ribblehead in foul weather. I said meet you in Horton. I got across there and the two of them had run over Whernside and Ingleborough in quite a quick time. They had navigated it really well in thick mist.' Joe: 'Once, when I hadn't done the Pen-y-Ghent bit, I did a run with some friends. We did Horton to Pen-y-Ghent and then Whernside, and then from the top of Whernside I ran home to Sedbergh, about another ten miles or so, through Dentdale. A brilliant run.'

They also briefly covered fatherly advice. Hugh: 'I can't remember giving Joe any specific advice on running the Three Peaks.' Joe just recalled: 'I think he gave advice along the lines of, "The race doesn't start till Ribblehead."' When I cheekily asked Joe why he hadn't run a faster time than his father when winning the Three Peaks, Hugh rescued him by quickly interjecting, 'I've got longer legs!'

Being a runner who thrived on confidence, Joe reckons his recent form saw him looking to win the Three Peaks in 2012. Asked when he thought he had that Three Peaks won, Joe calmly replied, 'When I won the Coledale Horseshoe two weeks previously. I was feeling really fit and really looking forward to the Three Peaks, to do something there. In the race itself it was on Whernside when I knew I'd win.'

Joe adds that 2012 was probably his most successful season on the fells, as he was British Champion. 'Having said that, my most successful single race was in 2007 in the Worlds (4th in Ovronnaz, Switzerland). I literally spent the whole year just thinking this is all I care about, in running terms. One 50-minute race. As a Junior doctor I often worked a lot of weekends and thus raced sparingly.'

For the 2013 Three Peaks Race, Joe had a marathon in his legs, and he had not done any fell training at all through the winter and spring. 'I sat in a lot more that year,' he chuckles. 'I got Carl Bell on Whernside again though! The rest of the race didn't feel so good. I was hanging on. Carl was quicker than me both years coming off Ingleborough, but I was second or third fastest there. In fact, I was quicker finishing off Ingleborough that year than the year before. Maybe there was a following wind!'

Hugh Symonds was not able to watch either of his son's victories, as he was on global travel trips both years. 'In 2012 we were tracking Joe from New Zealand (on a bicycle tour).

The following year we couldn't track him as we were on a ship crossing the Caspian Sea. We got a signal as we entered Kazakhstan, and heard he had won. My immediate thought was, could Joe win it three times?'

123. *Joe Symonds and Jasmin Paris with their winner's trophies, 2013*

Joe Symonds then returned to the Three Peaks after a year's absence in 2015 but he only finished in 12th place with a time of 3-09-57. It is just possible that Joe Symonds has unfinished business with the Three Peaks Race. 'I have not been back since 2015. I could still go back and get a third win,' Joe says quietly. That third win could still come, Hugh.

Joe finishes by summarising his feelings about the Three Peaks Race. 'On the start line of the Peaks very few people are in their comfort zone. There are many races that I'll do when I am absolutely in my comfort zone. For example, at the Sedbergh Hills race I know every hill and every gradient. It is what I like running on too. Many will stand there, at the Peaks, and think it is a bit long for me, or a bit fast.' Hugh Symonds adds that, 'At that time of year the weather can be very variable too. It can be a heatwave or snow.'

Joe Symonds reckons the Three Peaks Race is a fell race for a marathon runner, or a marathon race for fell runners. 'I mean it doesn't fit a category for pure fell runners or pure road runners. It is a wonderful event though. I suppose in my two victories I had a chance to approach the race from both angles: in 2012 as a fell runner and in 2013 as a marathon runner. Funnily enough I came out with the same position and a very similar time each way I tried it. John Wild, Jeff Norman and Kenny Stuart all went to the marathon from the fells.'

Chapter 36

LIGHT OF FOOT

2014

As 2014 was the race's diamond jubilee, there was a £500 bonus on offer if the women's winner broke the record time set by Anna Pichrtova in 2008. The winner for this year was Victoria Wilkinson, who finished in 17th place overall, the third highest overall ever. The highest-placed female in the race history is Angela Mudge, who was 11th in 1999, with Sarah Rowell the second highest in 1992 when she finished 15th overall.

Victoria Wilkinson (Bingley Harriers), who was 35 at the time, finished in 3-21-32 – more than 15 minutes ahead of Shona Robertson of Glasgow's Shettleston Harriers. Her time made her the fourth fastest lady in the history of the race at the time – behind Angela Mudge (3-20-17 in 1999), Sarah Rowell (3-16-17 in 1996), and Anna Pichrtova (3-14-43 in 2008).

Wilkinson said afterwards: 'I was pleased. I was aiming for a sub-3 hours 30 minutes, so to get 3 hours 21 minutes I was quite happy.' She had never expected to win the £500 bonus. 'The record is do-able on the right day, in the right conditions. But today conditions were pretty hard. It was fairly muddy, and I have only done it twice. It was pretty gloopy in places, and it was windy.'

Re-living the race, she added: 'Going up Whernside was fairly wet and there is that tricky bit coming down. You have walkers about and those steps, so that was probably the bit I did not enjoy. You have just got to get your pacing right and that is hard. It is a hard race because going up Pen-y-Ghent you are thinking, "I had better back off and not burn out, then you are thinking I had better press on to get a decent time." I was running with the men and men tend to be good pacemakers, so I was happy. There were a lot of good spectators out there and I had Bingley Harriers shouting me on.'

124. *Victoria Wilkinson*
at the viaduct, 2014

Chatting about that year recently, Victoria explained that it was one of the races that was on her list to do again. Between 2010 and 2014 she was doing more fell running, and thus less cross-country. 'This involved longer miles. According to my diary I ran it very conservatively. I didn't want to blow up again. You have to learn the race. The diary also had a note that says I knew I could run quicker than the 3-21 of that year.'

Victoria Wilkinson had started running early in her life. For her first race she was underage when she ran the Three Shires under-12s race. 'I daren't get a number so dived in and dived out. I started at the end of the road and pulled out before the finish. I wouldn't recommend that approach now! My dad was doing the main race.'

Victoria had a very successful Junior career, during which she says the highlight was winning the World Junior Mountain Running Champs in 1997 in Czechoslovakia, when she was 19. 'I started running in the BOFRA races, but when I joined Bingley (at 14) you weren't allowed to do BOFRA and FRA races, so I only did FRA races from then on. Then at 15 I gained an international vest in the Home International at Grasmere.'

In her younger days Victoria was equally adept at up and down, but she says, 'as I have got older, I have got less good at descending. You think more about your ankles and injuries then and are a bit more cautious.'

Victoria took to cycling from 2000 to 2005. She got injured running cross-country and hurt her knee in 1999 and couldn't run at all, so started biking more. 'I was always biking anyway from six years old onwards. I did my first National cross-country MTB series and came 5th. I got picked for the England Potential Plan and progressed to the World Class Potential Plan. That gave me five years of racing road, cyclo-cross and mountain biking. One of the highlights was doing the Commonwealth Games in Manchester, at mountain biking. I rode all over Europe and in America.'

She later got back into international running but has one big regret. 'I never got a Senior World medal in mountain running, which I will never forget. I won the World Masters last year. I also came 7th at Zegama in 2019. And did Sierre-Zinal three times, with a 5th as my best position.' Victoria adds a further

125. Personal drinks at Ribblehead

reflection on this point. 'I guess as World Junior Champion at 19 and World Masters Champion at 44, I can't complain. It is just that Elite Medal that I missed. But now in hindsight I'm so pleased and proud that my father got to see both those races. I wouldn't have won them without his, and my family's, support.'

There was also a £500 bonus on offer if the race winner broke Andy Peace's 18-year-old race record of 2-46-03. The money was unclaimed, as Ricky Lightfoot completed the race in 2-53-16. Salomon runner Thorbjorn Ludvigsen (from Norway) was running, with the tag of being the fastest runner to the top of the Empire State Building, but fellow Salomon athlete Ricky Lightfoot beat him convincingly.

Ludvigsen, who won the Empire State run in New York in February – taking 10 minutes six seconds for the vertical dash up 1,576 steps from the lobby to the 86th floor – came home in 6th place, 12 minutes 53 seconds slower than the winner on what was a slippery day.

Lightfoot, from Maryport (Cumbria), got a late entry for the Three Peaks on the Wednesday before the race and started off just hoping not to aggravate a knee injury, which stopped him running from the end of January to mid-March. The previous year had been very special. Not only did he become a father to a baby daughter, but he also finished first in the Borrowdale fell race, won the International Athletics Union Trail World title and the Otter Trail race in South Africa. Surprisingly, Lightfoot admits that he took the Three Peaks win off limited training. 'A hip injury was preventing me from doing a lot of training. It affected my hard sessions because that was when I felt it most. Although I was training, I was unable to get quality sessions in.'

Second place went to another Salomon International runner, Tom Owens, who had won the Three Peaks Race three years previously. His 29 minutes to the summit of Pen-y-Ghent was ten seconds faster than Lightfoot, but he came in three minutes behind at the finish, in 2-56-13. Third was four-times winner Rob Jebb, of Bingley Harriers, in 2-59-57.

Looking back recently, Tom Owens commented that this was the year after his first ankle surgery. 'I was fit and motivated and ran feeling more confident with front running it. I pushed on with Ricky. I felt he was hanging on, but then he showed his strength when I got dumped going up Ingleborough when it got steeper and couldn't get him back. He pulled away nicely. It was a change in tactics for me to go off more confidently.'

Prizes for this year's race, the 60th, were presented by Shirley and Dave Hodgson, who had been involved in competing or organising the race for more than 50 years and were both life vice-presidents of the Three Peaks Race Association. Race director and Three Peaks Association chairman, Paul Dennison, presented them with a specially commissioned painting showing Pen-y-Ghent, Whernside and Ingleborough and familiar landmarks including Ribblehead Viaduct and the Old Hill Inn to mark their commitment to the race and its organisation.

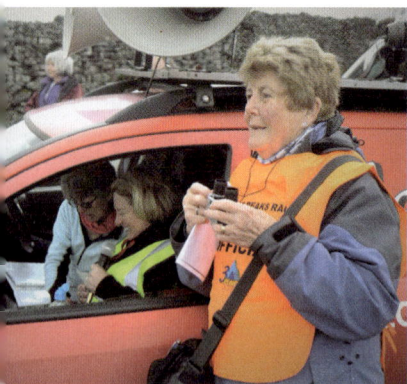

126. *Shirley Hodgson calling numbers whilst Clare Kenny and Denise Park do the race commentary at Ribblehead, 2014*

Chapter 37

I LIKE IT
BECAUSE IT IS HARD

2015

The record bonus was not claimed in 2015 either. Helen Bonsor, of Carnethy Hill Running Club, finished in 44th place overall in 3-27-24. Anna Lupton, of Black Combe Runners, was 2nd female in 3-34-46, and Caitlin Rice, of Glossopdale Harriers, was third fastest in 3-39-3. After a relatively dry week, there was heavy overnight rain, which turned to snow as the later runners reached the summits of Whernside and Ingleborough, where race marshals, electronic timing kit operators and radio teams were in place for up to six hours. Two of Bonsor's most notable wins have been at the Transalpine (2015) and the Salomon 4 Trails (2015), and she also set a new record time for Scotland's Tranter's Round in 2017.

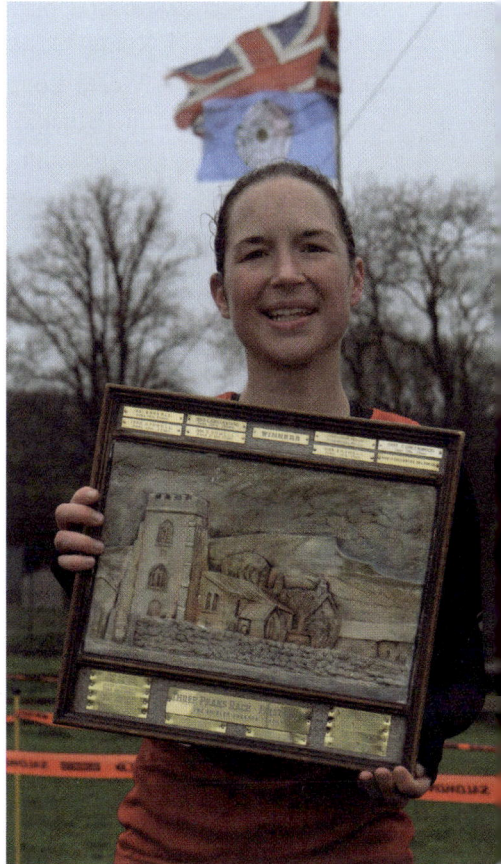

127. Helen Bonsor, 2015

Ricky Lightfoot continued his winning ways, after working a night shift in his job as a firefighter. The Salomon runner ran in to finish in Horton in a time of 2-51-42, just over a minute and a half faster than his winning time in 2014, despite running in heavy rain, sleet and cold conditions.

Lightfoot apologised to race organisers for not being able to stay for the prize presentation as he had to return to Cumbria for another night's work. 'I did the race and got away an hour after the finish and back home for 5.30pm and went straight to work. That was how it was done when you are a firefighter. We joked that I'd get a load of jobs that shift, and of course I did and was out pretty much all night. Car fires and all sorts.'

He claimed the £200 first prize and a Suunto watch in the 61st edition of the race but missed out on a £500 bonus for a new course record. Second place went to Welshman Andrew Davies (Mercia Fell Running Club), a former semi-professional footballer, who was World Long Distance Mountain Running Championship silver medallist in 2013. Davies finished in 2-53-53, after chasing Lightfoot around the course.

Ricky Lightfoot reached the summit of Pen-y-Ghent in 28-11 – only seven seconds faster than Davies. There was an 11-second gap on Whernside, but Lightfoot stretched his lead to 1 minute 6 seconds on Ingleborough. Third place was claimed by Andrew Fallas (Carnethy Hill Running Club), in a time of 2-57-51, pushing four-times Three Peaks winner Rob Jebb into 4th place. Jebb, 40, who was 3rd the year before, finished in 2-59-32. His time beat Karl Gray's v40 record by 18 seconds.

Ricky admits that he didn't change anything for the repeat win. 'I am not one for planning training. I do it day by day by how I feel. I've always been a self-determining athlete. I know I have to get the quality in there.'

Ricky Lightfoot has always lived in Cumbria. Early on he played a bit of football, but one day he was asked by the caretaker at his school if he wanted to do a race. He was hooked on running from that day. 'I got lost in that race and finished after 30 minutes on a freezing wet winter day down at Whitehaven. Something clicked and I enjoyed it. There were kids' races at the

128. *Friends and rivals, 2015. L to R: Andrew Fallas, Ricky Lightfoot, Andrew Davies, Rob Jebb*

January Jaunt organised by CFR, so I did that – I would have been 14/15 maybe.'

From that first run the caretaker [Brian] and Ricky became good friends. Of the people he encouraged Ricky was the only one still running three or four years later. 'He was a mentor for me, and we would go out running together. He gave me my first job in the school, working as a lifeguard for 18 months. Then I worked on the site maintenance team for 18 months and then joined the Fire Service. My work has not been a hindrance to training, and the only struggle I have had has been getting time off work to go to races. I get to use the gym in the mornings if I want. I work shifts which is just part of life now.'

Ricky has had a long international career, with one highlight being the Zegama mountain race. 'There were good people running and it was a breakthrough race for me. In 2009 I was picked up by Salomon and went over in 2009 and won at Zegama. I have never been to an event and partied so hard after a race as that time. Winning the World Trail Champs was also a highlight [in 2013].'

One other race that stands out for Ricky, this time locally but also in 2009, was winning the Blencathra fell race. Alan Bowness had held that race record since the 1980s. 'I knew I was in good shape and had come back from winning in Zegama in May. Zegama is up and down, over the marathon distance with 2500m of ascent. It is similar to races in the UK, and not unusual to get snow, hot summer days, hailstones, or anything. I was fortunate that year that Kilian didn't turn up. When I won at Blencathra I think I probably could have gone faster, I felt that good. I was only the second person to run under an hour and I had beaten Alan's time by about 90 seconds. I had always looked up to him when I was a Junior.'

For Ricky the Three Peaks Race is a great season opener, and he says it is good for flushing his feathers for the year. 'I like it because it is hard and is the type of race where you can get a 2-15 marathoner turn up and they can finish 20th in the field. It is runnable but you have to be an all-rounder. You have got to be good on fells, trails and the fast sections. Probably it is the ultimate race as an all-rounder. You have to be able to run hard on the first section so as to not get left behind, then run fast downhill too.'

Finally, Ricky Lightfoot talks about his ambitions. He reckons that he is not done with the Three Peaks yet. He has always wanted that third win. 'I feel as though it is there within reach. I have yet to get it right since 2017. In recent years there have been a couple of people who get a couple of wins and struggle with the third. I hope it is not some kind of curse. I am 38, but a v40 won it recently [Gary Greenhow] so there is hope. I had an injury in January this year, and I fell on Isle of Arran last week and hurt my knee, so I just want to be running consistently again. I would also like to represent GB again. The Three Peaks is a race that can have a stacked field at the front end, but people can drop off like flies. Then only three or four people stay the pace and I don't think there is any other race like that.'

Chapter 38

REFLECTIONS
FROM KAREN BRADLEY

Karen Bradley is a clubmate of mine at Barnet and District AC. With a marathon PB of 3-11-39 from 2006, she decided to do the Three Peaks Race a decade later, having walked the course with three friends in the summer of 2014. She recalls that, 'It was with my dog for a good part of it, the first and last summits actually. That didn't seem so hard. I was used to doing 15/20-mile off-road runs at the time.'

The rationale was that she was coming up to a big birthday (her 50th) and decided that doing the Three Peaks Race would be the thing to do to celebrate that milestone. 'I am not big on parties! I wanted something for my 50th year that would be a challenge. I thought it wouldn't need the full training that I might have done for a road marathon.'

In the year and a half between the walk and the race Karen did no running recces over any parts of the Three Peaks course. What she did do was quite a bit of training in the Peak District. 'It was just up, down and around on the hills, a day out in the hills with the dog. I also used to do repeat hill reps on the long hills in the Chilterns. I needed someone to make me do it, which is where my friend Steve Allen came in. He was willing to shout at me, "Do it again!". It doesn't need to be a big hill if you are doing it three or four times. Even round where I live, I could do laps of North Mymms Woods which has some good hills. I would try hard on the hills. I felt that training on the fells with the terrain changes, and on hills was going to be good preparation for the Three Peaks.'

Karen's qualification races were the Cardington Cracker and the Surrey Hills race. 'The two qualifying races weren't really to give confidence, more ticking them off to get an entry. They made me realise that everyone wasn't sprinting these races and that I was moving OK and not right at the back.'

Having left London in snow it was perhaps no surprise that they could see snow on the summit of Pen-y-Ghent as they looked up to it from the start field. But these were not conditions she either expected or prepared for, as she had what she described to me as a 'slightly amateurish' approach to the event. 'I had all the required kit, which included a tape-seamed top from the walking shop down the road. I wore Inov8 X-Talons which I was used to. It was cold at the start, so I was wearing leggings, a long-sleeve t-shirt and my Barnet and District AC club vest, and a buff and gloves.'

On the start line Karen was nervous about getting to the end, and also nervous about the temperature, which she hadn't expected to have to face. 'I was also a little bit nervous about navigation but actually it was easy. There is one bit of no-man's-land which I could have got wrong, but there were people around for all of the first two thirds or so of the race. As you approach the summit of Pen-y-Ghent you see the proper fell runners coming the other way. They are dressed in nothing really, shorts and a vest often, and a bumbag with all the kit in. They were careering down.'

On the road from the start Karen felt she may have been going too fast, but once she started chugging up the first hill she felt fine. All went well going up Pen-y-Ghent and across to Ribblehead, and she was in good time at the first cut-off point. 'As we were going up Whernside I was watching people and thinking I mustn't get wet through, as I will be cold for the next two hours. So, I put my waterproof top on, which was a good decision despite it being uncomfortable. It was soon a proper blizzard, and it was hard to see the tracks or anything. We just chose any way up. I had planned my eating for the summit, where I would have a breakfast bar and some water. But at the summit the marshals were shouting, "Everyone go through, you can't stop here, go through as fast as possible." They were worried about the conditions and wanted everyone off the top as soon as possible.'

Coming down was a nightmare and she spent a lot of time

129. *Karen Bradley dressed for the conditions in the 2016 race*

sliding on her backside in the thick snow. 'At the bottom there was a marshal saying, "You've got five minutes to get to the cut-off point." I sprinted as fast as I could. I legged it down to the checkpoint and there were a couple of people that hadn't realised and joined me in speeding along. I got there in time and my parents were there supporting me. I think I had a bit to eat and drink. I felt pretty good. Going up Ingleborough was tough, but I felt I could do this. I should have eaten more though. I can normally eat on the run and during marathons. I made myself stop and eat a bit. Coming off Ingleborough was horrible. You didn't know where to put your feet, jumping from rock to rock. It is goat territory. I got a bit demoralised there. I felt sick and dizzy. I ended up tagging along with another guy who was in a similar state. We talked our way down to the finish.'

Karen talks animatedly now about how the whole experience was what she called a total high. 'Immediately afterwards, and even now, I'd say I wouldn't do it again. My reaction was – that was hard. I didn't realise that I was going to have to go that deep. My first marathon probably left me almost as emotionally thrown as that. After that marathon I wanted to ring my husband and I couldn't remember his phone number. I had invested a lot in the Three Peaks. Everything was new, was a challenge and was fun. If I did it a second time it would be hard because I would be trying to go faster, and I'd know what was coming next and how hard it was. My relative lack of preparedness for the event may have made it easy – which sounds kind of stupid.'

Reflecting on the event now, Karen calls the Three Peaks a distance race. 'It is not just going up and down like a Lakes fell race might be. Fell runners will have an advantage though, particularly in coming down fast on the steep descents. But the boulder field coming away from Ingleborough is horrible. There was no obvious route that day, so you had to keep thinking where to put your feet next. Quite technical. I was also running on empty by then.'

In summary, Karen states that the race is right up at the top of her running experiences. 'It was a challenge that gave me a big buzz. I didn't really realise that people were going to be impressed that I had raced the Three Peaks. I also was quite pleased to be only minutes behind Wendy Dodds, who is a phenomenal runner who is way older than me.' Wendy was running in the w60 category that year.

Karen was too modest to mention that she was in fact the 5th w50 that day, finishing in a time of 5-29-37. She concluded our chat by saying: 'That evening I went for a meal with my parents, with a quiet beer. Having said I won't do it again I may find another physical challenge for my 60th in a few years' time [laughs].'

WILKINSON CRACKS
THE RECORD

2016

Victoria Wilkinson won for the second time in 2016, and set up a run of four successive victories. She claimed the women's prize in 35th place overall to beat ultra-runner Mira Rai from Nepal but was outside Anna Pichrtova's record from 2008.

Wilkinson finished in 3-26-47 with Rai nine minutes behind, in 65th place overall. Rai had won the women's 50K race at the Himalayan Outdoor Festival in 2014 and 2015 and had set a new record in the 2015 Mont Blanc 80K race. Helen Berry (Holmfirth Harriers) was in 3rd place and 71st overall in 3-37-20. The race had 800 starters, of whom 703 finished.

Victoria recalls that it was snowing on the tops that day. Her diary noted: 'Kept putting cag on, taking it off, and back on for each summit. Really crappy conditions.'

'I had done the Heptonstall race a few weeks before and had a heavy fall on to my knee. That curtailed three weeks of preparation. There was a lot of hype around Mira Rai, she was going to be the next best thing. She was a Salomon athlete as well. That took the pressure off me because it was supposed to be her that

130. *The presentation, John Calvert with Victoria Wilkinson, 2016*

131. Marc Lauenstein, 2016

132. Marc Lauenstein, 2016

was going to win it, maybe with the record. Then, to be honest, I don't think I saw her in the race at all.'

Marc Lauenstein claimed he was an orienteer rather than a fell runner when he first visited the Three Peaks Race in 2016. The report noted that Lauenstein, a dentist from Switzerland, won the event in a fast time on a course made challenging by four days of snow and ice, particularly for those less experienced in those conditions. It was 2-55 slower than the course record.

Lauenstein reached the 2,277ft summit of Pen-y-Ghent from Horton-in-Ribblesdale in 28 minutes 19 seconds – three seconds ahead of Lightfoot, but the firefighter then edged into the lead as it turned into a race with their Salomon teammate Tom Owens closely involved.

At High Birkwith only 42 seconds separated them with Lightfoot in the lead, Owens 14 seconds behind and Lauenstein 42 seconds in arrears. Lightfoot reached Ribblehead in 1-12-13 with Lauenstein, winner of the Pikes Peak Marathon in 2014 and the Marathon du Mont Blanc in 2015, still in 3rd.

But Lauenstein dug deep on the steep ascent to Whernside's 2,415ft summit, a climb made treacherous by the freezing conditions overnight. Whernside marshals normally lift a gate off its hinges to allow runners easy passage but struggled when they found it partly buried in frozen snow. Lightfoot knew the tricky descent down the natural rock steps to Bruntscar and reached the valley bottom at the Hill Inn checkpoint two seconds ahead of Lauenstein, with Owens now just over a minute behind. But it seemed to be the ascent of Ingleborough which made the difference. Lauenstein reached the 2,372ft summit 64 seconds ahead of Lightfoot, but the race was far from over and he and Lightfoot gave spectators a thrilling finish after the five-mile run for home.

Owens admits now that he tried front running with Ricky Lightfoot again that year, but that they couldn't hold off Lauenstein. Owens explains that Marc Lauenstein came past him going up Whernside and looking very strong. 'Ricky got close, but I never closed the gap and finished 3rd. Marc is one of the most talented international runners I've had the pleasure to run with – all-round excellence and a real gent. He was so strong going up Whernside, just jogging to the front of the race! Amazing on the steep and technical stuff. It was the flatter running he was a bit slower on, but a slower start meant he pulled through brilliantly. Ricky showed his class to keep it so close and almost catch Marc that year.'

Asked if he found conditions tough over what is billed as the marathon with mountains, Lauenstein said: 'Well, actually it is my first fell race. Really, I am an orienteer which is why I had some trouble running the section up to Ribblehead, but running up Whernside it was my terrain.' He also commented: 'On the way up Ingleborough I was able to get away from Ricky, but on the way down he was so fast. He is such an incredible runner. I really did have to push hard. When he was getting close, I was swearing. I used to think fell running was the thing to do and I always wished I could do it. Today was the day.'

Ricky Lightfoot thinks [*correctly*] that his time from that year makes him the fastest loser at the Three Peaks Race ever. 'It was one of my best runs at the race because I can remember being with Marc [Lauenstein] at the Hill Inn and he was such a strong climber and he pulled away from me going up Ingleborough. I got to the top and looked, and I saw the gap and knew I wouldn't catch him. I set off and must have felt good as it was one of those days where you feel your feet are barely touching the ground. I felt I was catching him. I pushed on and at the next stile I popped up and saw him again. Through the garden and across the road I thought it was on. He realised I was coming and put a big kick in and matched my speed. I lost by seven seconds after he had about a minute and a half at the last summit.'

Lauenstein, from Neuchatel, near Berne, has had success at a range of events. He won a silver medal in the long-distance category at the 2005 World Orienteering Championships at Aichi and silver at Aarhus in 2006. He also earned a bronze medal in 2005 as a member of the Swiss relay team. Lauenstein won the World Long Distance Mountain Running Challenge in 2009 at the Kaisermarathon, and also won the Sierre-Zinal race in 2013. In 2015, Lauenstein became the first runner to complete the Otter Run on South Africa's Otter Trail in under four hours. Later in 2016 he won Giir di Mont from Premana on a route altered by bad weather and followed this with a victory at the Matterhorn Ultraks race in the Skyrunner World Series.

2017

This year was the first time since a bonus was offered to break either the men's or women's course records (in 2014) that the organisers had to pay up. Months of training paid off for Victoria Wilkinson, who claimed the £500 bonus prize for breaking the women's record. Some of her training work is solo running, but Wilkinson had also trained with Martin Peace, Andy Jebb, Mark Roberts and her partner Darren Kay. Wilkinson knew she was ready for a record challenge before the race started. 'The results I have done in the past few months have been promising, but those races were much shorter, so they were in a different category. I know my training has been pretty good. I have been really lucky. I have not been ill, and I have not been injured. Not many runners can say that.'

Victoria Wilkinson, an ambassador for Inov8, finished in 13th place overall (a position only beaten by Angela Mudge with her 11th place in 1999). Wilkinson knocked a decisive 5 minutes 24 seconds off the time set by Anna Pichrtova, of the

133. Victoria Wilkinson celebrates her win in a new record time, 2017

Czech Republic, when the Three Peaks hosted the World Long Distance Mountain Running Championships in 2008. Wilkinson had predicted that Pichrtova's record was beatable, but knew it required the correct combination of near-perfect weather conditions beforehand and on race day, together with a peak personal performance.

Wilkinson, a remedial and sports masseur, had long held an ambition to bring the record back to Yorkshire. Doing it when the Three Peaks was the selection event for the World Long Distance Mountain Running Championships at Giir di Mont, Italy, in August, was even better.

She said after the race: 'If there was a guarantee of a record you would not need to run. A lot can go wrong in a race of this length, so you have to do it stage by stage.' The work had started months ago when she began a series of training runs over the course. 'I have done different sections six or seven times this

134. L to R: Nichola Jackson, Victoria Wilkinson, Charlotte Morgan, 2017

year, with different combinations of two hills, one hill, and the flat bits. I have done a lot of work on it.'

Asked how much more she thought she could shave off the record, Victoria Wilkinson said: 'I don't know. I was trying hard today. It is knowing how much you can push in the first half to be able to survive the second half. I tried to run it knowing that. I would have to change something in my training. I would have to reassess it and see what else I could do.'

After hundreds of spectators cheered her to the finish line, Victoria said she was very relieved to have broken the record to claim the £500 bonus price as well as the £200 women's prize, plus a £100 Inov-8 voucher, adding: 'I am very happy. Mission accomplished, and job done.' She was 39 that year.

Victoria Wilkinson, whose time was 3-09-19, was followed home by Nichola Jackson (Preston Harriers) in 40th place, recording 3-26-17. Third lady, claiming 49th place, was

Charlotte Morgan (Carnethy Hill Racing Club) in 3-33-19. Nichola Jackson said after the event: 'I've not done this race before and it's my first long race. I wasn't sure what pace to go, so I tucked in behind Julie Briscoe and got her coming off Pen-y-Ghent and then just tucked in with a group of men. Surprisingly I was passing people going up Ingleborough and then I just took it easy coming down because I do have a tendency to fall. The support out on the course was amazing. The crowds kept telling me I was 1st lady, but I knew that Vic was streets ahead.'

Victoria recently gave me a full and intriguing rundown on her build-up to the race and how she had felt within it. 'Throughout that winter I had recced sections of the route, way more than I might normally do. I probably did more road training miles as well, not racing but training. In hindsight, not realising it maybe at the time, my winter's training went really well. I didn't get ill or injured. Training and racing were going well. I run by feel, but I did know where I needed to be at certain times.' In her diary she noted: 'Top of PYG in 31 minutes, record was on.'

'I went out to win it that year and at that point I thought I might as well go for the best time I can.' She adds now, 'I remember Andy [Peace] came to watch and he rode his bike alongside me on the road section, and he was saying, "Are you alright?" I said, "Yeah, I'm OK." "Do you want anything?" "No. I am a bit worried that I feel alright." He said, "OK, keep it going." Rob Jebb had told me a couple of years before that, "The Three Peaks Race starts at Ribblehead. Get to Ribblehead in good form and in control, THEN you can start racing." I break the race into sections. Get Pen-y-Ghent done, then put it out of your mind. Then its Ribblehead, then Whernside, get the descent done, then I have various landmarks coming off Ingleborough. I had loads of people watching out for me that day. I worried about cramp and bonking, but they just didn't happen that day. In 2016 I cramped up going through Sulber Nick so walked for a bit. Back to 2017 Darren was there at that point and was panicking a bit. It was really slippy still and difficult to run over. Because I knew I was running at pace and had cramped there before, I was thinking, chill out, go slow. Get to the gate and set off again. Pushing up the last little hill towards the end you never know what might happen. It was a pleasure to get that time. If you could run it again knowing you were going to get the record you could love it all the way round, but within the race it is still stressful even with that end result. You could fall, or anything.'

The race was won by **Murray Strain**, of Edinburgh club Hunters Bog Trotters. He finished in 2-49-38, which was 3 minutes 35 seconds outside the men's record for the then current course. It had been quite a week for him, as he took a surprise victory in his second attempt at the Three Peaks. Strain, who finished 7th in 2016, said afterwards: 'I had an exam on Monday this week to become a qualified actuary. It has been a long haul for that. I have had a couple of hours running each day, which has been a break.'

A navigation error on the descent from Whernside probably cost 2011 winner Tom Owens the race. Strain beat him by 4 minutes 22 seconds, with Chris Holdsworth (Clayton-le-Moors Harriers) in 3rd place. But it was a surprise for Strain to discover he was in the lead going up Ingleborough.

Strain added: 'I knew I was a bit fitter this year. I had a strong winter. After running it last year it was always the plan to come back and have a good one and then when form started to come together, I thought maybe I might get a place.'

It was a bad day for Ricky Lightfoot. Strain commented: 'Ricky seemed to be struggling a bit on the hills. He was walking up Pen-y-Ghent, which did not look right.' Lightfoot, who had been running in the Himalayas with his Salomon teammate Tom Owens for the last two weeks, subsequently retired at the Ribblehead checkpoint. Lightfoot explains that it was a repeat of the injury he had in 2014. 'At the back end of 2016 I went to see a specialist in Cumbria, and they said sorry there is no appointment for you. I sat down and cried in the hospital. I found a doctor in Manchester who did hip surgery and booked a private appointment for the January. He said I should have a cortisone injection and if it disappears then we have solved the problem. It did go at first but wore off in six weeks, which was round about Three Peaks time. I was unsure whether to do it but turned up and only got so far as it was too sore. I was slipping about in the wet and it was like having a knife stuck in me. I stopped and asked for the operation as soon as I was back home. Three weeks later I was in hospital for a hip arthroscopy. I had the femur shaved and rounded.'

Strain, Owens and Holdsworth all checked in to the electronic timing equipment on Pen-y-Ghent summit in 28 minutes with Owens just in the lead. Strain was in 3rd place at High Birkwith, 1 minute 13 seconds behind Owens. The long valley-bottom run to Ribblehead put more pressure on Strain who arrived 3rd in 1-13-04, 36 seconds behind Holdsworth, with Owens over a minute in the lead.

Then came the punishing climb up the face of Whernside, which Owens reached in 1-39-38 with Strain and Holdsworth a minute behind. Down the rocky steps to the Hill Inn, Strain took the lead, reaching the checkpoint in 1-55-59. Holdsworth recorded 1-57-51 with Owens 12 seconds under two hours.

Murray Strain reached Ingleborough summit 3 minutes 31 seconds ahead of Holdsworth and nearly four minutes in front of Owens and, having been told that he was in the lead, pushed on to finish at Horton in 2-49-38. Owens finished in 2-54, with Holdsworth coming in less than a minute later.

Murray said: 'Apparently, Tom Owens shot himself in the foot. He missed the turning off Whernside. He was a minute ahead of me on the top. I did not know he had gone wrong. I thought he was away and gone. It was only halfway up Ingleborough that people were shouting that I had a massive lead. I thought OK, alright, where's Tom? I knew I had a chance of winning, so I pushed hard.'

Tom Owens recently told me more about that situation from 2017. 'It was brilliant conditions, really dry, good temperature, and I was very fit having had a really good winter and spring training. I led from the start and was by myself which I always found scary. I felt good and was running comfortably. I was relieved to get to the top of Whernside as I'm never sure of the best line up and tend to meander up this hill. The steep climb is always a case of damage limitation for me, but I was quite

135. L to R: Tom Owens, Murray Strain, Chris Holdsworth, 2017

clear at the top of Whernside and descended well. However, I missed the left turn at the bottom of Whernside (there is usually a marshal there but wasn't this year) and continued along the Dales High Way. It didn't feel quite right and I started to doubt myself and eventually met a group of walkers who told me I was wrong. I was so upset and angry! I turned round and ran back to the junction. I had lost a lot of time and re-joined the race in 5th or 6th place, I think. I must have run well over 1km extra. I have a tendency to lose my head a bit when front running, and I can get a bit overexcited.'

'I ran really hard to the road junction and start up Ingleborough – pacing had gone out the window but I was reeling people back in. I eventually got into 2nd place, passing Jack Wood and Chris Holdsworth on the Ingleborough descent, by which time I was knackered! Murray went on to win in a fast time. He had an excellent race and paced it really well. That was the year to get the record in those conditions. How embarrassing.'

Chapter 40

REFLECTIONS FROM JOHN OWEN

Leading v70 runner, John Owen, wrote a short article for the Barnet and District AC club magazine, of which this is a slightly edited version:[39]

It's one of the great races of the fell running calendar. I set my sights on it soon after I first ran in a fell race three years ago, at the age of 70. The modern race is highly organised by a big team, with high-tech control, and radio support. There is an entry limit of 999. In 2017, when I ran, 942 entered, 761 started, and 699 finished.

At race registration you collect a 'dibber'. You attach it to your wrist and insert it into the timing control box at each of the checkpoints and at the finish. Everyone's kit was checked. In fell races you must carry a map, compass, whistle, hat, gloves, windproof and waterproof trousers and hooded jacket, emergency food. Next, Race Director Paul Dennison gave his briefing, kicking off with, 'Welcome to the 63rd running of the Three Peaks parkrun.' Well, it's in the Yorkshire Dales National Park.

Three of the checkpoints are the three summits. The other two, at low level, have cut-off times. If you fail to make these within the time limit you must stop. Only well after I got into preparation for the race did I realise that these cut-offs would be very difficult for me. I did three trial runs over the first 15 miles to the fourth cut-off at the Hill Inn, which is after Whernside and before Ingleborough. The first time I got lost in mist, the second and third times I made it to the Hill Inn but failed to meet the 3.5-hour cut-off. I decided that, come race day, I had no option but to run it as a 15-mile race to the Hill Inn and make the best of it from there on.

---

39 Sadly, John Owen died in January 2022, just before research for this book started.

136. John Owen, 2017

Despite a fall on Pen-y-Ghent I was on schedule at the top and, after the descent, had a good run along the fairly flat section to Ribblehead, to below Whernside. Some runners were chatting to each other and didn't seem too worried about missing the cut-offs. But I couldn't relax and kept at it hard. I think the adrenaline kept me going. I was very nervous about the steep Whernside descent. People would come past me there. I reached the Hill Inn cut-off on 3-16 to my great relief but, on the steep climb up Ingleborough, I was really in trouble. I made it to the final checkpoint at the summit but, starting down, was struck by cramp and had to stop. After some rest I was able to start again, but by now all of the others who had made the cut-offs had gone past me. There was just one with me, an athlete from Nottingham called Paul who, very generously, said he wasn't bothered about a time and would run with me to the finish and make sure I was OK. We were joined by the official race sweeper, David, and the three of us set off together with about five miles more to go. Paul told us he had 'head-butted a dry-stone wall' the year before. David was jogging round the Three Peaks as light training for a Bob Graham Round in the summer. At the finish Paul and I ran in together, finishing just outside six hours. We thanked the marshals who had waited for us.

For me, coming in last was not in the plan. But I have no regrets. It was a privilege to take part in this great race. I think I was right to go all out early on to beat the cut-offs.

The David Scott trophy is awarded each year to the oldest finisher and, at 73, I was the oldest.[40] It was an honour to receive the trophy, an engraved decanter, from David Scott, who has completed 48 Three Peaks races. The race report, on the race website, records that I, 'became the oldest finisher in the race's history', which surprises me a little, in a time of 6-02-18. A wonderful race – organised each year by a brilliant team.

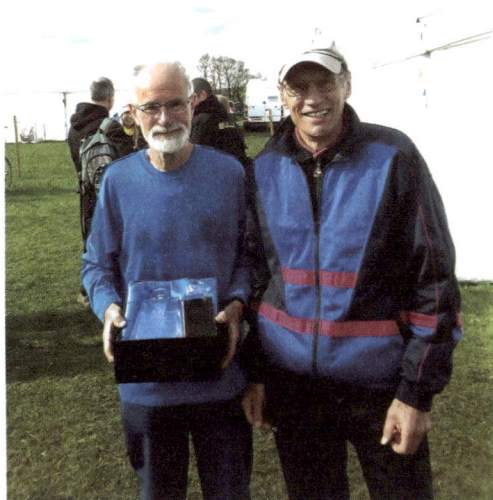

137. John Owen with Dave Scott

---

40 In 2018, for the second year in succession John Owen, of Barnet and District AC, was the oldest person ever to have completed the Three Peaks Race. That year he was 74 years and five months.

Chapter 41

FASTEST TO
THE FIRST SUMMIT

2018

The 769 starters streamed away from the race's starting field in 2018, past an articulated lorry trailer vinyl-wrapped with an image of **Victoria Wilkinson** and a fellow male runner. Victoria had knocked five minutes off the women's record to claim the £500 bonus prize in 2017.

The British International runner first claimed the women's title in 2014. Her 2018 win made it three in a row. The previous year Victoria dedicated months of training to beat the record. She had a totally different plan for 2018.

138. Victoria Wilkinson's image on the rear of a lorry

139. Victoria Wilkinson mixing it with the men, 2018

The Bingley Harriers athlete, who has represented Britain in six running and cycling disciplines, had her mind set on the World Mountain Running Championships in Karpacz, Poland, in June, followed by Skyraces in Italy and Andorra. She had paced her training for the World Mountain Champs goal and knew she was fitter at this point than the previous year. She came 5th at those World Championships.

Her dedication means Victoria was focused on her running and shut out other influences, including social media, where followers kept asking if she was attempting to repeat breaking the Three Peaks record. Immediately before the race, she looked at the 10ft-tall photograph of herself, which was seen around Britain on the CSH Transport lorry, but shut it from her mind.

'At the start I ran past without seeing it,' she said. 'My mind was set on the race. It was not a record-breaking attempt, which was a bit sad in a way, but I achieved what I set out to do.' She finished 33rd in 3-22-17, compared with 13th in 2017 in 3-09-19. Second woman was Georgia Tindley (Hunters Bog Trotters), 43rd overall in 3-26-02, with Beth Pascall (Belper Harriers) 3rd

140. Murray Strain, 2018

and 48th overall in 3-28-46.

Victoria's diary noted: 'Blowing up a bit going up Ingleborough. Not majorly but I was slower than I might have been.' She confirms her plan. 'I had my sights on the Worlds later in the year, in Poland. I was running it at 3-20 pace, so knew I wasn't ever on record form. I won by nearly four minutes, but you can easily lose that amount of time if you do get cramp. I wouldn't have known how far behind anyone was either.'

Tom Owens got it right coming off Whernside in winning the race for the second time, but was 3 minutes 5 seconds off the course record. The Shettleston Harrier finished in 2-49-08, which was 4 minutes 26 seconds quicker than his 2011 win. It also made amends for his mis-turn the previous year which lost him the race.

This year positions were reversed with Owens coming home 3 minutes 28 seconds ahead of his conqueror from 2017, Murray Strain. Owens, a Salomon International runner, said at the time: 'I was so relieved to stay on route and finish in 1st place. After messing up last year I was a bit scared to come back. This year

141. Tom Owens leads Ricky Lightfoot past Ribblehead Viaduct, 2018

there was a sign and a marshal at the junction where I went wrong, so I knew I was on track. But Murray is such a good runner. I remember glancing back on Whernside and thinking how close he was. Then he chased me off Ingleborough. He is super strong.'

Owens adds now that he had really wanted to make amends for the 2017 mess-up. 'I ran out in front the whole way again, but this time kept Murray Strain behind. I felt a huge relief at the finish. It was much wetter underfoot, but I had an excellent run, and it was my best time.'

Third place went to Ricky Lightfoot, who won the race in 2014 and 2015. At the finish, runners toasted their own efforts in a special edition Three Peaks Race beer from Northern Monk Brewery in Leeds, which had the event's history on a pull-off label, and each can signed by Ricky.

It was a comeback race for Lightfoot. 'I said to myself a top-three finish would be good because again there was a quality field. I got 3rd after rehabbing from my hip operation 11 months before then. I ran in with my daughter with a big smile on my face. I was back in the game again.'

This year the Three Peaks was the selection race for the World Long Distance Mountain Running Championships. Inov-8's Tom Payn, competing in the Three Peaks Race for the first time, finished 13th in 3-9-34 after starting strongly. Owens was on Pen-y-Ghent summit in 28 minutes 25 seconds with Payn only 18 seconds behind. But a week of training in the Dales was not enough for Payn. He was slower on the ascent of Whernside, part of the route which is out of bounds except on race day, and he fell further behind on Ingleborough.

2019

Victoria Wilkinson was back to win a fifth time. Achieving that win made her the second most successful competitor, with only Jeff Norman (with his six wins) ahead of her. Her winning time was 3-20-01. Her 32 minutes 47 seconds to Pen-y-Ghent summit claimed the women's prize of £100 for the fastest ascent and she also won another £50 prize for the 32 minutes 34 seconds she took to descend from Ingleborough to the finish. These were additional to her £200 prize for being the first woman finisher. Wilkinson was followed home by Annie Roberts (Todmorden

142. Victoria Wilkinson, 2019

Harriers) in 68th place in 3-41-02. Third woman was first-timer Katie Kaars Sijpesteijn (Keswick AC) who was 81st in 3-45-07. Victoria quietly points out that she was a v40 by then. Her diary noted it as an inconsistent race. 'My head was thinking, "You are OK, you are doing alright," and at other times I was thinking I was rubbish. Why so slow? Get your head together. I am not really sure what was going on that year. I didn't think about the prize on Pen-y-Ghent. If you went hard for that prize you might not finish!'

Brennan Townshend, of Keswick AC, was making his first attempt at the Three Peaks Race that year and showed his huge potential when he proceeded to win – beating past victors Ricky Lightfoot and Tom Owens. Townshend had planned to visit the Yorkshire Dales the week beforehand to reconnoitre the route, but his car broke down, so he just turned up and ran it on sight.

The 25-year-old reached the summit of Pen-y-Ghent in 27 minutes 53 seconds, which gave him the newly introduced prize of £100 for the fastest person to the first summit. Some may have thought that Townshend would burn himself out before the finish, but that was not the case. He was eight seconds faster than Ricky Lightfoot by then and was to stay ahead at every checkpoint except the Hill Inn where he trailed by two seconds.

Brennan Townshend climbed Ingleborough 1 minute 27 seconds quicker than Lightfoot and set off down the long run-in to Horton to claim another new £50 spot prize for the fastest descent to the finish in a time of 27 minutes 12 seconds. Townshend's winning time of 2-50-22 also banked him the £200 first prize.

Brennan missed the £500 bonus on offer to a record-breaker but plans to return. He said: 'I will definitely be back next year. It's a really nice course.'

It was a day of torrential rain, hailstones, sleet, changing visibility and strong winds. Lightfoot finished 2nd in 2-52-05, his second-best time over the Three Peaks. Carl Bell, also of Keswick AC, finished 3rd in 2-55-44, some five minutes ahead of Tom Owens.

Owens, who left it to the last minute to enter hoping to be

143. Brennan Townshend out on his own

fully fit, had been at Salomon's medical institute in Annecy in the Alps with foot and ankle problems and then suffered a glute injury two weeks before the race. He says now that he probably shouldn't have run that day.

Ricky Lightfoot certainly knew of Brennan Townshend. 'Brennan was a strong runner, and I knew he was good. I had raced him three weeks prior to this at the Coledale Horseshoe and had beaten him convincingly. I thought I could win the Three Peaks that year. But on the day the last climb got to me. It has been my nemesis over the years. I think Brennan pulled away and gapped me there. Brennan was sitting in earlier on and I think we knew he was waiting to go. He was just too strong on that day.'

Brennan Townshend didn't really start running properly till he went to college in 2008. He was brought up on Dartmoor, on a hill farm near Chagford. He says he did a bit of cross-country when he was at school and was in the top three in the county usually. But as his running progressed, he had an injury which set him back. Forced to move onto a bike, he joined the Mid-Devon Cycling Club and became good enough to win the Junior Tour of Wales. He progressed to being a professional rider, initially for Raleigh.

2018 was the start of serious fell running for Brennan. He set a new fastest time for the Abrahams Tea Round and won the Mourne Skyline race. 'I pushed the running training up then. At the time I entered the 2019 Three Peaks Race I had not won any Long 'A' fell races. I really didn't know anything about the Three Peaks Race either. I just turned up with the group I was running with, as I was now a member of Keswick AC. Carl Bell was one of the group.' Brennan had done no recceing, but had done the Coledale Horseshoe, coming 2nd to Ricky Lightfoot, not long beforehand. 'I had been out of action before that due to a virus. On the start line at the Three Peaks, I was excited but didn't know what to expect. Not knowing the route, I had to accept just following anyone in front of me. It might sound bad, but I was waiting for someone on the tops to be sure of which way to go. It was really cold, and I admit I used Ricky Lightfoot and Carl Bell's experience to help me. I had a really good race on the day.' He also admits that he went for the prize for first to the top of Pen-y-Ghent. 'My stepdaughter said, go quick so we can get to the pub.'

2020

Sadly, it was not possible to hold the race in 2020 due to the Covid restrictions at the time. Race Director Paul Dennison said: 'The decision has not been made lightly, but to put on this event we have to think about the safety of all the people of Horton-in-Ribblesdale, race marshals, first aiders, Cave Rescue Organisation, RAYNET radio operators, committee members and all competitors and supporters.'

144. Early morning on race day, 2021

Chapter 42

EXTENDED COURSE. NEW RECORDS

2021

Because of the Covid restrictions, the 2021 race was held 18 months after the 2019 one, with the date being changed to October.

The women's record holder, Victoria Wilkinson, was recovering from injury and did not enter. In her absence, the winner was the youngest woman in the race, 25-year-old Rose Mather (Morpeth), who had recently returned to fell running after competing in her teens. She finished 51st overall in a time of 3-47-38, almost three minutes slower than her mother Karen's 2nd place in 1984. Second female was Holly Wootten, in 3-50-05, and 3rd was Sara Willhoit (Mercia Fell Runners) in 3-50-33.

Gary Greenhow, of Ambleside Athletic Club, crossed the line first in a time of 3-05-22, some 19 minutes slower than the course record. It was the first time he had entered the Three Peaks Race, and he became the first over-40 male winner of the race. He finished exactly one minute ahead of Jonathon Cox

145. L to R: Sarah Willhoit, Rose Maher, Holly Wootten, 2021

146. Gary Greenhow, 2021

(Eden Harriers), who was also a first-timer. One of the pre-race favourites, Ricky Lightfoot, had to be content with 3rd place. Lightfoot admits to having had Covid two weeks before the race. 'I was in bed for three days. I was cleared of Covid before the race, but it is really the only explanation for the poor result I got that year.'

Alistair Thornton (Howgill Harriers) said he aimed to be first to Pen-y-Ghent summit, and he achieved his goal in 27-39 and won a £100 prize for his effort and ended up finishing in 13th place. The first five runners all reached Pen-y-Ghent summit within 29 minutes, with Tom Owens proceeding to pull out a short lead on the steep slog up the face of Whernside to record 1-49-06 at the summit. He continued to lead down to the Hill Inn at Chapel-le-Dale, but slowed on the ascent of Ingleborough where Greenhow and Cox were within three seconds of each other, finishing only 60 seconds apart.

Tom Owens recalls that the 2021 race was an especially odd race, because being in October the ground was heavy going and a lot of runners were rusty, having not raced much during Covid. 'I struggled to run fast on any technical ground after my latest ankle operation, but was really surprised to pop out on top of Whernside in 1st place. The front group went the wrong way in the Whernside clag, for once I chose a good route. I soon lost the lead at the base of Ingleborough, and rather shuffled in. The descent to Horton felt mega technical and was somewhat awkward for me.'

147. The presentation, 2021

2022

The race featured the 29th different women's Three Peaks winner, with Sarah McCormack claiming the title in her first attempt at the race. She had earlier broken a 35-year-old record at the 5.2k Rivington Pike Race on Easter Saturday. Having watched Victoria Wilkinson set the Three Peaks women's record in 2017 she was inspired to enter herself. Victoria, who was unable to race through injury, says she thought Sarah was a potential winner of the iconic race.

Victoria also explained her non-appearance that year. 'I was really up for it. I went round the whole route three weeks before the event and was very happy, although knowing I wasn't on record form. Then I got injured, with a partial tear to my Achilles tendon. That is one of the worst mistakes I have ever made. That was a major learning lesson. You really don't need to go round the whole route three weeks beforehand.'

Sarah McCormack (Ambleside Athletic Club) was originally a shorter-distance runner, but she had been entering longer races in the previous year or two to become comfortable with running for three to four hours. Victoria Wilkinson proved to be a good judge, as McCormack came home in a winning time of 3-23-21. She also won the £100 cash prize for the fastest woman to the top of Pen-y-Ghent, which is a climb of 694 metres, which she reached in 32-27. McCormack assumed control early on, topping Pen-y-Ghent with a lead of over a minute, an advantage she continued to extend. Such was her dominance that she clocked the fastest splits on all six sections and when she returned to Horton she had more than seven minutes to spare on her closest rival. Second female was v40 Sharon Taylor (Helm Hill Runners) in 3-30-40. Sharon joined Bingley Harriers at the aged of 12 and ran her first fell race when she was 16. Nichola Jackson, an Inov-8 ambassador, who was 2nd in the English Championships in 2019, finished 3rd in 3-31-56.

Sarah McCormack says she was pretty nervous about the race, due to not having done it before. 'It is also on the longer side of what I would usually do. I knew I was taking a chance by going off in the lead early, but I felt good on that first climb and thought

148. Sarah
McCormack, 2022

it would be a missed opportunity if I didn't make the most of it. I was really hanging on by the final climb up Ingleborough but found some life in the legs for the final descent.'

Expanding recently on her background Sarah surprised me by pointing out that she was born in Rockford, Illinois, in 1986. However, she has no memories of Rockford at all. 'I played football all throughout my childhood, as well as running track and cross-country from a young age. My parents were both keen runners and my dad also played a lot of football, so my sister and I just followed suit!'

Sarah's mother was from the Lake District and was a keen fell walker, along with the rest of her family. 'We would come over to the Lake District every summer and my plan was always to move there the moment I could. I grew up in a very flat part of Michigan, near Detroit, but I always wanted to be over in Cumbria rather than there, there was just no contest between the two. I moved over the week after I finished university, where I also ran track and cross-country. I didn't really have any job lined up when I moved over, I just moved in with my grandad and started applying for things. When I finally got a job, it was at Sheffield University, so the Peak District was where I first turned from a fell walker into a fell runner.'

Sarah has represented Ireland more than 25 times and won the Mountain Running World Cup in 2019. When asked if she is more of a mountain runner or a fell runner, she replied that she was a bit of both. 'I have done plenty of races on the continent and spend four to five months a year there in the campervan these days. I love both and I think it's so interesting how quite different cultures and traditions have developed around mountain running in different countries. The sense of companionship and enjoyment of the hills is the same, but the races themselves are quite different experiences.'

She was very proud to have got the course record at the Trofeo Vanoni international race in Morbegno, Italy. 'It attracts a fantastic international field and it's a race with a lot of history. The women's race is only 5k so you're just running flat-out at your limit for 20 minutes and then it's all over. The support on the course is intense, so you couldn't slow down if you wanted to!'

She explains her training and coaching arrangements. 'I am actually self-coached now. I like the independence of working on my own training plan, but I need to put it all into a calendar like I do with any of my (coaching) clients, to make sure I don't make spontaneous changes to it. I mostly do my harder sessions on my own, because I'm moving around so much. My dogs come with me a lot on my runs, even some of the harder ones, though they don't tend to look like they've noticed the change in pace.'

She concludes our chat with her thoughts on the Three Peaks Race as an event. 'I think it's probably one of the best-known fell races among non-fell runners, because the route itself is so famous. Within the fell running community, it seems to be one of the only events that will tempt people to do a bit of training on the road. The route really does have a bit of everything – you need to be conditioned to the long stretches of flatter running as well as the steeper slopes. The dramatic gradient and surface changes (alternating between steep, grassy fell and flat tarmac or path) can really catch you out, especially on a hot day when cramps are more likely. It's a great test of endurance and all-round running ability.'

Brennan Townshend (Keswick AC) won a second Three Peaks Race, in dry and sunny conditions. Townshend, the 2019 winner, was part of an elite group of four in the early stages of the race. At the top of Pen-y-Ghent and the summit of Whernside there was nothing between Townshend and eventual runner-up

149. Brennan Townshend, 2022

Billy Cartwright, with dual winner Ricky Lightfoot and Tom Adams just over a minute back. But by the time they summitted the final peak of Ingleborough the gaps started to appear – and then widen. It was Townshend, who was injured for a large part of 2021 and missed the 2021 Three Peaks Race, who took the win. He had only resumed training after Christmas, but proved strongest as he crossed the line in 2-55-34, over three minutes clear of Cartwright, with Lightfoot in 3rd. The race was also a GB selection race for the European Trail Championships. Ricky Lightfoot knew he wasn't in contention from the start. It did get him to the Europeans though as it was the trial for that event, so he was happy with the result.

Brennan recalls that he had a stress fracture in his left foot in 2021, and another injury to his shin. 'I had to spend a lot of time cycling. I have had coaches in the past but look after myself now and am now managing things better. Coming into the race

150. The top three, 2022. L to R: Billy Cartwright, Brennan Townshend, Ricky Lightfoot

in 2022 I didn't really think I had a chance. Off the back of six months out injured I had only been able to run for six weeks before the Three Peaks, so on the start line I didn't even know if I would finish the race. It was probably coming off Ingleborough that I realised I could win it. Billy Cartwright had got a big gap on the descent off Whernside, and I remember thinking that I just needed to keep running and see what happened. I could see him ahead and gradually got closer. You can sometimes tell from the body language of someone ahead of you as to how they are going, and whether there is hope for you. There was.'

Brennan Townshend's bike training is just road cycling, but it has crossed his mind to have a go at the Three Peaks Cyclo-Cross race. His stated ambitions are: 'To win the British and English fell championships and to focus on my best performances in long distance fell, mountain and trail races such as Borrowdale and Wasdale'. He concludes by saying that the Three Peaks is a real favourite race of his. 'The atmosphere and the number of runners, and indeed the history. It is a different style of race because of the amount of fast running you have to do, and it also has the big hills. Probably winning the Three Peaks is my running highlight so far. The second win was certainly a surprise.'

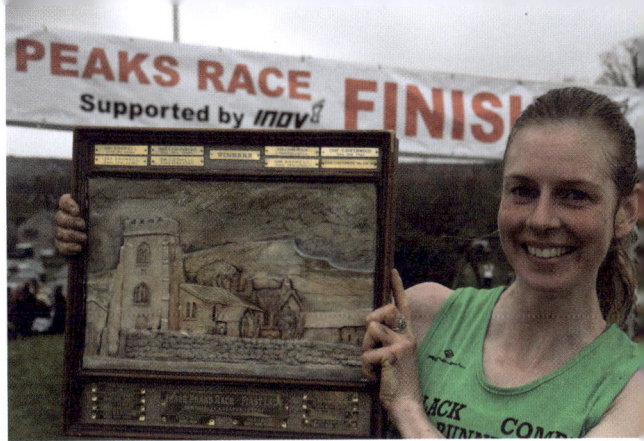

151. Cat Taylor, 2023

2023

The race also acted as a trial for the short trail event at the World Mountain and Trail Running Championships, being held in Innsbruck that June. The route was slightly increased in distance this year, which meant that two new course records were on offer.

In the women's race Helm Hill's Scarlet Dale was the early leader at the summit of Pen-y-Ghent in 34-24. A group including Victoria Wilkinson (Bingley), Martha Tibbott (Saddleworth), and first-timer Cat Taylor (Black Combe) were around 30 seconds back. At the Ribblehead checkpoint, Dale still led, but behind her just over a minute separated the next five runners, with Keswick's Holly Wootten now lying 2nd. Taylor was to prove the strongest climber to the summit of Whernside where she held a three-minute lead over Wootten and Wilkinson. This was in marked contrast to Dale who would drop out of the race.

At the top of Ingleborough, Taylor had increased her lead to seven minutes over Wootten. Cat Williamson (Loftus and Whitby) had moved into 3rd ahead of Wilkinson. Taylor didn't let up on the long descent to the finish at Horton, clocking 3-34-44. She finished over nine minutes clear of Williamson, who came through for 2nd in 3-44-03. Holly Wootten took 3rd in 3-45-15. Victoria Thompson came through strongly for 4th, with course record holder Wilkinson in 5th.

Victoria Wilkinson had learnt her lesson from last year and didn't run it all in training this time. She did do it in sections though. She explains the background to her run. 'Because of the difficult year I have had it was a totally different occasion. The

Three Peaks Race, for several reasons, has a special place in my heart and I particularly wanted to do it this year. I didn't need to win it, I didn't need to run a quick time, I just needed to finish the race. My partner, Darren Kay, started the race once but didn't finish it [laughs]. My dad did run it though. He had won the 3P cyclo-cross too, and I'd won the 3P cyclo-cross [the only female to do the double]. This year it was just a case of getting to the start line and then getting to the finish line. Again, I had great support all the way round the course. Close friends and Mum knew my aim this year, I couldn't have got round without them.'

When I interviewed her shortly after this emotional occasion, I asked her about further ambitions. 'I don't really have any at the moment. I will just see how it goes. Just keep running and keep enjoying the hills.'

She then gave her personal thoughts about the Three Peaks Race. 'It is high up there because this year I have been to hell and back and it was the Three Peaks I wanted to get through. It is a local race, there are always loads of people supporting me, people like to see a Bingley vest up there doing well. Bingley Harriers help organise it, there are a lot of them on the committee. I don't love the route though, although it is one of my favourite races! But it does have a bit of a continental feel to it, it has atmosphere, it has supporters, and there are always good guys to race against. I have spent a lot of time around it too. It is a special race to me.'

Victoria Wilkinson finished our chat with a very poignant thought about the race and one of its greatest supporters, another who is no longer with us. 'Another thing about the race is that when I think of Pete Hartley and the Three Peaks, I think of the location that he always took pictures from. When I pass that location I think of him, even this year. There are special people that I associate with certain locations, particularly on the Three Peaks route.'

First-timer Thomas Roach (Lewes AC) had assumed the lead by the summit of Pen-y-Ghent and had half a minute lead from the chasing group that included Sasha Chepelin (Carnethy), Finlay Wild (Lochaber), Jarlath McKenna (Tyne Bridge) and Chris Holdsworth (Clayton).

152. Thomas Roach, 2023

Roach held the lead across the trail section to the Ribblehead Viaduct checkpoint, with Chepelin and Holdsworth about 45 seconds down. Wild and Dan Connolly (Mercia) were another minute behind. On the long climb up Whernside, Roach maintained his lead. Wild had the fastest split up Whernside and closed to within 30 seconds, with Chepelin close behind. By Ingleborough Roach had extended his lead to almost five minutes over Chepelin. Connolly was now 3rd with Wild slipping back to 4th.

Roach ran a strong descent, and took the win in 2-53-28, shattering the previous best for the v40 category, even with the additional kilometre. Chepelin, despite an awkward fall on the descent, hung on for 2nd in 3-00-14. Finishing fast, Connolly recorded 3-00-30 for 3rd.

Brennan Townshend was 6th, missing out on a hat-trick. Possibly the pressure to win for a third time got to him, as he explains. 'This time I really focused on the race, and it played on my mind a bit, I think. The form was there but I think my mindset was putting too much pressure on myself.'

Thomas Roach is originally from Sussex but has lived in Austria for the last few years. He flew over from Austria and had not seen the course before but still dominated the race – although he admitted the route up Whernside proved the most challenging from a navigation point of view. His previous successes include a victory at Austria's Tour de Tirol, together with 15th place at the classic Sierre-Zinal race, both in 2022.[41]

Interviewed by RUN247 after the Three Peaks win, Roach said:

> It was my first time here, so the plan was to follow the leader as I didn't really know the course and I didn't know how well it was signed. But I always like to run my own pace and I felt like I could push a bit more on the first climb, so I took off! I lost my way on the second climb a bit, but I managed to find it again and then was able to finish it off on the last one.

Asked how much he'd enjoyed his first experience of this iconic race, he added: 'I absolutely loved it. This is my passion, so I'm always smiling. The aim today was to qualify for the Worlds, which is in my hometown of Innsbruck, so that's the next big target – and the Golden Trail Race series too.'

When discussing the latest course and record changes, Sarah Rowell commented: 'In some ways it is always changing. The top of Pen-y-Ghent isn't the same, we used to go down the little stream towards the bottom of Pen-y-Ghent, then we were able to take the corner off Whernside, which you can't anymore. Coming off Ingleborough it has changed. The gill straightening may have been for the Worlds in 2008 [*it wasn't until 2013*], and then the Whernside route changed, then not being able to take the diagonal off Ingleborough. Given the gradual changes, then maybe a clean slate is the right thing.'

---

41 After a win at World Masters Mountain Running Championships in September 2021, Thomas Roach failed a drugs test, which resulted in his disqualification from the event. He was banned for three months – for recreational cannabis use. https://www.athleticsintegrity. org/downloads/pdfs/disciplinary-process/en/AIU-21-164-Thomas-Roach-Decision.pdf

Chapter 43

SEVENTY YEARS OF
THE THREE PEAKS RACE

A notable feature of The Three Peaks Race has been its continual increase in popularity over the years. Having started from a very small beginning in 1954, it gradually increased its competitor numbers through the first three decades.[42] Women first competed in the race in 1979, although that was 25 years after the race was instigated. Sadly, it was not possible to hold the race in 2001 due the outbreak of Foot and Mouth, with the starting numbers for the year before having reached 491.

The numbers recovered quite slowly when the race resumed from 2002, but reached a new high of 756 for 2008 when the race hosted the World Long Distance Mountain Challenge, the first time it had been awarded to a UK race. With the organisers now accepting up to 1,000 entries, the start numbers peaked at 802 in 2015. The race's popularity then plateaued in the years up to the second no-race year, when it was not held due to the Covid pandemic in 2020. There was gradually a recovery in numbers after that, with 700+ again starting in 2023.[43]

Sponsors of the race come and go, but the race always manages to obtain more sponsorship to part cover (along with the race entry fees) the considerable cost of running such an event. The race probably has one of the highest profiles of any fell/mountain race in the country, having been sponsored for many years by a UK daily newspaper (*Daily Mirror*), and has had several TV documentaries feature it over the years. Doug Croft points out that, 'The *Daily Mirror* donated a cup to be awarded to the winning men's team. The *Mirror* sponsored the race for many years and gave us stability to grow the event from

---

42 The starter numbers first topped 100 in 1963, were over 200 first in 1971, and reached 400+ by 1978.

43 The full set of data for starter and finishers for each year is available in Appendix 5.

small beginnings. That trophy disappeared and caused me some embarrassment since I had been the MC at the presentation for many years and had to apologise for the missing trophy. I got fed up with the situation and donated the present trophy.'

The start venue had to be moved in 1975, which resulted in a change in the order the peaks were ascended, and a need to formalise the route from the start to the top of Pen-y-Ghent, which had previously been freeform, allowing runners to choose their line to what was now the first summit. Since that time there have been occasions where the route has needed to be changed, usually due to landowner requirements and/or work done by the National Parks team to alleviate erosion problems caused by the many pairs of trail shoes running over the course. Three times the route changes that have been instigated have made a significant enough difference to the distance covered for the course records to be reset from that year.[44]

The race organisation has taken on board many changes as necessary, whether it be for the safety of runners and officials, or to incorporate new technologies, such as online entries and computerised results, with split times given for each leg of the race. There is now an extensive list of awards and prizes,[45] with incentives available each year for the first to summit Pen-y-Ghent, and also for anyone beating either the men's or women's course records.

The race is now part of the World Mountain Running Association's running ranking scheme, which 'aims to highlight, showcase and reward the best mountain running athletes and races'.[46] It is also a UTMB Index Race, meaning runners can use their participation in the Three Peaks Race as part of their points total to claim, or go in the ballot for, an entry into races in the UTMB World Series.[47]

All the above has resulted in the Three Peaks Race being THE

---

44 Details of the route changes are shown in detail in Appendix 2, and the winning times and course records are detailed in Appendix 3.

45 See Appendix 6 for the list of trophies.

46 See: https://ranking.wmra.info/

47 See: https://utmb.world/utmb-index

mountain race that UK runners, at all levels, want to compete in, in a similar way that marathon runners want to run in the London Marathon. Some want to do it just the once, others strive to do it enough times to get the 15/21 completions award, and a crazy few keep doing it until they are no longer fit enough to make the cut-off times. It is perhaps worth repeating Jasmin Paris's quote from the top of Chapter 1: 'The Three Peaks is such an iconic race in the history of fell running, that I wanted to experience it for myself'.

Finally, whilst it is disappointing that the amazing course records set by Andy Peace and Victoria Wilkinson (in 1996 and 2017 respectively), and all the age group records, incidentally, are no longer valid, in 2023 the organisers had to make such a significant change to the route and its length that a whole set of new records have been recorded.

Hopefully, the accounts of the exploits of the various record holders, winners and many competitors, and officials, recorded in this book will give due acknowledgement to all that went before. It is a history of the self-proclaimed 'Marathon with mountains', and its many characters.

Appendix 1

ORGANISATION

In a long conversation I had with Dave Hodgson he explained some of the history of the organisation of the Three Peaks Race, which he had been very much involved in. 'The organisation has had several stages – particularly the Clayton phase and the formation of the Three Peaks Race Association (originally an amalgamation of Clayton-le-Moors Harriers, Lancaster and Morecambe Harriers, Bingley Harriers and Leeds St Mark's Harriers, in order to run the race). Alf Case was the first organising secretary, and Doug Croft took over from him, and used to do everything.'

As noted, Fred Bagley organised the first race in 1954, along with fellow Preston Harrier, Malcolm Withnell. For 1954 Fred Bagley had a team of Preston Harriers to help him as they put the event on as a club. Alf Case records in an article on the history of the event, '1956 saw Clayton-le Moors Harriers taking over as organisers, which task they maintained until the formation of the Three Peaks Race Association (TPRA) at the end of 1963, by which time the race had become more than one club could easily handle.'[48] Jack Bloor became chairman of the Association. The other Chairs have been Norman Thornber, Frank Travis, Dave Hodgson, Graham Maud, Paul Dennison, Martin Bullock and David Weatherhead.

Norman Thornber was critical to the successful running of the early events. He worked for an agricultural supplier and knew all the local farmers. He was able to go around them all and negotiate permissions to access the various stretches of farmland that the route went through. He also donated the trophy for the first male competitor to finish.

For the Race Association's first event, in 1964, there were over 100 starters, with 75 finishing. Alf Case also noted in his article: 'Safety of competitors has always been of prime concern

48 'The Three Peaks Race', spring 1972 edition of *The Fellrunner*.

to the organisers who have been fortunate enough to be able to call on the services of rescue teams from Bolton, the RAF, South Ribble, Cave Rescue Organisation for the fells, and the Police and British Red Cross for the lower reaches.'

In a profile of Alf Case, in *Stud Marks on the Summits*, Bill Smith gives a bit of Alf's background. 'A member of Clayton-le-Moors Harriers, Alf was a competitor in the first Three Peaks Race. He didn't even know about the event until the day before, when Stan Bradshaw came up to him and said: "I've entered you for a race tomorrow".' As a member of Clayton's committee, he became involved with organising the Three Peaks Race in 1956 and continued when the TPRA was formed. He carried on as secretary until the 21st race, in 1974, after which Doug Croft took over for the next 25 years, before passing over to Dave Renshaw. Other race Secretaries more recently have been Pat Philips, Megan Dennison and Linda Bullock. Alf Case adds, 'I was in at the start of the Fell Runners Association (FRA) and was its first chairman, hence my cherished membership number: 1.'

Doug Croft was never an athlete himself, as his *Stud Marks* profile reveals. 'At the time [of Alf Case's intention to retire as secretary] we were beginning to think in terms of limiting numbers and operating a first come, first served system. The feeling was that the person responsible should be seen to be independent and free from bias so that entrants could feel they were being treated fairly. My past experience was useful, and I was not a member of any club, and indeed never have been.'

In our conversation Dave Hodgson didn't hold back from offering some critical comment about the early organisation of the TPRA. 'It became a bit shambolic for a while, mostly because the race organiser was trying to do everything himself.' Although not in direct response to that comment, Doug Croft does accept in his profile that he had been criticised from time to time. 'Some of the action I have taken has undoubtedly been controversial. My philosophy has always been, and remains, twofold: to maintain the Three Peaks Race as *the* classic English Fell Race, and to give competitors the best possible competition.'

The obituary for Ted Pepper, who tragically died in the 1978 race, noted that, 'At the inquest the coroner recorded a verdict of misadventure and, in the interests of helping to prevent such a tragedy occurring again, suggested that emphasis should in future be placed on conditions which can be encountered and the need for adequate clothing and equipment.'

Doug Croft cites safety measures that had to be put in place after Pepper's death before the police would grant permission for the race to carry on. 'I took the view that the majority of competitors would prefer to carry a whistle, cagoule and overtrousers rather than not run at all. With the exception of a small vocal minority, I was proved right.' With hindsight he certainly helped to make the race the classic that it is, a point proved by many of the comments from competitors throughout this book. Doug also adds now that he felt very strongly about how the organisation needed to react in the aftermath of a death in their race. 'We introduced experience requirements from then on as part of the entry process. There was also a compulsory two-year disqualification introduced for anyone not complying with the safety rules. It has only needed to be enforced twice.'

Frank Travis was elected to the committee of the TPRA in 1972 and was its president from 1979 to 1981. Dave Hodgson took the job of Chair of the TPRA, a post he held for 15 years, and was succeeded by Graham Maud in 1997. Dave had a good feel for the challenges the organisation faced and how they should respond to the changing times. He gave me some background to his involvement in the race organisation. 'I was an outdoor pursuits instructor and I introduced several of my Venture Scouts to the Three Peaks. Jack Bloor said: "Without your help [*i.e. from the 9th Airedale Venture Scouts*] we couldn't organise the Three Peaks." We were manning all the summits. A lot of those lads stayed connected with the Association, including current Race Director Paul Dennison.'

From the mid-1980s onwards The Three Peaks Race Association introduced many innovations to their organisation of the race. The TPRA claims to be the first to operate a substitution system; the first to introduce a tag system (in 1986); the first to combine this with radio contact between Race Control and checkpoint; the first to use the labels system to display results; and one of the first to employ the SPORTident electronic timing system (with laptop computers on the summits of Whernside and Ingleborough).

Dave Hodgson said he was biased, but thought that the Three Peaks was the best organised race now. 'It is more difficult to organise than either the Ben Nevis or the Snowdon races, which are both straight up and down races. There are a lot of farmers we have to keep sweet on our circular route. Every year we organise a farmers' social and invite the relevant farmers and representatives of the land that we cross. It costs us about £600. I have done the Ben [*in 1964, coming 4th and being fastest newcomer to the race*] and been at the Snowdon race and I know what they are both like. I have never done any of the Lakeland Classic Long races, mind.'

The first thing Dave Hodgson did as Chair was to create a separate entries secretary post, a job his wife Shirley did for ten years. Later the entries task was handed over to Martin Stone's SPORTident (SI) company, then going online in time for the World Long Distance Mountain Running Challenge in 2008. 'My own view is that we helped SI get established. They were doing some orienteering events, and I think the Karrimor, but hadn't done very many fell races. We had a tag system in place – you took a tag to each summit and dropped it in the bin there to prove you had been up. It was a massive job to sort them, but we felt we would know roughly where someone went missing if they unfortunately did. When Martin first did it for us, I said I wanted to run the tags in parallel. Eventually SI did both entries and results for us.' The reason for running the tags in parallel was because there was a split at committee on making the changeover. That day, in 2003, the tags in the checkpoint bins were never looked at and the tag system was swiftly forgotten.

Dave Hodgson also commented: 'We tightened up safety arrangements after Ted Pepper's death. We introduced all the requirements about carrying gear and qualification. Subsequently, Paul Dennison and Dave Weatherhead have taken the Three Peaks to another level. The big marquee, a screen showing intermediate times, and improving the refreshments.' Hodgson added that it was accepted that it is a trail race with

153. Race certificate, 1987

three big hills in it, and that there is no navigation required now.

In the 2004 report it was noted: 'On the VIP guest list this year was the life member of Blackburn Harriers, George Kirby, who provided the race commentary for 35 years. Kirby commented. "Of all the things I've done in athletics, I think the Three Peaks has given me the most pleasure."' Around 18 years earlier, George Kirby had donated an eponymous trophy for the first Lancastrian finisher in the race.

In 2007 the TPRA started adding entertainment in the start/ finish area, in preparation for the World Champs the next year. For the Worlds in 2008 there was the introduction of stage prizes, for ascents and descents. After the 2009 event the setup was described in the online race report as 'a very convivial under-cover bar, food, live band and prize presentation.'

The prize-giving in 2015 saw Race Director Paul Dennison presented with an inscribed glass tankard to mark his 40 years' involvement with the Three Peaks Race. He began as a summit marshal on Ingleborough and Pen-y-Ghent before marshalling at Ribblehead checkpoint and then being promoted to race director.[49]

A special award is made to runners who have completed 21 races (men) or 15 races (ladies). The first six were presented with their award in 1989.[50]

As an organising body the Three Peaks Race Association is unique in fell running. Comprising representatives from the police, medical, communications and rescue organisations, the

---

49 Paul Dennison said in the 2023 race programme that he had had the pleasure of being part of the Three Peaks Race for 48 years.

50 The sixth person to achieve 21 Three Peaks Race completions was Bill Wade (later an active committee member for the Three Peaks Race Association), and the seventh (in 1989) was John Rawnsley, who was the founding father and long-time organiser of the Three Peaks Cyclo-Cross race and a member of Bingley Harriers. The cycle race started in 1961, seven years after the Three Peaks Race. John Rawnsley managed to rack up 45 cyclo-cross completions and also 30 Three Peaks Race finishes between 1966 and 1999.

154. The first six runners to complete the Three Peaks Race 21 times. Back row L to R: Alistair Patten, Dave Scott, John Huck. Front row L to R: Stan Bradshaw, George Brass, Alan Heaton.

local community, the National Park, and running clubs from the region, it is a diverse group.

Today the Three Peaks has the Inov-8 all-terrain specialist equipment company as its main sponsor. But there have been other long-term supporters, including the *Daily Mirror*, which sponsored the race for 28 years up to 1991. Other sponsors over the years, large and small, have included BT, Pace Micro Technology, Multiflight Ltd, Northern Rail, Hanson quarries, Craven District Council, Welcome to Yorkshire, TransLinc, Pete Bland Sports, CSH Transport, Northern Monk Brewery, Three

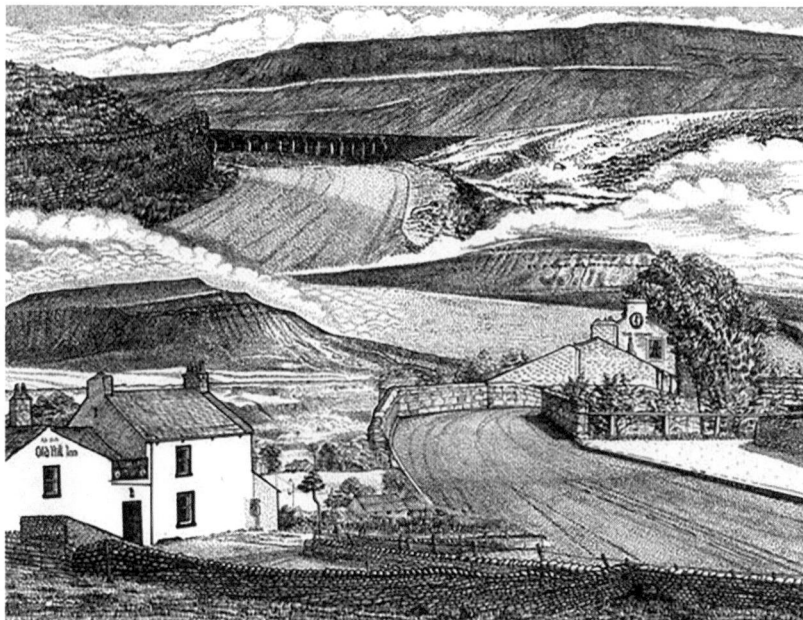

155. The image on the 15/21-year award

Peaks Bunkroom and Denise Park Chartered Physiotherapist.[51]
Such generous sponsorship enables a generous prize list,
including male, female and Vets team prizes, as well as an
abundance of trophies.

It should not be forgotten that the race could not take place
without the goodwill of farmers, landowners and the Horton-
in-Ribblesdale Playing Fields Association or the work of scores
of volunteers who marshal, carry out timing and provide radio
safety cover around the course in all weather conditions.

---

51 Denise Park is also a current committee member with responsibility for maintaining the
    sponsorship levels, and also has been the main race commentator since she took over the
    role from Clare Kenny in 2009.

Appendix 2

ROUTE CHANGES

It is important to recognise that the race has changed considerably since it started in 1954. In the first years it was best described as a long and hilly cross-country race; it is now a flagged trail race. There have been countless changes to the route. Some of the changes were very small – to stop corner-cutting for instance – others much larger. This appendix gives details of the significant changes, particularly where they demanded a re-set of the course records.

Bill Wade[52] recently offered some insights into the reasons for some changes and added a couple of anecdotes to help illuminate them. 'There are far more runners now, and account has had to be taken of the requirements of the Fell Runners Association (which was not founded until 1970), the National Park and local landowners – and it's become an extremely popular route for walkers and runners. I can't remember ever running on exactly the same route in consecutive years in the early days. When I first ran there were virtually no rules other than to visit the three summits, plus Ribblehead. In one very foggy year I remember running in a direct line from the Crown (in Horton) to the summit of Pen-Y-Ghent, reversing the route back to Horton and then running along the railway line to Ribblehead (and gaining several places by doing that). I never saw a train – it was a bad time for that line then and it almost disappeared under Beeching. When the HQ was at the Hill Inn the race started in the field above the Inn and finished in the field below it. Several versions of that particular part of the route have been used in years since then.'

Eventually the facilities and space at the Hill Inn at Chapel-le-Dale were not sufficient for the ever-increasing numbers of

---

52 Bill Wade was a long-time committee member of the TPRA. In his 50 years of running, he competed in the Three Peaks Race 41 times between 1962 and 2011.

competitors. From the six competitors in 1954, the numbers had increased to 112 by 1964, and 280 by 1974. Not only that, but there were also large numbers of supporters coming to watch, many of whom now came in their cars.

Dave Hodgson explains how the change took place. 'We had to move from the Hill Inn because it was too cramped there. Horton-in-Ribblesdale Playing Fields Association were very cooperative and helpful to us. The biggest field near the Hill Inn could only comfortably support about 80–90 competitors and it was becoming impossible to manage.'

So, the start was moved to Horton-in-Ribblesdale for **1975**. The big difference that starting from there meant was the change in the order of doing the peaks, with Pen-y-Ghent now first and Ingleborough last. Hodgson adds: 'From the Hill Inn the field was strung out by the time they got to Pen-y-Ghent. A lot of people had their own ideas of the best routes up Pen-y-Ghent, including myself. Starting from Horton we were forced to devise a separate route up from Horton to Pen-y-Ghent that all would have to use.' The new route added an extra mile-and-a-half, mainly due to the Pennine Way track being followed (first to the north and then east) all the way to Pen-y-Ghent instead of the more direct line over walled pastureland, as in previous years.

There was some debate about whether the new route was more interesting and more or less challenging. Bill Smith commented at the time that, 'The new venue provided a much more interesting run-in, for I doubt if anyone would argue that the long moorland trek over Sulber Nick is not preferable to the tarmac farm lane from Bruntscar. On the other hand, I must admit that the race somehow didn't seem as challenging without that final steep ascent and descent of Whernside, where the true fell runner could make up some places that he had earlier lost to fast road and cross-country runners.' As has been seen, plenty of runners have had cause to rue that long run-in when finishing on tired legs.

Dave Hodgson outlined further changes in the course that took place. 'For a few years we used the direct route off Pen-y-

Ghent via Black Dub, but then we were told not to run across the Moss. So, we then went down Sell Gill to Sell Gill Holes, to join the Pennine Way track. It was quite a tricky descent, but we did it for several years, until it was straightened out with a new path to avoid the Gill. We also used a more direct route up Whernside, going under the viaduct, to the farm and then straight up, turning right at the top for the summit. The farmer stopped us doing that though.'

A warning note from Dave Hodgson about the imminent possibility of route changes appeared in his race report for the 1982 race. 'I think competitors should be informed of some of the access problems which are an unfortunate feature of organising the race. Much of the recognised running route is not on public rights of way and we are dependent on retaining good relations with landowners. Regrettably, relationships can become strained and a fortnight before this year's race it appeared that re-routing would have to be carried out, which would add nearly two miles to the accepted shortest distance. Only strenuous efforts and skilful persuasion by a member of the organising committee enabled this year's race to be run over the usual course. The future is by no means certain.'

Indeed, in **1983** the first diversion in the Horton start course was implemented, as Dave Hodgson again explained in his race report for the year. 'The route change off Pen-y-Ghent imposed by local landowners probably added five minutes to the times of leading runners. At one time it was feared that three major route changes would have to be introduced this year. In the end only one was necessary as late permission was obtained to use the traditional route up Whernside. A last-minute intervention by the Police enabled us to retain use of the route into the finish, which crosses private land underneath the railway line.'

Bill Smith gives further detail of that change in the June 1990 *Fellrunner*:[53] The old direct route to High Birkwith and Nether Lodge, fording Hull Pot Beck *en route*, was replaced by a detour over Whitber into Sell Gill to rejoin the old route further along the Pennine Way. This is the tricky descent to Sell Gill Holes that

53 In an article entitled 'The Three Peaks Race: 1970–90'.

Dave Hodgson mentions above. That route remained in use for many years, including for the World Long Distance Mountain Running Challenge in 2008.

Bill Smith also notes: Four years later (in **1987**), the Whernside ascent from Winterscales was replaced by one further north, with the initial line from Ribblehead keeping to the right (east) of the railway viaduct, towards Blea Moor, before turning left under the railway onto the fell. This lengthened the course, causing another new record to be instigated that year.

The report for the **1989** race mentioned that, 'during the last 12 months the Yorkshire Dales National Park have carried out much anti-erosion work in the area. This has led to the construction of 1,500 metres of hardcore walkway over what used to be the peat bog approaches to Pen-y-Ghent and a similar stretch on the approach to Blea Moor. Whatever one's opinion of the effect on the environment, there is no doubt that the course is now faster, and it was no surprise to find new records in both men's and women's categories'. So, no change to the route, but faster running, with the records put down predominantly to the high standard of competition and near perfect weather conditions.

In **2007** the finish was changed to a safer but slightly shorter route crossing through the Rose family's garden to get to the road in Horton, but no record change required. The race also changed to the Saturday in that year.

Originally the course reversed the route off Pen-y-Ghent, which always ended up with runners going both ways on the same track, passing each other after the sharp turn on the last steep bit. From **2012** the descending runners took a higher line off the summit and rejoined the route further down. It still means a bit of congestion but not nearly so much.

In **2013** the Three Peaks Race was the first major event to use a revised route over Whitber created by the Yorkshire Dales National Park Authority to avoid a boggy section through Black Dubb Moss. The new path was opened and certainly pleased the farmer, whose land it crossed. This spelled the end of the use of the Sell Gill variant. Joe Symonds said: 'It was a joy to run. It is a really fast track. I know it is probably a little bit longer, but

I am sure it is quicker and it is a lot easier underfoot.' Again, no record change for either the 2012 or 2013 variations.

The route was slightly increased in distance in **2023** to nearly 39km, an extension of 0.6 mile (1km). This was at the request of the landowner, to avoid deterioration of the permissive path across his field from the Pennine Way to High Birkwith. The race website describes the change in detail: 'From the Pen y Ghent summit Checkpoint, descend via the summit loop to pick up the path again at the fingerpost and then follow the path over Whitber Hill to meet the Pennine Way at Jackdaw Hill, continue north on the Pennine Way (the Old Ing Loop) to High Birkwith Moor, at wooden farm gate turn West to continue on the Pennine Way Bridleway past Old Ing Farm to Fingerpost and then follow the path to God's Bridge. Continue past God's Bridge to Nether Lodge Farm to pick up the track past Lodge Hall and on to the B6479.'

Ever searching for improvements, current race organiser, Paul Dennison, has tried hard to get rid of the road section from where the runners come out from Nether Lodge to Ribblehead. Dave Hodgson points out why it has not been possible. 'There is a natural route on the left-hand side of the road but there is one farmer that won't let us go over his land. The reason he gives is that if the race uses it all the walkers will do so too.'

The final word on route changes and records goes to Sarah Rowell: 'Whoever ran this year (2023) would set a new record. And if they got within five minutes of the old records then they would earn the race record bonus from the organisers. I think they had added ten minutes to the cut-off at the Hill Inn.'

THREE PEAKS RACE WINNERS

Year	Winner	Time		
1954	Fred Bagley	3-48-00		
1955	George Brass	3-28-45		
1956	Jack Bloor	3-33-15		
1957	Peter Dugdale	3-33-50		
1958	George Brass	3-08-25		
1959	Frank Dawson	3-13-25		
1960	Frank Dawson	2-58-53		
1961	Geoff Hodgson	3-05-10		
1962	Geoff Hodgson	3-00-07		
1963	Dennis Hopkinson	3-18-37		
1964	Peter Hall	2-53-00		
1965	Mike Davies	2-47-00		
1966	Mike Davies	2-53-22		
1967	Mike Davies	2-47-19		
1968	Mike Davies	2-40-34		
1969	Colin Robinson	2-44-44		
1970	Jeff Norman	2-48-11		
1971	Jeff Norman	2-36-26		
1972	Jeff Norman	2-36-27		
1973	Jeff Norman	2-31-58		
1974	Jeff Norman	2-29-53		
1975	Jeff Norman	2-41-37*		
1976	John Calvert	2-43-59		
1977	John Calvert	2-51-04		
1978	Harry Walker	2-43-44		
1979	Harry Walker	2-53-11	Jean Lochhead	3-43-12
1980	Mike Short	2-43-32	Sue Parkin	3-35-34
1981	Harry Walker	2-56-34	Fiona Hinde	3-59-16
1982	John Wild	2-37-30	Jane Robson	3-40-54
1983	Kenny Stuart	2-53-34*	Carol Walkington and Wendy Dodds	4-08-01*
1984	Hugh Symonds	2-50-34	Bridget Hogge	3-41-00
1985	Hugh Symonds	2-49-13	Vanessa Brindle	3-38-10
1986	Shaun Livesey	2-56-40	Carol Walkington	3-49-12
1987	Hugh Symonds	3-00-01*	Vanessa Brindle	3-44-05*
1988	Ian Ferguson	2-57-29	Vanessa Brindle	3-37-16
1989	Shaun Livesey	2-51-45	Vanessa Brindle	3-32-43
1990	Gary Devine	3-00-51	Ruth Pickvance	3-44-18

1991	**Ian Ferguson**	**2-51-41**	**Sarah Rowell**	**3-16-29**
1992	Ian Ferguson	3-01-11	Sarah Rowell	3-19-11
1993	Gavin Bland	3-05-17	Carol Greenwood	3-39-50
1994	Andy Peace	2-56-52	Sarah Rowell	3-21-50
1995	Andy Peace	2-52-52	Jean Rawlinson	3-48-40
1996	**Andy Peace**	**2-46-03**	**Sarah Rowell**	**3-16-17**
1997	Ian Holmes	2-52-28	Carol Greenwood	3-34-39
1998	Mark Roberts	3-03-31	Carol Greenwood	3-34-16
1999	Mark Croasdale	3-04-48	Angela Mudge	3-20-17
2000	Simon Booth	2-52-43	Sally Newman	3-38-11
2001	Cancelled due to foot-and-mouth outbreak			
2002	Simon Booth	3-10-43	Tracey Brindley	3-46-12
2003	David Walker	3-06-27	Beverley Whitfield	3-56-40
2004	Andy Peace	2-55-46	Louise Sharp	3-39-40
2005	Rob Jebb	2-57-50	Sally Malir	3-59-56
2006	Rob Jebb	2-54-15	Helen Sedgwick	3-43-40
2007	Rob Jebb	2-51-49	Mary Wilkinson	3-30-22
2008	Jethro Lennox	2-53-39	**Anna Pichrtova**	**3-14-43**
2009	Rob Jebb	2-54-53	Anna Lupton	3-36-31
2010	Morgan Donnelly	3-02-34	Anna Lupton	3-30-45
2011	Tom Owens	2-53-34	Anna Frost	3-30-00
2012	Joe Symonds	2-55-58	Sarah O'Neill	3-28-46
2013	Joe Symonds	2-54-39	Jasmin Paris	3-33-04
2014	Ricky Lighfoot	2-53-16	Victoria Wilkinson	3-21-32
2015	Ricky Lightfoot	2-51-42	Helen Bonser	3-27-24
2016	Marc Lauenstein	2-48-58	Victoria Wilkinson	3-26-47
2017	Murray Strain	2-49-38	**Victoria Wilkinson**	**3-09-19**
2018	Tom Owens	2-49-08	Victoria Wilkinson	3-22-17
2019	Brennan Townshend	2-50-22	Victoria Wilkinson	3-20-01
2020	Cancelled due to Covid 19 restrictions			
2021	Gary Greenhow	3-05-22	Rose Mather	3-47-38
2022	Brennan Townshend	2-55-34	Sarah McCormack	3-23-21
2023	**Thomas Roach**	**2-53-28***	**Catherine Taylor**	**3-34-44***

Bold = course record. * = new record due to course change.

Appendix 4

CUT-OFFS

Race Director Paul Dennison explained in full in a *Fellrunner* article[54] in 2015 the need for and use of cut-off times at the Three Peaks Race. The following is a slightly edited down version of that article.

The reason for cut-off times at Ribblehead and Hill Inn checkpoints are twofold:

1 To safeguard competitors and marshals

The marshals are as important as competitors when I am making decisions about the race. As race director I am responsible for every person's wellbeing on the day.

Nobody is immune to exposure, especially marshals on the summits. By the time the last competitor has gone over the summit of Whernside and Ingleborough the marshals will have been out six or seven hours in all kinds of weather. They have a tent to provide some shelter, but once runners start to reach the checkpoint the marshals are all outside doing their job in helping to keep runners safe. The weather can change very quickly from calm and sunny to horizontal rain, sleet and snow with high winds, so we have to be ready for all conditions.

Competitors have to carry waterproof and windproof clothing and equipment for their own safety in case of injury or starting to get cold and wet. Marshals and radio operators have not only carried their personal equipment to the summits, but they have also carried up tents, laptops, SPORTident timing equipment, radios, aerials and spare batteries. In bad weather I have a responsibility to get them clear of the summits as soon as all runners are accounted for and safe.

---

54 'The Three Peaks Race: why and how we apply cut-off times', p.23 autumn 2015 edition of *The Fellrunner*.

2 To make this a race

This is a competitive race with entrants required to reach cut-off points before a certain time. These times are not difficult to achieve if you have done the correct training. The Three Peaks is not a race that you can just turn up and run. If you want an easier race there are plenty of challenge events around the Three Peaks.

How do I make the decision to call the cut-off time at Ribblehead and Hill Inn checkpoints?

Several things are taken into account when making these decisions:

- *The weather both on the summits and at the checkpoints. Race Control is in radio contact with all the checkpoints and other locations throughout the event, so we know the latest conditions around the course.*
- *How many runners are outstanding at the checkpoint in the few minutes leading up to the cut-off times?*
- *The location of the minibuses, which have to be in place and ready to bring runners back to Horton.*

When all these things are taken into account a decision is made.

Some years you may get a little leeway when I apply the cut-offs. In other years you do not. This is to give tail-end runners a chance if the weather is kind, or the race marshals, particularly those on the summits, a chance if conditions are poor.

The race website notes: The cut-off times (as of 2023) are at Ribblehead after 2 hours 20 minutes and at Hill Inn after 3 hours 40 minutes respectively after the start. If you are outside these times, you will be instructed to retire. Please respect the marshals' decision. In the event of a competitor being assessed as unsuitable to continue for medical or other reasons, the competitor will be withdrawn from the event.

Appendix 5

RACE NUMBERS OVER THE YEARS, AND SOME STATS

The graph below illustrates the gradual increase in numbers starting (and finishing) the race over the years. There is a steady increase in numbers from the first event till 1978, then something of a plateau in numbers from 1976 to 2000. With no race held in 2000 due to the outbreak of Foot and Mouth there was a gradual return of numbers for several years before reaching the peak years of 2008 to 2019. A break again for Covid in 2020 has seen runners returning to the race, which by 2023 had not yet reached the level of those peak years.

Starters (dashed line) and finishers (solid line)

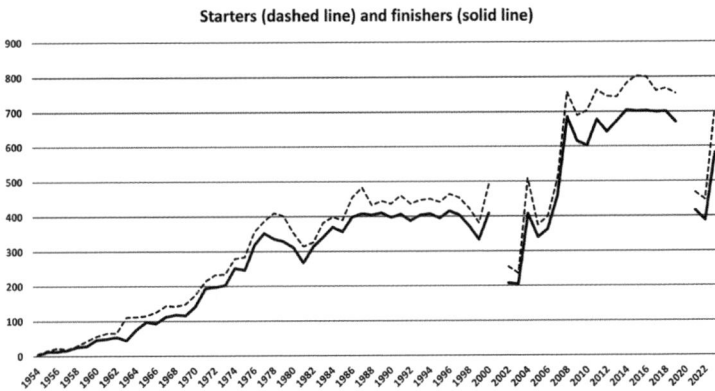

The numbers finishing, as a percentage of the starters, remains reasonably similar over the years. In the early years, with the small fields at the time, that statistic varied from the lowest year of 40.1% finishing in 1963 to a high of 89.7% in 1958. In more recent years the percentage has varied from a high of 96.3% in 1982 to a low of 80.1% in 2004. The weather on the day is surely a cause for that variation. For instance, 1982 was described in the report as 'sunny skies, becoming overcast, and with a coolish breeze' (good running weather for the year after the race was postponed due to huge snowdrifts) and 2004 as 'a boiling hot day'. A significant number of non-finishers will be those that are timed-out at the various checkpoints, which will be the fate of a good number of competitors on a particularly hot day. [See Appendix 4 for details of the cut-offs]

% women competing

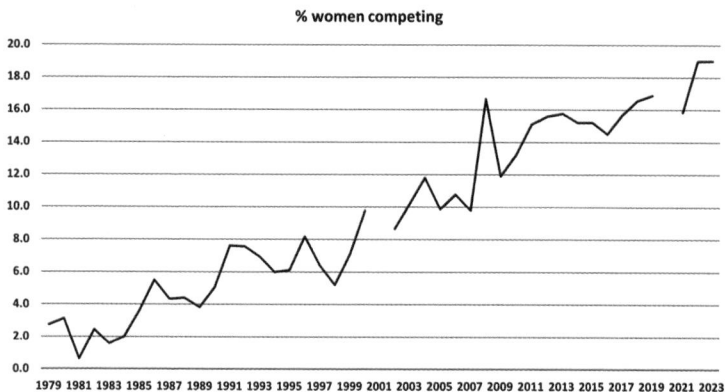

From when women first competed (in 1979) to 2000 the percentage of starters that were women increased gradually from 2.7% to 9.8%. Like the overall numbers the percentage of women recovered slowly after the Foot and Mouth break and soon was almost 17%, and three times reached 16+% before the Covid break. In the three years to 2023 the percentage has gone back up, to reach an all-time high of 19% in 2022 and 2023.

The percentage of women finishing each year was statistically unreliable as a measure in the first 7 years of their involvement, as the numbers were too small. Three times the ratio was at 100%, i.e. all starters finished in those years. From then on, the finishing percentage for women has varied from a high of 94.7% (1988) to a low of 68.0% (1986). [For neither of these years was the weather significantly good or bad enough to get a mention in the race report.] This is a lower top value than the men and also a lower bottom value. The fact that a lower percentage of women starters finish the race than men is confirmed by averaging both the women's and men's finishing percentages for all the years from 1986 (when women's numbers become statistically significant) to 2023. This gives average finishing percentages of 84.6% for women and 88.6% for men.

The following table shows, respectively, the numbers of starters, and finishers[55], and then the percentage of the starters that are women for each year (in Part II).

Year	Starters	Finishers	% Finishing
1954	6	3	50.0
1955	16	13	81.3
1956	23	13	56.5
1957	19	17	89.5
1958	29	26	89.7
1959	44	29	65.9
1960	57	47	82.5
1961	65	49	75.4
1962	66	54	81.8
1963	111	45	40.5
1964	112	75	67.0
1965	115	97	84.3
1966	126	93	73.8
1967	144	112	77.8
1968	142	118	83.1
1969	149	116	77.9
1970	175	142	81.1
1971	214	193	90.2
1972	232	197	84.9
1973	234	202	86.3
1974	280	251	89.6
1975	284	246	86.6
1976	357	319	89.4
1977	387	352	91.0
1978	410	336	82.0

---

55 The raw data is from the race website at: https://www.threepeaksrace.org/history with further data manipulation being performed by the author.

Year	Starters	Finishers	% finishing	Women starters	Women finishers	% women finishing
1979	402	328	81.6	11	8	72.7
1980	353	311	88.1	11	9	81.8
1981	314	267	85.0	2	2	100
1982	326	314	96.3	8	3	37.5
1983	381	341	89.5	6	6	100
1984	398	369	92.7	8	8	100
1985	389	356	91.5	14	13	92.9
1986	454	399	87.9	25	17	68.0
1987	483	408	84.5	21	16	76.2
1988	432	404	93.5	19	18	94.7
1989	444	410	92.3	17	15	88.2
1990	436	397	91.1	22	18	81.8
1991	460	406	88.3	35	29	82.9
1992	436	387	88.8	33	29	87.9
1993	447	404	90.4	31	27	87.1
1994	450	407	90.4	27	24	88.9
1995	441	395	89.6	27	21	77.8
1996	464	415	89.4	38	31	81.6
1997	453	404	89.2	29	22	75.9
1998	423	372	87.9	22	21	95.5
1999	380	333	87.6	27	25	92.6
2000	491	409	83.3	48	41	85.4
2001	No race					
2002	254	207	81.5	22	15	68.2
2003	235	205	87.2	24	22	91.7
2004	508	407	80.1	60	43	71.7
2005	375	340	90.7	37	31	83.8
2006	399	363	91.0	43	40	93.0
2007	510	459	90.0	50	43	86.0
2008	756	685	90.6	126	109	86.5
2009	689	615	89.3	82	74	90.2
2010	703	602	85.6	93	79	84.9
2011	762	677	88.8	115	95	82.6
2012	744	641	86.2	116	82	70.7
2013	742	672	90.6	117	103	88.0
2014	782	704	90.0	119	105	88.2
2015	802	702	87.5	122	92	75.4
2016	800	703	87.9	116	92	79.3
2017	760	699	92.0	119	110	92.4
2018	767	701	91.4	127	107	84.3
2019	752	670	89.1	127	104	81.9
2020	No race					
2021	467	416	89.1	74	65	87.8
2022	447	387	86.6	85	74	87.1
2023	704	581	82.5	134	111	82.8

Appendix 6

PRIZES

Trophy	Awarded to	First presented
Norman Thornber Trophy[56]	Overall winner	1958
Stan Bradshaw Trophy	First m40	1971
George Rhodes Rose Bowl	First m50	1980
9th Airedale Ventures Trophy	First Scout	1981
Jack Bloor Trophy (Curlew Plaque)	First newcomer	1986
Shirley Hodgson Trophy	First woman	1991
Clayton-le-Moors Bowl	First m60	1991
Peter Wadsworth Trophy (Tankard)	First runner representing a Yorks Club	1992
George Kirby Trophy (Tankard)	First runner representing a Lancs Club	1992
Mike Hetherton Trophy	Veterans' team	1994
Jenny Vesey Trophy	First w60	2009
Alf Case Trophy	Women's team	2011
Bill Wade Awards	Youngest male/ female finishers	2013
Doug Croft Trophy	Men's team	2014[57]
David Scott Award	Oldest finisher	2015
3 Peaks Salver	First w40	2022
3 Peaks Salver	First w50	2022

---

56 The oak wall plaque includes two of the Three Peaks – Pen-y-Ghent and an outline of Ingleborough – as well as the Ribblehead Viaduct on the Settle–Carlisle railway and Horton-in-Ribblesdale church.

57 The original *Daily Mirror* team trophy went missing and the present trophy (presented by Doug Croft) was awarded for the first time in April 2014.